MULTICULTURAL REFLECTIONS ON "RACE AND CHANGE"

featuring archival interviews from the
Race and Change Oral History Collection
Broward County African American Research Library
and Cultural Center

Compiled and Edited by
KITTY OLIVER

BORDIGHERA PRESS

Library of Congress Cataloguing-in-Publication Data

Multicultural reflections on "race and change" : featuring archival interviews from the Race and Change Oral History Collection, African American Research Library and Cultural Center / compiled and edited by Kitty Oliver.
    p. cm. -- (Fuori collana ; v. 1)
    ISBN 1-884419-79-8
    1. Florida--Race relations--History--20th century--Anecdotes. 2. Pluarlism (Social sciences)--Florida--History--20th century--Anecdotes. 3. Social change--Florida--History--20th century--Anecdotes. 4. Community life--Florida--History--20th century--Anecdotes. 5. Florida--Social life and customs--20th century--Anecdotes. 6. Florida--biography--Anecdotes. 7. Interviews--Florida. 8. United States--Race relations--Case studies. 9. Pluralism (Social sciences)--United States--Case studies. 10. Social change--United States--Case studies. I. Oliver, Kitty, 1947- II. African American Research Library and Cultural Center. III. Series: Fuori collana (Boca Raton, Fla.) ; . 1.

F320.A1M85 2006
305.8009759--dc22

2006044037

Printed in the United States.

Published by
BORDIGHERA PRESS
Languages and Linguistics
Florida Atlantic University
Boca Raton, FL 33431

Fuori collana 1
ISBN 1-884419-79-8

Acknowledgments

Thanks to the Florida Humanities Council for initial research funding to develop the Race and Change Project and archive; to the scores of Florida Atlantic University Communication and English students who dared to become explorers with me in this work over the past few years; to the great staff of the African American Research Library and Cultural Center, and Special Collections in particular, for professional guidance and resource assistance and enthusiasm for the potential of this material; and, with love, to B.J., for valuing history and helping to preserve it for others.

*All photos, as well as recordings and transcripts of
oral histories excerpted in this book, are housed in Special Collections,
African American Research Library and Cultural Center, Fort Lauderdale.*

CONTENTS

FOREWORD

RACE AND CHANGE: AN HISTORICAL LOOK

African American Research Library and Cultural Center

Racism has been a part of the daily life of America from its beginning. As a result, it has had a negative impact on every citizen, both Black and White, and has affected communities and caused a blight on America's historical image that can not be erased. Black men, women and children were relegated to less than human conditions, bought and sold as commodities on an auction block, used as laborers with little or no wages and treated with no dignity. They suffered family separations caused by the masters and were often whipped as animals, many times in public and in the presence of their family members. They were disenfranchised from the political process, had no say in their livelihoods, could not attend public schools to earn an education, and when change came after the Emancipation Proclamation of 1863, which was supposed to free the slaves, in essence a different kind of enslavement resulted.

Poor schools with hand-me-down books and materials, separate water fountains and restrooms — one marked FOR WHITE and one marked FOR COLORED — racial slurs, trumped up legal charges, lynchings and other acts all marked the life of the African American. While the brutality of these events was inflicted on Blacks, White citizens also suffered as well. Some were forced into silence; others who dared to speak had to do so through undercover means. Liberal-thinking Whites were restricted from actively and openly speaking out against the racial practices of the day. At the same time, there was also a festering of hatred among many other Whites that consumed their very being.

But change had to come. In 1909, the National Association for the Advancement of Colored People (NAACP) was born, giving hope. From that hope emerged people with self-confidence, with talents and valued human relationships. This was put on display during the 1920s and early 1930s as the Harlem Renaissance, showcasing poetry, prose, music, theater, dance and comedy and providing dynamic artistic depictions of the life and times of the African American. By the 1940s, the NAACP came into its own, and formed the Legal Defense Fund to attack racism through the legal system. The success of the 1946 case of *Smith vs Allwright* came when the US Supreme Court ruled that Black citizens had the right to vote in state primary elections, and in 1946 in *Morgan vs Commonwealth of Virginia,* the US Supreme Court ruled that bus segregation in interstate travel was unconstitutional. These rulings paved the way for the successful 1954 Supreme Court decision in the case of *Brown vs the Board of Education* (Topeka, Kansas) that declared "separate but equal" to be unconstitutional. This mammoth decision affected every school, every community, every household and every citizen. Now America was facing major change — a change that was not easy to embrace, but change just the same.

History tells us that change did not come "with all deliberate speed" as the ruling commanded. In this volume of writings, students in classes created at Florida Atlantic University and taught by Professor Kitty Oliver sought to understand the dilemmas met by grassroots community residents as they faced the desegregation process. You will find yourself immersed in the lives of the writers and the South Florida narrators they encountered. Through the medium of oral history, they interviewed or conducted research in the archives of recordings of those who participated in the Race and Change Project, presenting those raw experiences in the language of the interviewees, and adding their own reflections. These revelations provide us with a vivid picture of how communities dealt with forced integration and the medium used to come to terms with the removal of the barrier of race.

You, too, will begin to visualize your own approach to race and change and realize that each one of us must find a comfortable plane on which to live equally with our neighbors, without regard to cultural backgrounds, religious beliefs or the color of our skin. The Broward County African American Research Library and Cultural Center here in Fort Lauderdale, Florida, is excited to add these oral history interviews to its collection for historical information and further research.

Julie V. Hunter
Executive Director; Broward County
African-American Research Library and
Cultural Center; Fort Lauderdale, Florida

Field interviewers at Belle Glade City Hall in front of statue commemorating deadly 1928 hurricane. Author Zora Neale Hurston wrote about it in Their Eyes Were Watching God. *Photo by Natasha Pierre-Louis*

Field interviewers in Delray Beach, Fl. Photo by Claudina Souther.

Introduction to the Collection

I am a fortunate university department chair who spotted a talented faculty member who wanted to make the university classroom a whole community. "Go ahead and do it, " I said; and Kitty Oliver went ahead and did it, and her students had the best learning experience of their lives. A safe environment was created where students and community members learned from one another and, in the process, celebrated life in all its complexity.

Most teachers are not as brave. Most of us like to stay in a familiar place and not take too many risks. We don't like it when we don't have the answers. But the best teachers are willing to be students themselves; they are unafraid to accompany their students in the learning process; they enjoy modeling an open mind and a creative spirit. The Race and Change Project is an example of the best that higher education has to offer. This book will give the reader a taste of what's possible.

Dr. Susan Reilly
Chair, Department of Communication;
The Dorothy F. Schmidt College of Arts
and Letters; Florida Atlantic University

Editor Kitty Oliver,
founder Race and Change Project and
Collection. Photo by Claudina Souther.

Kitty Oliver is an author, oral historian and television documentary producer special-izing in race relations and cul-tural diversity issues. She is also a veteran South Florida journalist. Her book, Voices of America: Race and Change in Hollywood, Florida, *a col-lection of oral histories on race relations experiences of Blacks, Whites and immi-grants, and the companion PBS TV documentary,* Crossings of the Racial Divide: Hollywood Stories, *which she produced and wrote, are used widely in the public schools along with her collection of autobiographical essays,* Multicolored Memories of a Black Southern Girl. *She is founder of the "Kitty Oliver Oral Histories Collection on Race and Change" (also known as the Race and Change Oral History Project) in Special Collections at the African American Research Library and Cultural Center in Fort Lauderdale, Fla., featuring over 100 interviews collected in South Florida by her and Florida Atlantic University students she has trained. A member of the national Oral History Association and the International Oral History Association, she has presented her Race and Change work at their conferences. Her consulting company, Kitty O. Enterprises, Inc., conducts workshops and projects nation-ally. She is currently writer-in-residence at the African American Research Library and Cultural Center.*

"THE RACE AND CHANGE PROJECT": CREATING A NEW DIALOGUE

Kitty Oliver

The first burst of daylight fanned across the empty parking lot as I pulled into a faculty space close to the building, far from the street. Force of habit. I had my pick of spots — it was Saturday morning, too early for the weekend working academics and their students. But I needed time before my class arrived to compose myself. They say you teach what you need to learn; I was taking a group of 16 men and

women on a journey of discovery in a new course exploring race relations, and the next few months were going to be a new adventure for
me, as well.

The basics had been worked out with careful planning and a prelim-
inary on-site visit. Our caravan of vans and cars would assemble on the
Davie Campus, just west of downtown Fort Lauderdale, FL, by 7:30 a.m.,
and head north along I-95 through densely-populated Broward and Palm
Beach Counties for a pickup at the main campus in Boca Raton. Then
we'd cut west across the state to a rural part that many natives, including
me, had never seen. Circling the massive Lake Okeechobee — the Seminole
name means "Great Water" — we would find the lookout point and stop
for a quick walk along the pier to get a speechless panoramic view. It's a
natural wonder carved out of the Everglades, the source of drinking
water for southern Florida, struggling to suckle the increasing demands
of relentless urban development. We'd take an ecological tour of the
Kissimmee River outflow to the protective Hoover Dike, then pile into a
bungalow at a wooded retreat center for an overnight stay. There, the real
expedition would begin.

Like any reliable navigator I had created a road map to share with
them, based on my research that created the Race and Change Project.

It began in the late fall of 1999 as a series of questions I had been pon-
dering for awhile after years of work as a diversity consultant doing
cross-cultural sensitivity training and years before that as a journalist
with The Miami Herald writing about communities where racial and ethnic conflicts often reared their heads. With the new millennium approaching, I thought, why not get a different type of reading on race relations,
beyond the political rhetoric and the opinion polls, and look at the issue
in a more inclusive way? The elderly with the longest links to the past
would be included, of course, but so would other untapped voices ready
to take a place in adding to the historical fabric of American life. A generation of Blacks and Whites that came of age with the passage of the Civil
Rights Act of 1964 and made the transition from segregation to integration would makeup a large portion of the interviews I ended up conducting. And certainly, the aftermath of the Civil Rights Movement had global effects — especially on immigrants to this country. So, why not ask the
same questions of a cross-section of people — not only Blacks and Whites
who are "natives" of various parts of this country, but residents from a
variety of other countries and backgrounds as well, and see what paral-
lels, or clashes, emerged from their views?

I wanted to explore their personal histories in the context of their
times, the places and people who influenced them from childhood onward,
the experiences that shaped them — the ones *they* considered most significant in their lives. The questions could be posed in a way that
encourages detailed memory. The writer in me envisioned richly-tex-
tured stories pouring forth: scenes of encounters etched vividly in the

mind; warm recollections of daily life in times long gone; reflections on the sometimes subtle ways that they — and we, as a society — have grown and changed over time. And, if it was all recorded for the historical archives to be shared with others, those treasured memories would continue to live.

Few places in the United States provided the goldmine of cultural diversity found in South Florida. Since Hollywood, FL, located between Miami and Fort Lauderdale, has been cited nationally as having the racial and ethnic demographics of what the US will reportedly look like by the year 2025, the city became the ideal study area for the first group of 42 Blacks, Whites and immigrants, or the children of immigrants, from various Hispanic, Caribbean and Asian backgrounds who were interviewed. A book, teacher's guide, TV documentary and a series of performance presentations were developed in the aftermath to highlight the stories and promote community dialogues on race.

That first Saturday morning in 2001, however, as I sat in the Florida Atlantic University parking lot, I was heading into uncharted territory. I knew the students would be trained in the theory, ethics and techniques of conducting oral history interviews and they would spend part of the semester in the Lake Okeechobee area recording narrators; eventually, I would train and supervise other groups of students to collect stories in other areas. What concerned me most on that day was how I would manage to keep them engaged for the rest of the term, after the field work ended. I wondered how I could make history relevant, a living thing for them.

Slowly they arrived, a couple driving up together, and they piled into the vans mostly as strangers. Even I had not met many of them. During our after-dinner orientation at the retreat house, I decided on a round of introductions, just to get acquainted and learn names and find out why each had enrolled in the course. By the time the final student shared, I began to sense where this excursion might lead. I discovered that they were Florida-born and transplants from various parts of the US, from South American countries and islands in the Caribbean. The majority was well over 30, and they had lived through major shifts in racial attitudes. There were more Whites than Blacks — a trend that would continue. But, one-by-one, encouraged to talk about their backgrounds and perspectives on race relations, they opened up like live wires sparking ideas and reflections so fast it was difficult to cut them off so that everyone could get a turn. Some of them even stayed up and carried on the conversation long after lights-out for the rest of us. I decided not to end the classroom exchange, but to capitalize on it. During the three-month semester, they were assigned to talk and write and share their personal experiences around race and ethnicity and dealing with differences as a requirement of the course, drawing on the eclectic mix of narrators' stories in the Race and Change Project as a catalyst. In the process, some close bonds were formed.

In 2002, I began working with students in a different way. In the course, Writing Across Cultures, they used the archival Race and Change collection as a research tool to fuel their intercultural communication and creative writing work. Discussions of autobiographical literature from various cultures provided models and laid the groundwork for writing about their own personal experiences from childhood on, and the shifts and changes that have occurred in their perceptions of others. Perusing oral history recordings, they discovered narrators who resonated with parallel or contradictory memories. Interviews or "encounters" with others in the course added another layer, another contemporary perspective to consider. All those voices were then incorporated into their personal stories of exploration and self-discovery. Interestingly, several ended up taking the field course later and using oral history techniques further in their academic work or in their careers.

Little did I know, that Saturday morning, where all this would lead. The first group of students conducted interviews with residents of the small struggling agricultural communities of Belle Glade, South Bay and Pahokee along the southern rim of Lake Okeechobee. In the years since, teams have converged on the coastal town of Delray Beach, which is growing fast and increasingly multi-cultural, and smaller projects have been conducted in Boca Raton and parts of Fort Lauderdale. The field-work has resulted in a tapestry of reminiscences that shed light on lost or little-known aspects of community life and rituals in various cultures. The stories of narrators also recount painful and poignant experiences of being "the other," and memorable interactions with people who are different. Over 90 narrators are featured in the Race and Change Oral Histories archive in Special Collections at the African American Research Library and Cultural Center; another 30 audio recordings of residents of the Black communities of Liberia in Hollywood, FL, and the North Fork of the New River in Fort Lauderdale, FL, use the same format of questions. The Lift Every Voice Project, which presents oral history and writing workshops for residents in culturally diverse communities, also uses the Race and Change interview strategies and goals.

Meanwhile, an array of creative work has been produced by students in the FAU courses — work that is also housed in the Race and Change archive. Included are: videos, photographic displays, radio programs, and even a reader's theater script. At the core, however, are the essays of personal experiences. Some are written by creative writing students; some by students who were challenged to experiment with a new form of written expression. The stories offer a candid look at where we are and how far we have come as Americans in terms of race relations.

This collection features some of those stories, chosen for the range of racial and cultural perspectives: southern and northern parts of the US; European; Latina; Jamaican. The approaches to autobiographical writing vary as well. Glenn Malone makes a novel, philosophical examination of places significant to Lake Okeechobee residents which actually serve as metaphors for racial division in the area's past. Clarence Bornstein and Kami Barrett, on the other hand, stretch the boundaries of point of view using creative nonfiction techniques to explore the pain of prejudice. White writers look at naiveté and ambivalence to racial issues; Black writers discuss family, community and challenges in interracial as well as intraracial relationships. Other topics include religion and faith in Black and White cultures; responses to one-on-one encounters with differences, seeing themselves through others' eyes; and views of race from the perspective of people whose worlds have expanded because of their ethnicity or international travel. The writers were free to use different techniques for blending in the oral history voices from the Race and Change collection, but the narrators are presented as full-fledged characters whose stories also unfold in the course of the essays, staying true to their inflections and dialect. Many of the photographs were also taken by students.

In the editing of this book, some narrators are used by several writers so their voices have been edited to reduce repetition. The essays are presented as they were written, although some editing has been done for space and continuity. One writer has chosen to use a pen name; her story, however, is true. Presented together, the experiences of the writers and the narrators they include create a unique dialogue across racial, cultural and generational lines. In the final essay you'll find some how-to tips about conducting a Race and Change project.

The words "Black" and "White" are capitalized when they as used as racial descriptions of people. Many of the narrators also self-describe themselves in that way. The terms represent the most obvious physical differences which cause negative reactions and behavior, but they are just metaphors for the separations that we create among ourselves as human beings, in general, and the troubles that result. The problem is global, and it occurs no matter how seemingly homogeneous a community, or country, appears to be. We build walls to divide us and then end up having to find ways to tear them down by creating new ways to dialogue.

That Saturday morning, years ago, waiting uneasily in the parking lot for my first group of students, my big concern was how I would keep them interested in the class for a few months. I had no idea how many people would be touched by the Race and Change Project, and how much we all would grow and learn.

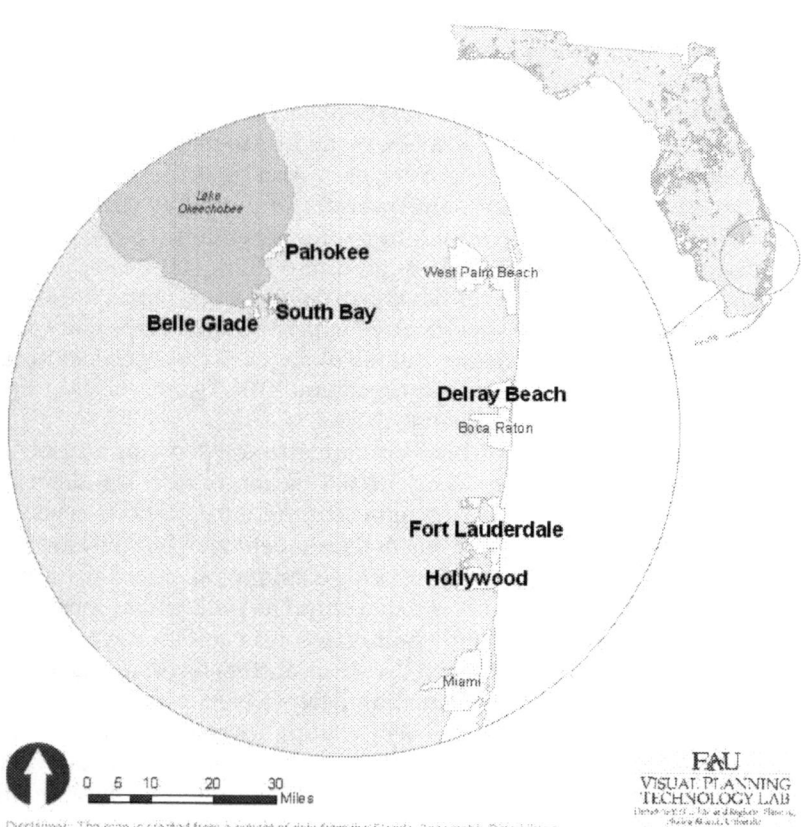

Florida Study Area

Lake Okeechobee

Pahokee

West Palm Beach

Belle Glade   South Bay

Delray Beach

Boca Raton

Fort Lauderdale

Hollywood

Miami

0   5   10   20   30
Miles

FAU
VISUAL PLANNING
TECHNOLOGY LAB

Created Dec 2006
By: Jennifer L. Rosenberg

Disclaimer: The map is created from a subset of data from the Florida Geographic Data Library GIS database. The creator makes no claims, no representations, and no warranties, express or implied, concerning the validity, the reliability or the accuracy of the GIS data.

WRITINGS ABOUT RACE FROM THE FIELD

INTRODUCTION

These writers were part of teams that conducted Race and Change interviews for projects in the Lake Okeechobee, Delray Beach and Fort Lauderdale areas. In the classroom, the potential interviewers learned the theoretical and practical elements of oral history collection and studied the racial and ethnic demographics of the designated community and the issues raised by those changing cultural dynamics. In the field, they opened themselves to new ideas and change. After the memories were collected and transcribed, they set to work finding ways to blend aspects of their lives and personal reflections into some of the narrators' stories.

Vernon Dexter with interviewer Beverly Walker.
Photo by Natasha Pierre-Louis.

Glenn Malone is a Florida native who grew up in the Miami-Ft
Lauderdale metropolitan area. He received all of his education in
Florida's school system and is currently pursuing a Master's
degree. He dives, fishes and enjoys Florida's natural beauty when -
ever he can, which is never often enough, he says. He curses devel -
opers and the politicians they own. He also roots for alligators and
sharks in all of their encounters with humans. Go Greens!

Romanticism and Reality:
The Geographic Metaphor and Race

Glenn Malone

The majority of people, when they picture Florida, envision a state of
palm trees and beaches, high-rise hotels and golf courses, theme parks
and shopping meccas. They don't usually picture rural hamlets and large
tracts of farmland, with the occasional distant memory of a citrus grove
as a possible exception, but Florida is and always has been more than a
tourist destination. From its beginnings Florida has been an outstanding
combination of the exotic and the domestic, the cosmopolitan and the
provincial, the old and the new. Florida's history includes Conquistadors,
Pirates, various tribes of Native Americans, colonists, slaves and their
descendants, carpetbaggers, immigrants, migrants, land swindlers, cap-
tains of industry, refugees, astronauts and, yes, tourists. But no matter the
nature of the group or individual that inhabits the land, it is the geography of Florida that has had the most influence on its development.

Make no mistake, humanity itself is a group of beings forever defined
by physicality. At the core, each of us is a separate unit with a boundary
called a skin. We first define everything in terms of whether or not it is
within us or outside of us. Inner or outer, that is the essential model on
which we base the beginning of all our perceptions from infancy. Like
water, our perceptions flow to fill the ever-expanding vessel of our lives.
As we grow, we project this in-out paradigm on our surroundings, not
merely filling the vessel, but changing its shape in the process. We move
in and out of our cribs, in and out of our houses, to a wider environmental and social model that places us in and out of our community. Even if
there are no definable natural barriers, we create them. If the natural
geography isn't enough for us to quantify our relationship to the outside,
we make a road, a lake, a field, a canal or a building, which becomes the
symbol or metaphor for how we identify ourselves. Whether the bound-

ary is natural or fabricated, it is geography that provides the most constant of reference points for the definition of self in humanity, for how we see ourselves as a people, for how we see ourselves as a community.

As I set out to examine the metaphorical structures in the small rural communities surrounding Lake Okeechobee, a student researcher, collecting oral histories in a project sponsored by Florida Atlantic University, I was confident about the nature of the metaphorical patterns I would encounter. I would be taking an analytical look at the state I had lived in all my life — a comfortable little examination among the familiar and domestic images that I had seen, heard and been taught about all my life. As a "tail-end baby-boomer" born in the early '60s and raised in the eco-conscious and ethnically diverse environment of the Miami-Fort Lauderdale metropolis, I was self-assured and even somewhat arrogant in my expectations of what I would find. After all, I was a native. I had swum, fished, camped and boated in Florida all my life. I knew the plants and animals. I could name exotic birds for the ever-present visitors from the North. I could give reasonably accurate advice on fishing and diving. I could tell numerous stories about the local history and sometimes I could even get away with a tall tale or two. Skunk ape and shark stories are my favorites.

My parents, teachers, neighbors and friends had gone to great lengths to make me aware of the environment and community that surrounded me. For as long as I can remember, not a year went by where I hadn't been regularly exposed, indoctrinated if you will, to the environment and history of Florida. I was politically astute, socially progressive, environmentally aware and steeped in a mythic tradition that included Crane, Rawlings, Hurston, Hemingway, Stoneman-Douglas and countless other artists that made Florida their muse. I was a Romantic in the most expansive use of the term. Real Floridians were a part of the land. The ocean, the Everglades, the rivers and hammocks were what helped us to define ourselves. The spectrum of geography and climate that Florida offered, the range of races and ethnicities that have made Florida home, Florida's history and possible future were all an open book to me. I was naive. I was simplistic. I was wrong. As I was given an orientation to "The Glades" area and Lake Okeechobee, both areas that I had visited numerous times, I found an even deeper love and respect for the land. Tours of the Kissimmee River restoration project and lectures about "The Glades'" area reinforced the romantic notions that I had adopted as my own and had assumed others shared. But in the course of several interviews I found that a people that lived in the closest proximity to one of the largest geographic features on the North American continent, Lake Okeechobee, were able to gloss over the subject with the most perfunctory of comments. As Barbara Bell-Spence put it, "I knew nothing of the lake."

My God! The lake was everything. The lake was "The Beast" in Zora Neale Hurston's most famous novel, *Their Eyes Were Watching God*. The lake was the center of one of the greatest environmental and political issues of the last two decades. When pressed about the lake there were some admissions about a use of the lake for recreational fishing, but there was no all-consuming metaphorical relationship between the people and what I had perceived to be the center of the community. I had expected a string of magical pastoral metaphors with Lake Okeechobee as both the creator and the destroyer. I wanted an arcadian mythos adapted to the flat grassy expanses and the smooth blue waters of what was arguably one of the greatest natural wonders Florida has to offer. I wanted wise old farmers, intrepid fishermen and prophetic rural wisdom. What I had missed was that it is the community that creates the metaphors that define it. I was in the midst of a community, in the heart of the state, that had a greater interest in survival and defining itself economically and socially than in any high-flown mythic metaphor that a White boy from the outer skin of east coast had read about in his air-conditioned classrooms or seen on weekends and vacations.

The geographic metaphors were there to be found; that fact was true enough. However, the uncomfortable truth was that the metaphors that I found in the greatest profusion were geographic abstractions that I had never personally experienced and had conveniently relegated to the category of a wicked and shameful history. The population of "The Glades" area is predominately African American, southern, rural and composed of people who have lived and continue to live with the insidious metaphor of the color line. For me, color lines had always been historical, remote and devoid of any of the hurtful reality that they had in the past. Now, here were some of those lines, tangible, vivid and alive in the memories and lives of the people who survive with them, fight with them, endeavor to overcome them, and refuse to forget them.

Beyond the "Twenty Mile Bend"

On the southern edge of Lake Okeechobee lie the two small communities of Belle Glade and South Bay. Historically, both have deep roots in what the locals call "the muck," the rich black soil that makes the area ideal for year-round farming, and farming is still an essential part of the local economy. "Her Soil is Her Fortune" is a motto that both defines and limits the two communities. Agriculture as a primary source of employment is poor competition for more lucrative and less backbreaking work found outside the geographic boundaries of the communities. The major geographic boundary and metaphorical pattern that separates the communities from other outside communities is "Twenty Mile Bend." Essentially, "Twenty Mile Bend" is a curve in US 27 that is used to separate Belle Glade and South Bay from the coastal communities of Palm Beach County. Local resident Virginia Walker, one of the Race and Change narrators, explains "Twenty Mile Bend" as: "the way to West Palm . . . according to the County Commissioners it would be western Palm Beach County because the districts are set up in such a way that that is part of it."

The distance between the communities seems somewhat insignificant when traveling at 70 miles an hour from Fort Lauderdale to Belle Glade today, but when used as a geographic metaphor in the memories of a young Black girl's recollections of her father's confrontation with someone outside the community, the power of the landmark's symbolic meaning becomes evident. Barbara Bell-Spence, Assistant to the City Manager of Belle Glade at the time of her oral history interview, relates the following story that shows the geographic metaphor's power as a defining symbol of both the community's physical and social boundaries:

> *"As I said, my father was very active in the community, and my mother was very community-oriented too but she worked mostly through the church. She was a Sunday school teacher, an old mission society woman and she visited people. I mean she did all those things that most Christian-hearted women would do. She was a strong woman in herself, and she always taught us to be self-sufficient and independent. By the same token, my father was somewhat the same way, and he would tell the people that worked for him, 'When you go past Twenty Mile Bend on the other side and you listen to this stuff that people are telling you, don't bring that mess back with you past Twenty Mile Bend.'*
>
> *"He was very bold in a sense in telling people how he felt. As a matter of fact, Autrie Williams, who you probably will interview later on, will tell you of an instance where a deliveryman was bringing vegetables and stuff in and he asked to speak to the person in charge. When my father came down, [the delivery man] made a sly remark about, 'there's no White man here?' or something to that effect and he got 'put out.' I'm saying it nicely but it wasn't so nice the way he got put out. My father was the type of person who was self-assured, and he didn't take no crap off of nobody no matter what their race, color or creed was. He instilled those characteristics in me."*

The use of the "Twenty-Mile Bend" as a means of drawing a line between the Belle Glade/ South Bay community and the rest of the less agricultural, more commercial South Florida coastal communities is confirmed in later interviews with other long time residents such as Harvey J Poole, Sr., local radio personality and activist, and Lexie May Childs, retired housewife and Sunday School teacher. In answer to questions about changes in the community Poole comments on the expansion of economic interest from the outside with a reference to "Twenty Mile Bend": "They're moving this way . . . You see they've built up practically to 'Twenty Mile Bend' and they're going to make 'The Bend' heading this way. They've got no place else to go." Lexie May Childs confirms the existence of "Twenty Mile Bend," but sees the landmark as simply a spot on the highway, although she does hint at some other significance.

"I never knew nothing but it was the 'Twenty Mile Bend' . . . That's all I know. Now there were people here ahead of me that knew if they made it out to 'Twenty Mile Bend' they may have been out of the water or something like that but to me it didn't mean anything."

"Twenty Mile Bend" is clearly significant by virtue of the fact that it is recognized as an important means of identifying the area outside of the community by the community itself. In the metaphorical structure of "Twenty Mile Bend," the physical structure of a part of the highway leading in and out of the community is being used to conceptualize the nonphysical in terms that are physical. In essence, the clearly delineated piece of highway is helping to make clear the social and economic barriers that exist outside the community. Furthermore, "Twenty Mile Bend" serves to define not just the exterior barriers but helps to define the social unit of the community. Interestingly, the "Twenty Mile Bend" metaphor is cross-cultural in that it is recognized by members of the community and outsiders as well as by all the different ethnic groups within the community.

Obviously, Bell-Spence's concept of "Twenty Mile Bend" has more emotional and cultural significance than those of the other narrators because racism is associated with the metaphor. However, the "Twenty Mile Bend" is the mildest of the "color line" metaphors that were encountered in this project, and it is significant to note that because of the sweeping geographic nature of this metaphor, all racial groups are subject to its lines of delineation. It would seem that the less discriminating a "color line" line is, the greater the probability that the symbol may be rehabilitated into a source of positive community identification. Both Belle Glade and South Bay are communities that are striving to "get a sense of themselves" and a clearly defined metaphor such as "Twenty Mile Bend" may be just the type of tool that can be used to build a system of defining metaphors to aid the communities in this process.

Crossing "The Canal"

The clearest geographical metaphor that serves as a "color line" is found in the form of an irrigation canal that bisects the city of Belle Glade. Although it is no longer a barrier of any true significance, "The Canal" is clearly a historical symbol of racist policies that predate the Civil Rights Movement. Every community has a vestige of "The Canal" in some form or another, and as a metaphor it is unremarkable. When asked about the racial composition of the city of Belle Glade during her youth, Bell-Spence characterizes the city as, "Mixed, depending on the 'side of the tracks' or the side of the canal. The canal was basically our divide." There is a certain matter of fact presentation on the part of all the interviewees when questioned about "The Canal" and one gets a distinct impression that the rendering of "The Canal" to an empty and powerless symbol of past racist policy is a matter of triumph and pride. On two separate occasions with two different residents serving as guides around the city, "The Canal" was brought to the attention of the research group.

Lexie May Childs has a particularly utilitarian account of how she dealt with the issue of "The Canal" as a color line: "As I said, didn't bother me. If I worked for somebody on that side, I went on over there and worked. Nobody bothered me and I didn't bother nobody. And hey, I did my work and came back home." The particulars of segregation are often hard to relate to younger generations, according to Childs. She goes on to state that it is difficult to explain to her Sunday school students that she ate in the back of restaurants because they are too far removed from that time. "Because they were born in the '70s and '80s they can't see that, but it didn't bother us because we had done it for all our lives." The accounts of both Bell Spence and Childs give an indication of a metaphorical structure that is losing its potency due to a lack of shared experience. While individuals born in the 1970s and 1980s are certainly subject to and suffer the deprivations of racism in some form or another, a metaphor such as "The Canal" serves only as an historical reference point that may or not be related to present experience.

It would be a grave error to dismiss the metaphorical nature of "The Canal" as a representation of the "color line," however, just because there is no means of drawing a correlation between the historical example and current examples. Admittedly, the insidious nature of today's' "color lines" makes it more difficult to do. Childs may have been able to deal with "The Canal" because it was clear and defined. Today, the assigning of a credit rating, certain hiring practices or criminal profiling are highly abstract concepts that can easily be used to conceal institutional racism. If there is anything to be learned from the example of "The Canal" it is that the abstract concept of racism can easily outlive the rudimentary metaphors that were once used to symbolize it.

From "The Project" to "Uptown"

As stated before, the Belle Glade/South Bay area is a historically agricultural community. Because of the agricultural history, a metaphorical pattern has formed that draws a line between residents based on the type of employment that earlier residents found. In the African American community, the largest demographic group, the line is drawn between agricultural workers and business owners and professionals. Economic changes over the last 30 years have reduced the level of agricultural employment in the community as a whole, but the geographic metaphor of "The Project" and "Uptown" still exist. In fact, the issue is a rather contentious one for some narrators. Bell-Spence is the one interviewee that gives the most detailed description of "The Project" during her youth:

"At that time [it] was basically where all the farm workers lived; it was for farmers and people who worked in agriculture, and both of my parents at that time were farm laborers. The way we grew up we did not have, at that time, the luxury of in-house bathrooms or running water and things of that nature. We had what we called a "washhouse" which was a big building that had bathrooms in it. It had shower stalls, and it also had tubs and things that women used to wash their clothes. As time progressed, we were able to move to what we called a 'labor home,' which was really more of a duplex. That particular place had two bedrooms, a living room area, a kitchen area and we had a bathroom. We were able to get what I thought was a total luxury — a wringer washer — so at that time we were in 'hog heaven.' Then we moved to . . . they did what they called 'urban renewal' and redoing 'The Project' area and they took some of the old wooden houses, the one room type houses, and tore them down and actually built regular houses and we were able to move into a three-bedroom house."

While a considerable sector of the community lived in "The Project," there seems to have been some stigma attached to living there, she says:

"Among Blacks we even had our own class structure. Growing up, and being from 'The Project,' we were not as involved in community things as those that lived here in town. Very seldom did someone from 'The Project' become a debutante or [take part] in some of the elitist type of social groups that the sororities sponsored . . . things like that . . . [S]o we had our own little class system."

There was, however, a tight sense of community shared by the residents of "The Project" as witnessed by Bell Spence's description of holiday events:

"As far as my family was concerned, everyone was a neighbor. Everyone knew everyone. We knew everyone around us. A good example is on Christmas. We would cook all kinds of things and we would go house to house just to sample what 'Miss So and So' cooked here or what somebody cooked there . . . or somebody would have oranges here or apples there or maybe somebody would have pecans. Then, about 10 or 11 o'clock during the day, we would all congregate on this one road in 'The Project,' a real smooth road, and all the kids that had got new skates and bicycles and things like that would all get together and the bicycles would pull the skates. It was just one big happy family. Everybody, most of us, attended the same church, and we were all more like sisters and brothers than just neighbors. It was a selfish kind of thing because we really didn't share that experience with the ones in town."

Other residents see "The Project" as a geographic metaphor for community advancement and empowerment. Harvey J. Poole, Sr., administrator of the "Okeechobee Center" — also referred to as "The Project" — portrays the cluster of housing and recreational facilities as the center of a "renaissance" for the African American community. For Poole, issues between residents of "The Project" and "Uptown" do not exist. Indeed, collective community efforts are born of a collective geographic metaphor according to Poole. His details of the formation of The Belle Glade Interracial Council detail the benefits of collective action on the part of the African American community:

> *"We realized what the Whites were doing . . .who had all the economic security; they controlled it, but with all that they couldn't pick all those beans. They couldn't cut all that cabbage or all that cane. They needed the Blacks to do the work. We decided they were going to treat us right. So we formed the Belle Glade Interracial Council . . . It was to bring about a mutual understanding between people."*

Unlike Bell-Spence, Poole's use of "The Project" as a metaphor involves the definition of political and economic power. For Poole, "The Project" is not so much a place to live as it is an area in which to recruit and organize political and economic power.

Not all residents of the Belle Glade/South Bay area see "The Project" in such a positive light, however. Lexie May Childs's attitude toward "The Project" is indicative of the "Uptown" perspective. When asked about "The Project," Childs hints at the schism between the "Uptown" residents and "The Project" residents that is detailed earlier by Bell-Spence:

> *"I never lived in 'The Project.' I never lived in the center. When I left that two room shack down there, I moved to my own house. And that's been 40, 50 years ago. I never lived in 'The Project,' so a lot of people, you knew them and that's that. You see them, you saw them, but that's it."*

Childs's attitude towards "The Project" is characterized by an individualism that places a premium on personal action:

> *"I always been a kind of . . . I guess . . . 'get up and go.' [Poole] might have had some information I needed, and I go around to 'The Project' and asked him about something I needed to know. But just to be around in that environment — that wasn't me."*

Clearly, perceptions of "The Project" as a metaphor vary with the individual's experience in the structure of the metaphor. Bell-Spence associates "The Project" with home and community, Poole sees it as a metaphor for community and collective political/economic action, and Childs sees it as a sometimes useful, but relatively undesirable encroachment upon her individualism. Despite the differing views exhibited towards this geographic metaphor, "The Project" maintains metaphorical coherence as a center for the entire community. All references to "Uptown" are made in relation to "The Project," thus subordinating "Uptown" to a secondary metaphor that encompasses a group within the community.

The importance of the opposing metaphors of "The Project" and "Uptown" lies in the implied expansion of the community, allowing individuals to define themselves within a growing collective body. The primary basis for this division is an economically driven need to exert independence and move beyond the comfort of the collective existence that is characteristic of agricultural communities to an entrepreneurial and professional model that favors individualism. Belle Glade and South Bay are striving to grow and expand beyond the agricultural structures that have limited them in the past, while attempting to preserve the rich history and culture that is based in a rural tradition. The competition between the geographic metaphors of "The Project" and "Uptown" are a precise illustration of this dynamic. My recognition of the need for progress and change in these communities is in part due to my awareness of the impact of racist policies that perpetuated the imposition of an outmoded agricultural economy upon the residents of Belle Glade and South Bay. Agriculture is vital; this is true, but a progressive and forward thinking populace cannot rely upon a single resource to ensure the continued survival and growth of a community.

I come from an urban area and from a family that has not had a significant involvement in agriculture for at least fifty years. My elders have pleasant memories of idyllic rural bliss, and my limited personal experiences as a child reinforce this romantic myth. I'm sure if I were able to interview members of my family three generations back I would lose some of the misty-eyed bucolic visions. If I were to add to that infusion of the realities of agricultural life the oppression of racism, I am sure I would race back to the suburbs at a speed that would be alarming. But I still envy the people of Belle Glade and South Bay in their evolving rural communities. Somehow I think that the need for progress will not completely dominate that which is best about the natural splendor of the land around them, and that the metaphorical structures that embody the evil of the "color line" will also evolve into historical symbols that remind, instruct and enlighten the posterity of Belle Glade and South Bay. Perhaps there is room for a little romanticism.

Beverly Walker received an A.A. degree in Elementary Education from Miami-Dade College and a B.A. in Arts and Humanities from Florida Atlantic University where she earned an M.A. in Liberal Studies with a focus on Ethnic Studies. Her experience in the Race and Change oral history project made her realize the importance of preserving people's stories and encouraged her to share her own.

FAITH, CHURCH AND THE MULTICULTURAL COMMUNITY

Beverly Walker

As far back as I can remember, church was always a part of my life. I have only two memories of myself at age three or younger. In one, I am sitting on a chair in the narthex of a church, just inside the front door, and my mother is tying my shoe. When I recounted my memory of this as an adult, my mother told me I could have been no older than three because we joined a different church around that time. We moved a few times during my childhood, but my mother and I always belonged to a Catholic Church wherever we lived. By the time I was seven, my three sisters were married and living in Connecticut and my parents and I moved to Florida. My father never attended church with my mother and me, which I just accepted as something he didn't do. But his lack of participation influenced how religion affected our daily life. When I was young, my mother would pray with me before I went to bed and teach me songs like "Jesus Loves Me." But we never prayed before meals or had any religious discussions that I can remember that involved my father. From fifth through eighth grade, I attended the school at our church — all of my friends went to the same church and school. My fondest memories are of our Christmas programs and singing in the choir. This was probably the most intense period of faith formation of my life up to that point. In an environment where God was being discussed and prayers said on a daily basis, I became increasingly more aware of God's presence in my life.

My mother became more involved in the church also at this time, including becoming a "Fisher." The name comes from the biblical account of Jesus calling Simon and Andrew and saying, "Follow me and I will make you fishers of men." What she did was "fish" for families who were listed as church members but the children were not attending religion classes. Through this, she encountered needy families whom she helped by giving rides, buying food, and providing other financial assist a n c e. This had a lasting influence on me as we were not well off. After I graduated from eighth grade, I spent two years in a Catholic high school and two years in a public school. These years brought new friends and activities but I continued to attend church and began teaching first grade religion class. Teaching deepened my faith in some ways but also made me begin to question some of the things I had learned. The issues that I had were not related to anything biblical, but rather, practices and rules of the Catholic Church such as confessing sins to a priest, the ban on birth control, and praying to saints. Although I lived at home while attending community college, I joined a different Catholic Church that had a very upbeat service with guitars, modern music, and a dynamic pastor and this seemed to satisfy my doubts — for the time being.

After I got married and started a family, it was important to me to teach our children about God and to belong to a church. But as my doubts — which began in high school — kept resurfacing, I began to explore other Christian denominations. My husband, although baptized Catholic, had not attended church as a child. I read the Bible and studied different denominations to find a place where we would both be happy. We chose a United Church of Christ Church, a liberal denomination, near our house in North Miami and joined in 1976. For our family, the church was our extended family. Our two youngest children were baptized there. Our baby-sitters were teenagers from the church. Both my husband and I became very active in the church, which was very much involved in social ministry to an extent I had not been exposed to before. Prior to coming to this church, my previous worship experiences had been almost completely with other Whites and Hispanics. But by the time we left in 1982 to move to Broward County, we probably had four or five Black families who were members. I don't remember that anyone ever commented on this fact or thought it unusual and I assumed that other churches were becoming integrated, also. But I was surprised that the new church we began going to had no Black members at all.

While I was appreciative of the emphasis on social ministry in our former church, I felt something was lacking spiritually and when we moved we chose a Lutheran congregation. This church had a stronger emphasis on spiritual development and I began attending weekly Bible classes and reading the Bible at home on a daily basis. I became active in a number of committees and groups as well and my children attended the church run school. All that changed four years later. The church's school closed due to dwindling enrollment and the pastor began a movement to sell the church and move to western Broward; at the same time, some of the members began moving out of the older eastern neighborhood and buying new homes further west. The issue caused a division in the congregation between those of us who felt that our mission was right there and those who wanted to sell the church and move.

The proposal was voted down and the church remained in the same location but the congregation was depressed and angry from the battle. We were unable to focus our attention away from the internal problems caused by the division in order to successfully minister to the community. The church continued to lose members. A few years later, a merger with a Hispanic congregation that had been meeting at another church brought about 20 new members, but they were not from the surrounding neighborhood. By the time I left in 1999, there was an average attendance at the English language service of about 12 people, while the Spanish service had grown only slightly and maybe one or two of the surviving members, besides the pastor, still lived in the neighborhood. There were few activities besides Sunday Service and Sunday School.

When I became involved as an interviewer in the Lake Okeechobee Race and Change Project, I began reflecting on my own religious experience and chose religion as the focus of my study. The Race and Change Project consisted of conducting oral history interviews with residents of Belle Glade, South Bay and Pahokee, an area of adjacent small towns at the southern rim of Florida's massive Lake Okeechobee. From our scores of narrators I selected the oral histories of people of different ethnic backgrounds including two African Americans, two Jamaican Americans, one White, and one Filipino. I wanted to see how their faith experiences as children and as adults had influenced their lives. I was also interested in how their churches interacted with the community and what kind of changes they had seen in the church they attended. I found, in the process, that I learned a great deal from them.

I always thought you had to travel to another country to be a missionary, but Gloria Williams, an African American who was born in Belle Glade and grew up in Bean City, a migrant area, describes her early life and how the influence led her to be a missionary right in her own community. She is a member of The Greater Union Missionary Baptist Church in South Bay:

> *"We would come together, every Sunday morning in my family. My parents would cook biscuits, steak, eggs, and coffee and you had to be around the breakfast table on Sunday mornings for prayer and it was a must that you be in church starting with Sunday School, and you were not late. I'm thankful for that part of my life because it has kept me to be the person that I am, I believe, today because of that background early in life, knowing who was in charge of our lives.*
>
> *"Community life around the lake was a life of family because even within your family, when you would visit the different neighborhoods from Belle Glade, South Bay, Lake Harbor, Ritter, there was a connection because it was very religious-oriented. On Sundays and Wednesday you would always go to church. And there were always church suppers and other activities which brought the*

community together. . . . My parents were my role models. Outside of what they taught me, the only role model I have is Jesus.

"The churches, they have different ways of helping. I know the church in Belle Glade that I was a member of, Mount Calvary, to assist with needs of the community has what they call Heaven's Breadbasket where they feed the families a hot meal on Monday and give them a bag of groceries. I've been instrumental in giving them clothes for their church. We have the different mission societies. If there is a problem in the community and the churches know about it, the churches reach out to help those families. The churches work together closely with different programs . . . to make sure all the other churches' needs are being met.

"The churches have different services letting members and the community know that to be judgmental against one another is not the way God wants us to live. They are preaching that togetherness is what we should have because in a time like the crisis that we are in now, the churches are telling them . . . to continue to do what God has asked them to do — to pray for one another, to help one another. Not to hate, because hatred for one race or the other brings about the things that are going on in the world today. So, I think the churches are being instrumental in teaching God's word so that people will understand that if we hate one another then we will destroy one another.

"As a missionary, I don't see people of color. I just see people. Because God says, 'Love ye one another as I have loved you.' It's not easy to love everybody, but then I think about, in spite of everything that I've done in life, He still loves me. So I got to love everybody. And if you mistreat me, I got to ask Him to help me to . . . love you regardless. And so as a missionary and accepting Jesus into your life, you can look at people as yourself and you won't show any distinction between races. You won't like what they're doing. He didn't tell me that I had to like everything. But he said I had to love you in spite of . . . And, so that's just the way I come out of my shell, because Jesus loves me. If he loves me, I got to love you, also. You don't have to go around telling everybody that you're a missionary, that you're Christians, or wear a sign. He said, 'Let your light shine so others can see a difference in you' . . . It's the life that you live, it will speak for you. And so that brings me out of my shell knowing that the person that I used to be, that person is dead."

Bazil Anderson is a 62-year-old self-described Jamaican American from South Bay. Like my mother, his parents also were generous in sharing what they had with others:

"My earliest memories in . . . Jamaica were my parents and the impact my parents had on my life as well as the other eleven siblings in my family. They were Christian people. Ever since I knew, my family, church, and Christianity was a very intricate part of their life and so they instilled it in us as kids. At eating time we ate together. There was always grace at the table. We woke up with a

prayer service in the home and usually we go to bed having prayer together. Very often as young people it didn't fit in our itinerary, but it was their way or no way.

"Discipline in our home was going to be there every time. It was unquestionable — whatever dad or mom says was what we did. Wrong or right. So we were always wherever they wanted us to be whenever we were supposed to . . . I had maybe two or three good friends. . . . We stood out as young boys who were just seven eight, nine, 10 years old and we were looked upon as being different. For some reason the other kids thought we were different. Maybe we were. These were other boys who go to church . . . and as their parents were as strict on them as they were on us, that maybe was what kept us together.

"During my growing up period, my parents had been a part of the church. My dad became the pastor. My mom was . . . always accounting for the money, always writing the minutes of the different organizations in the church. I remember vividly how helpful many of the members of the church were to my family, and as I grew up more I realized that a part of the reason for that was because my parents had been so helpful to so many people in the community. Whatever we had, they felt that other kids should have the same thing, and sometimes it sort of made us as young people upset because we felt that there were things that we should have had that they were giving away and we thought we needed it. But they knew that we could do without it, so they gave it away — if it was a worn shoe or some worn clothing or whatever, or sometimes new clothing. Food was always in our house. And Mom would be always preparing some to go. Sometimes we weren't too happy because we were planning on what we were going to do with that food later on. So those are some of the things that I remember that Mom and Dad really got us involved in early and somehow we have all come to try to give back to the community something."

Anderson moved from Jamaica to South Bay in 1979 and joined Mt. Zion A.M.E. Church in nearby Belle Glade. He has been a member ever since.

"I think [Christian upbringing] laid a lot of groundwork for discipline that parents enforce and the church enforce, so you go through life thinking, Why should I do something which society is not going to accept? Do I really want to do that? I've been taught all along. I've been reading the Bible. I've been preached to by the preacher and he says it's wrong. Do you really want to do that? No. So that has sort of built a strong sense of what's wrong and right within me. And not just in stealing something. But even at work people think you're different . . . because you do what the company expects you to, what your employer expects you to do, and even a little more, if you can. You try to be as honest as you can be. [Mt. Zion A.M.E. Church has] a health fair . . . we have a feeding program, we have a literacy program, a tutoring program. The young people have stayed away from the church and the men, especially, are not in the church as much as they used to be. Every effort we get we try to recruit more men to be active."

I remember the fellowship and camaraderie I experienced as a youngster working at church fairs and dinners, but my church never had a "toe party" like the one Harvey Poole, Sr., an 88-year-old African American who came to "The Glades" in 1931, remembers:

> *"I've lived in some larger communities in my moving about, but the church has always been the cultural development center of the communities where we lived. . . . We had entertainment for our kids which they laugh at you now when they hear about it. I'll tell you about a toe party. You would fix a box that you would take to this party with enough food in it for two people. Then I would buy a ticket and pull a ribbon, you'd have a ribbon tied around your toe and if I got the ribbon that matched your toe then we ate together. That's called a toe party. That's the way churches used to raise money. And it had our young people involved in it that way. It gave them something to do."*

Christianity had a profound effect on Poole's life after a traumatic event. As he explains: "I witnessed a lynching in front of a house there in Georgia in 1919. So that created a lot of ill feeling in me. But thank God, in 1923 I accepted Christ as my savior and removed all the hate out of my heart."

Like Anderson, he also is a member of Mt. Zion A.M.E. Church. He has been there since 1939.

> *"Well, even with single parent families nowadays, you still have some folks that are still trying to be role models, male and female. You take in our church, we have a group that is known as Men of Adam and they go about and do things for youth in the community. Not necessarily in the A.M.E. Church . . . but in the community and other churches. They meet at other churches [and] put on programs . . . trying to bring kids around to get the right perspective in life. And we need more of that."*

Vernon Dexter is 77 years old, White, and was born in Salt Lake City, Utah. He moved to Belle Glade after World War II in 1948 and he talks about friendships back in those days:

> *"I think people back in the early days tended to develop friendship based on their religious affiliations — because they would have more in common . . . I think that basically those people here pretty much did things along either the civic activities like your social clubs or your churches because that would be where you would come in contact. . . . Certainly, I would not say that all my friends were of my faith per se, but naturally many of my good friends were, and I would think the same for other people. In the earliest phases of Belle Glade as I remember, from then up until the '60s, the churches were very active. Again, one has to recognize . . . the lifestyle changes that have occurred. Back in those early days there was no television, and there was not other things to draw you away.*

. . . There really weren't the distractions that we have today so you had a stronger community of activity within the framework of the population here that you do not have today."

Dexter belonged to St. Mary's Catholic Church in Pahokee until St. Philip's opened in Belle Glade in 1951. Like me, he has witnessed segregation in the church. He talks about this and the demographic changes that have occurred in the area:

"I would say probably up until, oh probably 1960, then it started changing. And I think basically the reasoning for the change was the population began to change, as we had a change in the Cuban government down there and the people started migrating away from Cuba. The crop and farming situation was in a state of flux at that time where it had gone from — up to and through the war — vegetables of various types, leaf crop, beans, celery, what have you. After the war, the economics being such, that product didn't sell too well so many of the farmers went into cattle . . . and we had through the early '50s, we had the largest cattle market in the state of Florida out here north of town. . . . But cattle then began to drift away when they discovered, with the advent of the Cuban government change, [that] sugar cane would grow here as well as it did. Many of the farmers moved their cattle off and went back into sugar cane. . . . And that changed the makeup of the community. . . . So we had a lessening of the population in here, a change, in other words, a state of flux here that was some of them leaving and some coming in. Now, what generally came back as they would leave, what would come in here would be basically the Cuban national that had immigrated from Cuba to here that was sugar-oriented, that had knowledge of sugar — how to grow and how to cut and how to process. Those people came in, so you had a change from a pure Anglo-American to a mixed group of people in here and much today the community is of that origin.

"There's been a slow down in the number of people attending [church] . . . other things to occupy their time. The people who have come in [to Belle Glade] have not filled that void. . . . [The churches] are still segregated, by choice, not because it has to be, but people want to be associated with their own kind . . . St. Phillips has a strong Cuban and Haitian influence but some of the other churches don't have that. Of course, the Episcopal Church is integrated, but the Presbyterian Church has closed and the Lutheran church is ready to close. There are lots of little mom and pop churches, mostly Black and Hispanic."

Natividad Perez was born and raised in the Philippines and moved to Pahokee, a few miles to the north of Belle Glade and South Bay, in 1991. Like me, she was raised Catholic and she describes the influence it had on her:

"It made me a better person . . . I am a Catholic by birth and I was brought up in a Catholic school. That's why whenever there is a time that they need my serv-

ice, I am there. I am the organist in St. Mary's Catholic Church. I teach
Confirmation on Saturday for the little kids who are taking catechismal instruction, from the sixth graders. And on Wednesdays I have my seventh and eighth
graders for the Confirmation class. And that might be the reason why I want to
stay in Pahokee, because I have a mission to do."

St. Mary's reaches out to the community and, Perez says, that is
what she likes most about her church:

*"We participate in every community festival and the Christmas parade. . . . [We]
opened a preschool and afterschool program. We built a clinic in 1994 or 1995
when the hospital closed, a free clinic for migrant workers. It has a dentist and
x-ray room. A doctor comes every other Saturday to check the migrant workers."*

Reverend Clifford C. Davis, is 70 years old and moved from Jamaica
to the Lake Okeechobee area about 43 years ago. He has been the pastor of the Wesleyan Community Holiness Church in Belle Glade for
twenty-three years. My church debated the issue of the location of our
ministry. Rev. Davis considers his ministry to be right where he is. He
has seen positive changes in the church and describes how his church
ministers to the community. Davis begins by talking about his childhood in Jamaica:

*"We attended St. Faith's Elementary School and St. Mary's Jr. & Sr. High
School . . . I attended the Catholic Church. We were very religious people . . . we
have Whites and we have Blacks in both schools but we never have any kind of
segregation, nothing like that. We sit together, we eat together, play together. .
. . My mother, she kept a Sunday School every evening and all the neighborhood
would come and my grandmother does the same. . . . If we failed to show respect
to anybody, especially someone who is your elder, we would be reprimanded for
it. . . . You had to show respect to people. As a matter of fact, we're taught that
at home [and] we're taught the same thing at school.*
 *"I have seen some changes in the churches. In 1959, those were during the
Civil Rights [Movement] years when segregation was very high, the churches
were segregated, the schools were segregated and other public places, and these
five men went to a certain church and they were not expected to be there and
they did not verbally tell them to leave but they were cold toward them. So the
next Sunday they went back. But when they went back, they were flogged, they
were beaten. They used some strip from tires and they flogged those men, and
nothing came of it. Later on, so many years after, I was living in Belle Glade
then and this young lady she was trying to write a paper on the culture of the
different churches, the Black and White. And she went to a church in Belle
Glade. She sat through Sunday School and when the time came for the service to
start the minister told her, he said, 'I'm sorry you have to leave because the congregation doesn't mix.' And she had to leave the church. And there was a big*

write-up in the paper. . . . Those are the negative things. I have seen now where Black people now are members of White churches and White people also attend or have visited Black churches. It never used to be like that. So this is one of the big changes that really took place. . . . Now, I have seen White people even come to my church because we are friends and we get along real good. I invited them and they come. . . . As a matter of fact we have what you call a Fifth Sunday Community Service. I am a member of the Belle Glade Ministerial Association and every fifth Sunday we go to one of these churches, Black churches, white churches, all of us come together as a congregation in those churches and we fellowship there. And the Ministerial Association meets at Belle Glade in the conference room and people of different color belong to the association . . . I've always said that if the proper changes are to be made, they will be made only when the people of God, the churches, come together and be a part of this and these are some of the things that I can see happening.

"What we do as a church, and of course I am a part of this also, we does a lot of outreach. Outreach in ministering to people. Outreach in visitation. Outreach in benevolence. We have a place in Belle Glade called the Lighthouse Cafe where we feed the needy people. Every morning, that happens six days a week, Monday through Saturday, six o'clock in the morning it opens up. . . . The Ministerial Association, we pay our dues and it goes into a treasury, has some funds for emergency uses. What we as a church does in that area . . . we have street meetings at the loading ramp in Belle Glade that's between Fifth and Sixth Street . . . and we invite the community. We set up platforms and speakers . . . not just my church but the churches in the community . . . and speak to them and we give out literature to the people and we try to counsel with them . . . sometimes we cook and prepare food for them. As a result of this we have seen people come into the church. I'm centrally located in Belle Glade. I could have moved from there because the headquarters asked me if I'm ready for an appointment somewhere, but I said no . . . I believe that the ministry is right here and I want to serve the people who are in need and this is a needy area."

When my church voted to remain in the same location, those of us who were in favor of it felt that our mission was right there, but we did not see ourselves as missionaries like some of the people interviewed. I think the expectation was that the people would come to us. As these narrators told their stories, I realized that each of their churches reach out in one way or another to their community. This is not solely for humanitarian reasons, but as part of their religious beliefs. Jesus says in the Bible "for I was hungry and you gave me food, I was thirsty and you gave me drink, I was a stranger and you welcomed me, I was naked and you clothed me, I was sick and you visited me, I was in prison and you came to me. . . . Truly, I say to you, as you did it to one of the least of these my brethren, you did it to me" (Matthew 25: 34–36, 40).

One afternoon when I was taking a snapshot of St. Philip's Church for this project, a priest came over to speak to me. I told him what I was doing and he told me that the church is too small to seat the people and they have to set up chairs in the aisles to fit everyone in. I asked, "Well, that's a good thing, right?" He nodded in agreement. The church had responded to the need in the community with both Haitian and Hispanic ministries. If they had not done this, they may not have had to worry about the extra chairs. Whether it is feeding the hungry, providing health care, youth activities, or preaching the word of God in other languages, these congregations are finding ways to bring people together.

I am now a member of a Lutheran church where the pastor believes that each member should have a ministry. The members are constantly challenged to "go outside of their comfort zone" and reach out to those outside the church. Ministering to those in prison, feeding the hungry, and providing shelter for homeless families are just some of the many opportunities that members have to serve others. As I listened to the recorded oral histories and wrote about these narrators, I realized how much I was learning from them. It is easy to overlook the need in a community because it can be overwhelming. It is difficult to forgive those who have hurt you and challenging for most people to share their faith with others. Ministering to people of different ethnic and racial backgrounds in an area that is often neglected can be difficult. But these people have shown that this can be done. Their stories of service and how they share their faith are helping me to redefine my mission in the community and hopefully, like them, I will work through my church to help make some positive changes.

Clarence (Clare) Bornstein is completing an M.A. in British and American Literature from Florida Atlantic University in the Spring of 2006. His plan is to teach part-time while he returns to, and pur - sues a neglected dream to develop and build real estate. Writing, however, will remain a major objective. He says that the oral history work, "remains an unforgettable experience. Something opened up in me which, heretofore, was inaccessible prior to the Race and Change project. Without the encouragement and support and train - ing [I received], writing would not be the important part of my life that it is now."

ANTI-SEMITISM AND BLACK RACISM: BLACK AND WHITE IMAGES

Clare Bornstein

The man and woman are near their four-score biblical life span with the end in sight, yet short of being contemplated. Irene is financially secure in her retirement and lives what appears to be a calm, serene, and giving life driven by service to others. On the other hand, Clare lives a stressful life that eludes a calm agenda and any retirement dreams. But both of their life experiences, in some way, were shaped by unpleasant racial experiences. They met as narrator and interviewer in the Race and Change oral history project in the Belle Glade, FL/Lake Okeechobee area.

Irene Clay is a retired African American educator. She is self-confident, dignified, and exhibits a sense of assuredness about her value and place on the plant. It is surprising how her moral strength and spiritual resolve have evolved *from* her experiences with racism. If her own encounters with the Jim Crow laws in Florida, in the '40s weren't enough, she endured the effects of those same laws on her two bright, strong daughters in the early '60s. But she seems to have no anger, no remorse, just respect and love for herself and others.

> *"I'm the most important person in the world, and you should be too. I tell my girls, if you don't feel good about yourselves, why do you think I am going to think well of you. From that position I can only respect and value each person I come into contact with in my daily routine."*

Clare Bornstein is a retirement-age White Jewish male who has just resigned after three and a half years of teaching high school. Listen to his musings and sense an articulate and introspective man who isn't convinced he has earned the right to occupy his place on the planet:

I scratch out a living with no retirement in place and am confused about my future. Living in Canada, when I was a child, I endured physical and emotional attacks from my mother and father. As I was to learn later, these brutal attacks were triggered by their inherent instability and a reaction to the ethnic slurs from their customers who tormented my parents and who then vented their rage upon me. I am confused where I can go with the rest of my life: I wrote in my journal a few weeks ago, I ain't worth a shit, just to see if I really believed what I have been telling myself all these years. It certainly didn't feel good to say it but I wanted to get it out of my head and spoken. My parents taught me that I was stupid and incapable of anything.

The worthless script influenced the rest of my life. I believed I had no skills to be successful, just a talent for creating chaos and confusion in my life. I was a latchkey child, which meant I came home from school, around three, no one was there. I would get the skeleton key from under the coco mat at the back door, let myself in, and run upstairs and hide under the blankets on my bed because I was afraid to be alone. They worked at the store, and if I saw them, it was about 7 or 8 pm. After school, when I was a little older, I would walk downtown to the train station and sit on a bench in the depot and hope that someone from the debarking four or five late afternoon trains would take me home with them and care for me. I searched for a loving, inviting face that would whisk me away from my unhappy world. No one claimed me. I thought I had been given to the wrong family and it was up to me to find the right parents who would guide, teach, and love me. Even now, many years later, I look at a pretty woman's face, hoping we can have an accepting, supportive, and loving connection.

It got worse for me after the war when my mother was home a little more. She was always angry with me. She continually had something bad to tell my father about me. He would come down to the basement where she threw me almost daily, and he would punch and kick me. My mother and father ran a small men's wear store during the Second World War in a Canadian ghetto populated, in the main, by immigrants. The clientele was eastern European, people who came to Windsor to work in the car factories. They sure didn't like Jews. A few years ago, I was told in a Shame and Guilt workshop that often Jews who were victims of racial inequities and verbal violence took out their pain, anger, and frustration on their children in physically violent and emotionally destructive ways. The immigrants abused my parents and they discharged their frustration on me. By the time I got to grade eight, I was convinced that I was worth-

less and bad and deserved the treatment I was getting. I believed I was incapable of doing right. I was a good Pavlovian dog.

Irene's aunt, on the other hand, raised her, her two sisters, and her one brother in West Palm Beach.

"My mother and father didn't want us, so my aunt, who considered us a blessing, adopted the three of us. My auntie protected and kept us away from the degrading actions of the Whites as much as she could. The neighborhood had a circle of protection that provided activities, through the churches, after school and on the weekends, to keep the children occupied and involved with their own kind. The modus of the circle was to try and avoid, and filter out racially unpleasant experiences that the children might encounter. When my husband and I had our own family, we had a circle of friends and we did the same thing Auntie had done, and the whole group was protective of each other's family. We would plan activities for the children to do our events in a supervised area, and nothing was done haphazardly. We did not run into the racism too often, only when we went into town to pay bills. From time to time we would encounter it and feel the harshness of the White man's hatred. In town there was Black and White fountains and I would drink from the illegal fountains. I don't know why, I just did it.

"In our Black enclaves we shielded family and friends. We isolated the children from some of the angst of the Florida Crackers. I remember attempting to eat at the restaurants and the waitresses were not willing to serve African Americans. The upshot was that when we traveled we packed brown bag lunches to circumvent the indignities when we interacted with the Whites. In the main, it was important that we didn't make trouble and knew how and when to keep our mouths shut."

Irene tells of a specific memory of racial encounter that stands out for her.

"I have always tried to overlook the separateness that racism promotes. When I was fifteen, I volunteered to work at St. Mary's Hospital, in West Palm Springs. It had to be around 1943. I thought differently about race because you did not see race there. I was able to have friends among the younger people. They would come to my home and I would visit theirs and I think that prepared me for what was coming later on. I acted as if what was happening between the races was not existent."

As for Clare:

My encounters with my racial foes were not quite as empowering as Irene's. Paul White, a school buddy, and I had a symbiotic relationship. We walked to school sideways, back-to-back protecting his Black ass and my White ass. If we hadn't we probably wouldn't be here now. Ethnics like us needed to, literally and figuratively, face our realities and protect our posteriors. So, back-to-back, we walked to school sideways and that way we had a commanding 360-degree view of our Jewish and Black realities. At 15, Paul was 6'2" mulatto, drop dead gorgeous; his biological father must have been Errol Flynn. I, on the other hand, at 12, was 5'2" and rotund, handsome by most standards, and sturdy mind you, but rotund. Once at school nobody bothered Paul. He was quiet and serious looking and he managed to keep his stern-looking face to the maddening crowd and they left him alone. For me it was a different story. I was fair game and the day's entertainment. The bigger boys would approach me and push me down. They had a way of shoving me on the chest so that I always fell backwards and the back of my head would hit the concrete. I would reach back and wonder why my head wasn't split open, it hit so hard.

On my neighborhood streets my mother told me to kick the Gentile boys who picked on me. I kicked them in the shins, when I was threatened, and then ran like hell. I wondered why my mother advocated the kick-and-run strategy, rather than punching the big bully in the face, surprising him, putting up a fight, getting a bloody nose, proving my mettle, and winning the day like the bully scenarios in the movies. I guess dirty Jews were cowards and didn't fight. That was the message I got. It was a strategy that didn't build my self-esteem and I remember how turning tail always bothered me. I was not a responsible confrontation and it sent the poorest of messages to my adversary and me. I wanted to face the results of my actions and grow from the experience. I was developing instincts but there was no logic to this current mess called my life.

My Bar Mitzvah training was another kind of torment. I was occupied four days a week and all day Saturday with memorizing and learning the Hebrew chants for the ceremony. The speech after the religious rituals was designed to acknowledge and honor the role my parents played in my life. The words that Rabbi Dubitsky gave me to memorize for my little speech almost make me sick. The facts were so far removed from reality. After the ceremony my father took me in the kitchen of our small synagogue and relieved me of my Bar Mitzvah money, stripping the bills from the cards that had my gifts in them. He used my presents to pay the caterers, and emptied the envelopes in front of me. A couple of years later I ran away from home, so fucking battered I was punchy.

Irene was more fortunate. She got her Bachelor of Science degree from St. Augustine College in Raleigh NC.

"After I got my degree in teaching I came to Belle Glade to teach for a year or two and I met and married my husband. We had two daughters and both of us were interested in protecting them emotionally and teaching them how to survive the racial oppression. We did everything we could to shield them from racism's ugliness. My husband and I were affiliated with different churches. He attended an all Black Methodist church and attended and all White Episcopalian church. I remember when I arrived on Sunday morning; a core of White males

stood up and left the service, making their White apartheid statement. I remained and made my all-of-humankind-are-created-equal-stand, equally clear. It was obvious to me that racial climate in Belle Glade was the same as Chicago or any place in the country.

"As I mentioned before, I followed the strategy my aunt had established for us and sheltered the young ones and minimized their contact with the White community and kept them focused on positive things. My husband and I managed, to a large extent, and kept the children insulated from the outside world. We always wanted to support the children and develop their interracial skills so they would be better prepared to enter and function, in a positive way in Whitey's world. My husband would drive our daughters to the poorest ghettos and show them the shacks and the degradation of the Blacks that were trying to survive at the lowest economic level. He then explained to them that this is not the world we prepared you for, and this wasn't what your mother or I expected for you. He was more dictatorial than I was, but he was sensitive to the children's troubles and seemed to always have time to listen to them.

"My husband was very supportive of me. When I was working on my master's, we agreed that I would go off to different parts of the country to attend classes when I was working towards my master's. He said I could go wherever I wanted to go during the summers and I would pick different schools so I could see the world. One summer at Northwestern University in Chicago was the worst summer I spent in my life. No one talked to me and there were no Blacks, just Whites all over. If I talked to someone, it was like talking to the wall.

"Another experience that I remembered with pain was a bathroom stop that I made on a road trip with my then six-year-old daughter. I asked the attendant for the keys to the Black-only bathroom that my daughter needed to use. The bathroom was so utterly filthy that my little girl told me, Mommy I don't have to go any more. I was pained and heart-broken so I put my baby back into the car and turned around and brought her home. Later my other daughter attended Kent State University. She said she went into the lounge at school and there were a group of Mexican immigrants working there for peanuts and she heard them say, 'I don't know what these girls come up here for. She's probably on welfare.' My daughter felt awful. Ironically, one of my daughters has a master's and the other has a doctorate. The world is a confusing place but I don't go to bed mad, although I could have a lot to be mad about.

"A pervasive problem [though] that has serious impact is that all discipline has been taken out of the schools. Parents can't tell their children what to do. The kids are out of control. When I taught I made sure every child who left my classroom could read. I don't know what happened, but the reading scores have gone down and that bothers me. Something is happening to our educational system; I don't know what it is, but it needs to be remedied. Even though I was in adult education for the last ten years prior to retirement, my formula for success in the classroom is to give the parent back their authority.

"The United States is going downhill and White Americans stay back in their ethnic groups. An even more destructive behavior is that White folks are not aware that they make racist comments when they chat with you. I haven't seen them myself, but people tell me the Ku Klux Klan meet regularly on the coast in the wooded areas. We now have Black and White commissioners in Belle Glade and they have managed to hire a Black native son as city manger. The police department now has some African Americans on staff. [But] to tell you the truth, there haven't been many changes. Racially, improvements are hard to see, very delicate. The Whites are tolerable but not wholly accepting. There are a few of them that are, but the majority are not."

In Clare's case:

Anti-Semitism has been with me a long time. My first job was doing cleanup work for a fledgling VW dealership. That was in the early '50s and I believed that menial job was all I was qualified for. All the mechanics were ex-German soldiers and officers and one salesperson was an ex-Luftwaffe pilot. They wondered what this young "Jude" was doing sweeping floors. I felt out of place and I knew they thought I should have been one of the exterminated six million. The job didn't help my self-esteem.

I did some real estate sales and after that I decided to learn the construction business because I knew I wanted to build and develop. I worked for a developer-contractor, a German immigrant who made good and surrounded himself with German and other Eastern European tradesmen. He took on but people kept me at a distance and clearly tolerated this White Jew that management was training to be a superintendent. It was an uncomfortable time for me and one carpenter, a very big man sensing my discomfort with some of my Teutonic co-workers, rolled up his sleeve and showed me his SS tattoo and laughed in my face. Putting it mildly, I felt very uncomfortable, inadequate, and frightened being an unpopular minority.

I earned my high school diploma in 1993, my BA in 1996, and my teaching credentials in 1997. I have been teaching since then, but recently resigned my position. No support for new teachers, enormous workload, and no payment for the major preparations that new teachers have to do. I was almost working for minimum wage. Leaving teaching feels good to me. In fact, nothing has felt so right in a long, long time. Teaching is not fun. The senior teachers, close to retirement, are counting the minutes until they are free. The administrators indulge the students, give very little credence to teacher input, and take a student's word over the teacher. In my case, I had an abusive Black assistant principal who owned little in the way of leadership skills. For me, in the end, the ineffective administrator was a blessing in disguise, however. Teaching, in the main, is classroom management, and has not been satisfying. It was time for me to no longer accept overt and covert abuse in my life. I feel free as the wind and liber-

ated. With some work at the Community College and at the local University, I am confident that I will recreate my paycheck. I also have made a new beginning.

Yesterday when I was writing in my journal, out of nowhere the words "Clare, I love you" wrote themselves on my page. I was dumfounded. I smiled; the words energized and inspired me. I have come a long way. Irene is already there, but that's okay.

She says, "I'm the most important person in the world and you should be too . . ., if you don't feel good about yourselves, why do you think I am going to think well of you."

Her profound message has imprinted itself on my psyche.

Jacki Holland is a second-career student who left the legal field as a court reporter and received a bachelor's degree, graduating magna cum laude in English. She plans to pursue a Master of Fine Arts in creative writing. She says: "I have always had, it seems, a desire to play guitar, to learn sign language, and a yearning to draw. And always, I read. I have a deep love for words. Although I never learned guitar, never pursued my interest in sign language and recognized I lacked the talent to draft or sketch, I could give life to words. A poem I wrote entitled, 'Little Boy Lost' appeared in a campus pub- lication. An introduction to creative nonfiction opened up a new genre of writing for me. The Race and Change oral history class evoked a newfound desire, a desire to explore my own familial his- tory, the history of a socially deprived but culturally rich family who persevered and overcame seemingly insurmountable obstacles."

GENERATIONAL EXPERIENCES ACROSS THE COLOR LINE

Jacki Holland

"To everything there is a season, and a time to every purpose under the heaven. . . ."
Ecclesiastes 3:1a

As I slowly swing back and forth — one leg under me on the patio glider, my eyes focused on the gentle movement of the lake behind my home in Pembroke Pines — I find myself in a reflec- tive mood. The homes I grew up in were certainly different from this one. I remember one in particular, a big rambling house in Hollywood, Florida. After a severe storm, I would step off the porch and look out over the backyard, covered with murky water several inches deep, fat earth worms and croaking frogs in their element. In those days, my family loved to fish. We would gather up our cane poles, our pails and fish worms, and make our way to a favorite canal. All up and down the bank Black men and women, boys and girls, in floppy straw hats, would cast out and pull in. If we had a good catch, on Friday night we would have a neighborhood fish fry. Now as I look back, two generations ago, I ask myself, what else has changed for my people?

Way "back in the day," when my siblings and I were growing up, my mother stayed at home. She cooked and cleaned and cared for her many children. I was the second youngest of 15. Dad was a sharecrop- per and would work the fields; he also was a barber and would cut hair on our enclosed front porch. Three or four of my oldest sisters and my two oldest brothers were required to catch the bean-field truck. The truck would come through and make designated stops. Black males and females from age eight to 70 would be loaded up like a herd of cattle and transported to White-owned bean fields where they would toil from sunup to sundown for 40 or 50 cents per hamper. Every once in a while, they would work in a Black-owned bean field, and the wages were a little better.

"A time to plant, and a time to pluck up that which is planted." Ecclesiastes 3:26

At a young age, I remember going door-to-door selling bags of okra and tomatoes from the field my father sharecropped. We younger children would go in dyads. My sister, Regenia, a year and a half older than me, and I would go as partners. We would knock on the resident's door and chime out, "Would you like to buy a bag of okra? Only 25 cents." The older ladies almost always bought something, just out of the goodness of their hearts. Skipping along, the quarters jangling in our apron pockets, anticipating the treats we would buy with the money from our sales, we were content.

However, I also remember a time when we were treated as lower-class citizens; a time when we were segregated; when racism flourished: a time of inequality, of hatred; a time of pain. Interviewing residents of Delray Beach, Fla., for the Race and Change Oral History Project is the catalyst that triggers these memories. One rather unique narrator was Butch Harrison, 69, who is White. Harrison lived in Delray Beach for close to half a century before moving to another part of Florida, and he still spends lots of time there. He had many Black friends, he said. Whereas the color line was bold and severe for my family, it was close to invisible from Harrison's perspective.

He is a professional storyteller and self-described "real Florida cracker" — the name originated from the cracking of the whip used to work cattle, he explains. Now a resident of Live Oak, FL, he talks about his early years in Delray Beach, his positive interactions with Blacks, and the changes Delray has undergone. Harrison is still looking for the paradise he perceived Delray Beach to be when he was growing up:

> *"Yeah, we had an absolute paradise here. It was a paradise. I wish that we had it again today. I left about 23 or 24 years ago. I left and moved up, trying to find a paradise that we used to have, but the paradise that we used to have here will never return.*
>
> *"[During] my childhood, my mother was a stay-at-home mom. And there was a Black lady back in those days, her name was Hattie L. Smith, and she was a retired schoolteacher. And she used to take care of me. I have been very fortunate. I've always had as good a relationship in the Black community as I*

had in the White community. Had no problem whatsoever. I always had as many friends in the Black community as in the White community. We all lived together for many, many years. I mean, they had their own community, and we had our own community, but we intermingled. We worked together. We had friends together, you know. Had no problem.

"We fished together, sometimes, off the beach, back around 1950 until about 1954. We played all kinds of sports — where we sit this morning was a football field — when I was growing up. Of course, there was segregation back then. Carver High School was the colored school, and the old Delray High School, where Old School Square is today, part of it was where the Whites went to school. And on Thursday nights, during football season, the Blacks played on this field. And we'd all go watch them play on Thursday nights, and Friday nights they'd come watch us play.

"There was a gentleman here in the Black community, his name was Spencer Pompey, and Spencer Pompey was the coach at Carver High School when I was playing football. And Spencer Pompey was my friend. [He] paid me some of the nicest compliments that have ever been paid me, and I always was very comfortable with him. Spencer Pompey [prominent educator and civic activist], on several occasions, said that the two best high school running backs that he'd ever seen were myself and Charlie Wynn. Charlie Wynn [was a great football player], and I never felt that I was that good. But I thanked him. And it was really neat.

"[As] far as racial attitudes, you had people on both sides of the fence that had attitudes, racial attitudes towards the different ethnic groups. Myself, I never had a problem with any of that; I was never radical. As an example, right this morning, before I even walked in, [Alfred Straghn] started hollering my name. And that must stand for something. [But] I think everybody lived by the attitude, 'live and let live.' I knew a great many people in law enforcement and what not, and we never had much trouble — I mean, somebody would go out and get drunk on Saturday night, you know. And then if the law was called, the law would go out there and do whatever they needed to do. But it wasn't near as bad here as in a lot of different places.

"[There's] been a lot of changes. I'm amazed today. In fact, this morning, I walked into the McDonald's and the only language I could hear was the French Creole of the Haitians. And there are so many of these different people that are moving in here. I understand that Delray is a Haitian capital of Florida. And, I mean, I have no objection to that, you know, but I think things are changing."

Like Harrison, I, too, have seen changes. However, during some of the same years that Harrison was living in "paradise," my family, many times, was struggling through a virtual netherworld. When I was about six, we lived in a big wooden home that we called "the big house." The kitchen was at the back, and I remember times when one of my older sisters would stand at the sink washing dishes, while Regenia and I would sit at the table caught up in the stories she told: ghost stories about a friend's mom who died and whose ghost came back to haunt her daughter's foes, and fairy tales about living in a mansion with a full staff and fine cars and money enough to buy anything our hearts desired. She never told us about the painful racial memories. It was many years later before I heard the sad but true stories about an era of blatant racial discrimination:

My oldest brother Gene worked for a big manufacturing plant called Plant City Steel. All the Black workers worked outdoors, in the fiercely beaming sun, while their White counterparts, trained by the Black employees, worked inside. Despite the unfair treatment, though, there were good memories sprinkled here and there that gave those days a tasty flavor. I still remember Plant City Steel's annual company picnics: croaker sack and three-legged races; horseshoe and tug-of-war games; chicken and ribs; baked beans and corn-on-the-cob; intermingling of Blacks and Whites for a time of good, clean fun.

Nonetheless, the racial discord overpowered the perceived harmony. One of my oldest sisters, Bernestine, reminded me of this White lady that she worked for on the other side of the tracks. One day my sister took me to work with her and as I sat outside on the back step, her employer's two young daughters came and sat next to me. Within minutes the three of us were whispering and giggling like new best friends. Immediately, the mother admonished her two girls; socializing with me was not permitted. As I now look back I realize we were not only young and innocent; at that tender age, racism was being imbedded in us.

Gene, who is 17 years older than I, told me about the mixture of joy and pain of segregation. He was a teenager during the early '50s. On Friday nights, he said, young men in the neighborhood would usually go courting; visiting their girlfriends, they would sit on the porch, holding hands and stealing kisses. The tone of his voice shifted and changed as he told me that during football season they played high school games on a normal playing field; however — and here his voice was deep and smoky with memory — they did not enjoy the luxury of a gym. Their basketball games were played on asphalt slabs, and they marked off the sides. There they would engage in a game of "open court" basketball, and in the winter, they would place big fire barrels around the court, in an attempt to keep warm. The warmth went beyond physical comfort; there was an inner coziness with the knowledge of being one with your brother, the closeness of sharing the hard times.

Gene also shared with me that he was once instructed by a White man to address the man's young son as "sir." My brother could not understand why he should address a boy his own age as sir, and refused to do so. This attitude of white supremacy and social hegemony was prevalent. Bernestine tells the story of the time she took a bus uptown. This was one of the occasions she had me with her, and since there was only one available seat, she placed me on the seat while she stood. A couple of stops later, a white woman got on, looked around, and ordered my sister to remove me from the seat and allow her to sit. My sister, grudgingly, acquiesced. That was the law.

"A time to keep silence, and a time to speak." *Ecclesiastes 3:76*

We were a family of radical genes, however. Long before the Civil Rights Movement of the 1960's, we began asserting ourselves. One day way back in the '50s, my mother went to the post office and was pushed by a White man who told her, "Move out of the way, Nigger." Mama hauled off and slapped him, then ran for her life, knowing that once she got home to Papa she would be safe. Another time Bernestine slapped a White lady in Pic-n-Pay when the woman snatched a pack of meat out of her hands. And Gene once punched a White man after the man walked into a Royal Castle and found Blacks sitting who refused to yield their seats to him, and loudly commented several times: "A man can't even find a seat for Niggers." Years later, when a young White man attempted to supplant himself before my children at a Miami Seaquarium exhibit, I "read" him. We were there first and when we were ready to move on, we would, I said. Down through the generations, that radical gene continued to surface: A White man told my young son that, "Billy" (referring to his own son) "has permission to smack you." My son's quick retort was, "And my dad has permission to smack you." When the story was recounted to me, I remember thinking that the fruit really doesn't fall far from the tree. A product of a new age, my son was asserting himself.

Nevertheless, the era of in-your-face racial prejudice was a long season. The story was told of the time when a Black man would walk in his own neighborhood, minding his own business, and a White policeman on road patrol would call him over: "Come here, boy. Stick your head in this here window." The keeper of the law would then roll up the window and slowly drive a block or two with the Black man walking alongside the patrol car, his head caught in the window. No harm was intended, the officer would claim; he was just having a little fun.

Still fresh in my memory is the time when my son was arrested, a few blocks from home, as he took a shortcut on his bike, through a predominantly White condominium complex, a wrench in his pocket to adjust the slipping bicycle chain. The charges lodged against him were loitering and prowling and possession of a burglary tool. I made the trip over to the Juvenile Detention Center, signed papers guaranteeing his appearance in court, and took my son home, concerned about the outcome. We never heard anything more about it; obviously the false charges were never filed.

One evening, years later, I was at home enjoying a glass of wine when my stepson called me from a public phone. As we talked, I could

hear a police officer approach him and threaten to arrest him for loitering and prowling if he didn't hang up the phone and move along. My
stepson told the White officer, "I'm on the phone with my mom. I'm not
doing anything." The officer left, but we quickly concluded our conversation, and I advised my stepson to leave the area immediately. From
generation to generation, the color line continues to exist, sometimes
subtle, oftentimes camouflaged, real nonetheless.

Alfred "Zack" Straghn, a native of Delray Beach, has vivid recollections of racial injustices. He, too, was once subjected to unjust treatment
by law enforcement. The color line for Straghn was clear and prominent.

Straghn has always lived on the west side of Swinton Avenue, in an
area that has now become prime land for redevelopment. But, born in
1928, he has many memories of growing up in what was then Delray
Beach's Black community. He remembers his school days, and he also
remembers Blacks being treated as second-class citizens, having to
"walk the chalk line," and being the last to "get the crumbs" in the job
market. Straghn has owned a funeral home for many years now and he
has witnessed an evolution in Delray over the years:

> "[During] our school years, we wondered why we had to use second-class books,
> the books that were in the White schools; they were hand-me-downs, some of
> them were raggedy, but they enforced us, 'please take care of the books.' The first
> time I became aware of [the racial climate is this day] I went out to the bean
> farm and the man that we picked beans for . . . had a son. He told me one day . . .
> you know you have to call him Mr. Buck. Then I wondered why I had to call
> [his son] Mr. Buck when we were playing together. And I never did call him Mr.
> Buck. . . . [But it was] then that I realized that somebody was trying to instill
> something in us that just wasn't there . . . I've always taught my children . . .
> that there is no person that's better than the other person, [that] you are just as
> good as anybody that breathes on the face of this earth, and don't ever feel infe-
> rior to anybody. And that's the way I felt.
>
> "I went fishing [one day], and I drove my boat up to Atlantic Avenue
> Bridge. I got out of the boat without a shirt on. I walked up on the bridge. By
> this time a police officer came by, and he stopped. He asked, 'What do you mean,
> walking out here without a shirt on?' And I said, 'I have my boat down there.'
> He [then replied], 'You must think you're a White man, walking here without a
> shirt on.' I didn't say anything, because by that time I had pretty well swelled
> up inside. . . . He said, 'Well, I'm going to take you down to the station' . . . He
> took me down. . . . When my uncle came to get me, he said, 'C.B., I want you to
> talk to that boy there, before I put my foot [up his behind].' And that's when it
> really let loose in there. I said, 'Yeah, and you will be walking with a track and
> a dot (meaning a peg leg because Straghn would take off his real leg) [if] you
> kick me.' And that's the way I left it.
>
> "[As far as jobs were concerned,] we were the last to get the crumbs. I
> always resented that. [But in the funeral business], we ran an ambulance serv-

ice . . . and they called me out on 441. There were two ladies ran into a ditch and drowned. The sheriff department was there when I got there . . . A Puerto Rican fellow . . . was diving. He came up with the lady's pocketbook. And when he came up, he held it up, he said, 'Here's the pocketbook.' The sheriff said, 'get him out of the water, get him out of the so-and-so water' . . . As soon as he got up on the bank, the sheriff kicked him. Boy, that boiled me. I just couldn't take it. I spoke out. And I told him, 'You didn't have to do that to that man.' That hurt me in my heart. [This incident] I think turned the table . . . [and later the sheriff and I] ended up being good friends.

"Let me tell you [about] the changes [in Delray Beach]. I was part of many of the changes. I was part of integrating the beach; I was part of integrating the restaurants in this area; I was part of integrating the laundromat. But the thing that has struck me the most [is once] in this same building, on Martin Luther King Memorial Day, a lady . . . was [reciting excerpts] from [MLK's] speech. As she was speaking, and the same man who . . . took me to the station [because I wasn't wearing a shirt] . . . was standing next to me. He was captain then. And as she was giving the speech and she got to certain parts of that speech, it moved him. I saw the tears [running down past his chin]. After that, he and I were talking. He said, 'Zack, you know, I've been somewhat of a tyrant' — and he was. He said, 'I never did stop to think that people went through things like this. I tell you what, my life has changed, and I'm going to try to correct all of the wrongs that I have caused Black people in this community.' That's when I said, 'Boy, this thing is really going places.' He became chief of police; I was instrumental in having him for the Chief of Police of Delray. . . . We had seen the worst part of this man, so make him chief and let us see the best part of him. And he was good. . . . He started integrating [the police officers' territory]. He started giving Black police officers promotions. And from that point, I know what could happen with change."

"A time of war, and a time of peace." Ecclesiastes 3:8b

At the close of our third and final Saturday round of interviewing Delray Beach residents, I make my way to the van for the trip back home. One of my classmates — a tall pleasant White male with a unique sense of humor — is driving a group of us. I choose, once again, the back coach seat. My intention, as it had been in the morning, is to enjoy a modicum of solitude, and to reflect on the day's interviews. As I ease my weary body onto the seat, he asks, "Jacki, would you like to sit up front? You don't have to take the back seat, you know." I am sure he means it differently from the way I take it. But feeling sensitized by the stories I had heard and flashing back to my own family's experiences, I feel a momentary sting. The comment grates on me a little. But then, just as quickly, I feel an overwhelming sense of peace. "Thanks," I reply, "but I'm okay back here."

Nancy Speed is currently a Language Arts teacher at Stranahan High School. She says, "All the oral histories collected during the Race and Change Project were heartfelt and enlightening, but the narrators reflected in this essay seemed to resonate with some of the experiences that I encountered. I felt an amazing connection with these articulate, successful women. The tumultuous times actually made us want to make the world a better place. I am blessed to have taken part in this project. I have related many of the experiences to my students. Hopefully, they will touch them as much as they touched me."

SCHOOL PICTURES IN BLACK AND WHITE

Nancy Speed

I always felt my parents were two very mismatched people; my father was a suave New Yorker and my mother was a farm girl from Maryland, yet they avowed their romantic love for each other throughout my childhood. What they did agree on was their version of the American Dream. They wanted to bring their children up with all the luxuries they never had. He was the first generation of immigrant parents who taught that work comes before play, she fled the farm mentality and lifestyle for Washington D.C. suburbia. They lived an idyllic life: parties, movies, and Sundays filled with lovemaking. Fate seemed to deny them children and their first eight years of marriage were filled with fertility treatments, miscarriages, and infant mortality but they fought back until I was born: Nancy, named for the Sinatra song with a smiling face. I was followed by two more girls and a boy. The design of the dream worked — until 1960 when the constant flow of alcohol eroded it and the beautiful couple and their lovely family fell apart. Their solution to keep the family together was to give up the lucrative job, house, neighborhood friends, and relatives and move the family 3,000 miles away to California. During the next year, I would attend five schools while in the third grade and start fourth grade in Hollywood, Florida.

The first people I encountered that were not like me were the Seminole girls that could run so fast nobody challenged their superiority in athletics. Their hair was beautiful: straight, black, and shiny. They weren't my friends. I was shy, chunky, and a bookworm. Hardly athletic. We lived in a boxy house I wouldn't bring anyone to anyway. By that time, while we were not exactly poor, there wasn't much money. The car was repossessed, and I had learned to go to the neighbors to call the police because my parents' arguments turned into fist fights. In the middle of my fifth grade year we moved to Ft. Lauderdale. Riverland Elementary was segregated as was New River Junior High, but when I started Stranahan High School in the 10th grade the push for desegregation was in full force.

I was so scared that I would be bussed to a Black school that I wrote a letter to Supreme Court Justice Earl Warren. I had learned in Civics class that this was a democracy and that your voice could be heard. I decided to give it a try. It is uniquely ironic that I was begging for desegregation plans to be set aside so I could go to school with my friends. That is the fear that was instilled. I didn't want to be bussed. I had just started to make friends and to be able to talk in class without turning red. The fear was about going somewhere new, not about Black kids — I didn't know any, but television gave a window to view the militant issues surrounding desegregation. I didn't want to go to school where there were hostilities between people. School was my escape from the drama of my house.

I entered Stranahan High School. No bussing yet. Whew! That was all I cared about. Not about Black kids or fairness — just me. There were Black kids that year. I have since learned that desegregation was accomplished if a course was not available that a student wanted to take at their school; they had the option of transferring to a school that offered the course. The first Black kids I met were Charlie Wilkerson and Ruben Carter. Carter became one of Stranahan's outstanding alumni — a star football player who received a scholarship to the University of Miami, was drafted and played his entire career for the Denver Broncos, coached with the Howard University football program and the New York Jets. He is now head coach for Florida A & M University. Ruben was too busy preparing for a game against the Miami Dolphins that was played in New York to come to our 30th high school reunion. (Miami lost.)

Both Charlie Wilkerson and Ruben Carter sat behind me in Mr. Tosh's biology class. I liked them because they could get Mr. Tosh to talk about fishing and we didn't have to work. A Walking Catfish would get you an "A" for the quarter. Walking Catfish were new phenomena (a fish that could move from one pond to another when water was low). We were school friends with common goals — getting a good grade. Charlie was funny and Ruben was a star. Together they were popular and invincible. I was shocked at dinner one night when I related I had exchanged school pictures with Ruben and Charlie. My mother's reaction was to say that now that they had my picture they were going to tell everyone I was their girlfriend. I told her she was wrong. I was testing my limits and rebelling against my mother because I grew up with her stories and her racism.

I had always known my mother's attitude toward Black people, but never thought anything about it. She had torn me away from a water fountain that had a "colored" sign above it and related a story of her not realizing she was sitting next to a Black person in a movie theater until the lights came on. She was raised in a time when racism was tolerated. "They got off the sidewalk when a White person passed," she said. I finally knew some Black kids and they were like me. I did not get my pictures back. We never passed beyond our in class friendship; however, I found out at the 30th reunion that Charlie had once called my house on a Saturday when we were teenagers and my mother would not let him talk to me. She said I was too busy doing chores and could not ever talk on the phone on Saturdays. Thirty years. How sad. I don't remember if I ever got the message because she made it clear to him not to call any more. I don't think he told me at the time, but he never called again. Even when Charlie told me this, 30 years later, I did not initially think the worst of my mother — that's too difficult; but I knew her racism had hurt him then, and now. I loved running into him when he managed the Sports Authority, occasionally in the mall, and at least once every 10 years at the reunion because the friendship and joy of high school life still spark fond memories of school.

I'm still there, too. I teach at Stranahan with its long legacy in the city of Ft. Lauderdale. High school is a powerful learning experience for more than just facts. Integrating the schools was a wonderful step towards breaking down the fear, but there are still ethnic differences that exist, tension between ethnic groups, not between people. The students tend to stay within groups, but they cooperate without rancor when necessary and when there is a common goal. The ingrained fear and hatred is not instilled — as a rule. They make their own judgments. The same theme was echoed in the reflections of the residents of Delray Beach during the oral history interviews I helped conduct for the Race and Change Project in the spring of 2004.

The reflections of Susan Hurlburt and Yvonne Odom on their high school life resonated with some of the same feelings and struggles that were a part of my growing up during the desegregation of schools in this nation. Hurlburt was receptive and involved in the school-related activities that carried over into her desire to keep the races together during the three decades of reunions since graduation. Odom forged new ground by being the first Black student at Seacrest High School. Her story is a testament to the strength of innocence. We are three women who felt more than understood the greatness of the moment in history.

Hurlburt has lived in Delray Beach since the early '60s, and attended Seacrest High School during the desegregation movement. Her memories as a White person are focused around a boring Delray (they called the city "Dull-ray") Beach, but safe existence growing up and attending high school in a small town. She relates her experience of forging friend-

ships with Black kids at school and special functions that did not, however, carry over into her private life.

*"[A]bsolutely, the town was segregated. No doubt about it. It was segregated in
a way, and I'm sure there were sure some unhappy situations and it isn't all the
way I see it through a kid's eyes. But it was segregated, I thought in neighborhoods. This is where this group of people — whether they had to and didn't have
a choice — nonetheless, this is where this group of people settled and built up
their neighborhood around where they settled and lived and this is where the
other one was. [L]ike I said, I'd walk around with a Black woman holding my
hand since I was five years old. . . . I'm sure she felt anxiety, but basically I
think she was treated with a lot of courtesy for being a woman, for being a lady,
for being a person.*

*"I do remember one time my mother getting very upset. She was in a play
at the Delray Playhouse and she gave tickets to Yvonne, our housekeeper at the
time, and her husband, Willie. W]hen they came to the playhouse all dressed up
[Yvonne] said there was this old guy at the [box office] and he wouldn't let them
in. He started giving them a hard time because there weren't other Blacks there.
[I]t got back to my prima donna mother backstage and she comes out and starts
making this fit and everything [saying], 'Oh my God, I'm sorry, I'm sorry. We
weren't paying attention. We didn't realize what he was doing over here.' It
was one person's attitude that he probable had been brought up with. So as
wrong as that could be it was only . . . ignorance. It was wrong, but nonetheless, it wasn't personal. It was ignorance. But there was a whole other crowd of
people that made it right. Of course [the scene] probably embarrassed the hell out
of poor them. I felt sorry for them.*

*"But that was part of the changing. Slowly, but surely you come down to
a tiny little town in the South. . . . [A]s a kid I didn't see a lot of that. I'm sure
if we spoke to Yvonne or Corrine I'm sure they could say we saw plenty more
and were uncomfortable but I bet you [the Black people] could tell you some nice
things too. Where they [were] loved and appreciated; about other people that
didn't think twice about what color they were, and it goes both ways.*

*"I can remember being at a high school football game after I graduated and
going back and, who did I see — Sammy Taylor. . . . And I knew Sammy from
high school: 'A' because he was drop dead gorgeous and we were all crazy about
him and 'B' he was a big flirt. [H]e had already graduated. So he's there at the
fence and I yelled, 'Sammy!' I go over, he gives me a big hug. Well, he's got these
two Black girls next to him talking. One girl's holding the other like she wants
to come after and get me and I see him over there and he's saying, "Shut up,
what's going on over here?" She just didn't like me over there being a White girl
over there talking to him — and [he] wasn't [even] her boyfriend.*

*"When I was in fifth, sixth grade, somewhere in there, just out of no where
I got elected to be vice president of the Junior Red Cross and go to these county
meetings once a month. . . . [T]he secretary was Cheryl Pompey. . . . [Her father]
was the former principal of Carver [High School] and he was a big advocate for*

minority rights . . . Cheryl was the secretary and I met her way back when and when we got to junior high and high school she was always involved like I was. So we were kind of like buddies and we had the same birthday. So every year I'd send her [a] card she'd send me [a] card. Even now, I still get birthday cards from her.

"You know, in school you pretty much hang around the people you live near and that go and do the things you want. But I always had friends in every class that, you know, I'd mess around with and what-have-you, but we were pretty segregated socially. When . . . homecoming would go on we'd get the homecoming committee and you'd have volunteers . . . a whole group of people outside your own little community. [W]e'd all get together and have meetings. . . . [T]hat is the time you would see people you didn't normally see except in school. We had this whole crowd of Black kids that were just involved in these extra things. . . . And all of a sudden . . . now it's at night time or after school, and here's these friends from school there. So I can remember that. [T]hat was always fun."

The activities surrounding school functions were always a safe environment for students of different races. The reality of outside criticism when you moved away from those activities was very real. In my case, I could go to any school function and not have to relate to who was Black or White. We were there for a purpose. But just as Hurlburt found out, any hint of a bi-racial relationship outside the safety of school could stir up prejudicial feelings.

Yvonne Odom is a Palm Beach County school teacher. She was born in Daytona Beach and come to Boynton Beach, near Delray Beach, in 1959 when she was in the eighth grade. She is one of five children raised by her father, a single parent and a Baptist minister. She was the first Black student to attend Seacrest High School and shares this in her oral history:

"I remember my father never mentioning anything about race. I went to a private boarding school . . . in Jacksonville for colored girls. I did have a couple of White instructors; prior to that everything was segregated. My father shielded us from a lot of [racism] in the fact that we drove a lot. He had a car and we would travel a lot. We moved here in '59. At that time I was going into the eighth grade. [I was] very disappointed, coming to Boynton as a child.

"The day came [to transfer to Seacrest]. They told me to arrive at about 10:00 a.m. My father brought me in the car. My first day of school was in English class. But one thing that disturbed me on my schedule, they did not put me in P.E. class . . . I had incidences of name calling but, the adults around these other children were able to minimize it so it never got out of hand. I was the only [Black] student in the whole campus for a full year . . . I had made my mind up that I wasn't going to avoid any situation. I made it my business . . . to go to wherever; if it was a party, if it was an assembly, if it was a dance, I was determined.

"They went over my schedule and at the time I had already missed my first hour and I think most of the second hour. [My English teacher] had a seat picked out for me. . . . He was a very pleasant teacher. I was introduced. There was a young lady — I don't remember her name — she apparently was told to tell me the assignments. She wore glasses, those big-rimmed glasses . . . and she explained to me where [the assignments] were. I could see [the other students] were looking at me . . . I guess I was a curiosity. I had questions asked of me like, "Did we burn [in the sun]?" [During the P.E. class the next quarter, my presence] dispelled the rumors about Black people having tails, so . . . the girls realized that my body was just like their body and I realized their body was just like [my body]. Children had these myths about what you looked like based on stories they were told.

"What I learned when I went over there [to Seacrest] was that . . . I know a lot more than a lot of these kids because we were told that all the White kids were smarter than we were; that all White kids did everything right. I'm thinking [to myself] 'these kids [are] skipping school . . . they had a smoking area.' [That is] unheard of on a Black campus . . . because of the high standards. What I learned more than anything is [that] bad is a balance [because] what I've [also] found in my students is that students tend to hang based on likeness [not because of race].

"The bad students hang together, the honor students hang together, thugs hang together, [and] dope smokers hang together. [Y]our race might initially get you to get that feeling [of friendship], but what will keep you going is whether you like this person or not. . . . We've been fighting this battle [of racism for a long time]. It is not won yet."

Students aren't afraid to explore the unknown: biology, algebra, or history. It is part of the everyday world — learning something new. An added benefit is exploring human relationships. For students during desegregation we had the opportunity to explore beyond the outside layer of skin to find that we were the same on the inside. If we had the same focus, we forged friendships. Nevertheless, whether we came together as friends or not, we dispelled any falsehoods bred from a legacy of racism.

Students aren't the only beneficiaries of the change that has occurred. Mom has made major changes in her belief system. She is retired and plays tennis every day and competes in senior tournaments. When she returned last week from competing in a Mississippi match, she called to tell me she was safe. During the conversation, she announced that she had extended an invitation to a Black couple to stay at her condo this summer during a tournament. They have accepted the invitation and I know she will make them feel right at home.

Gaye Lawrence received her undergraduate degree in Communi - cation from Florida State University and is currently pursuing a Master of Arts degree. Her goal is to be a college professor teaching courses in Public Speaking, Rhetorical Theory and Intercultural Communication. She says, "I enjoy exploring human nature and different cultures. I have chosen a field of study I feel passionate about. I learned so much about the significance of oral history and I experienced great gratification participating in the Race and Change Project. The wonderful people I met and the lives I had an opportu - nity to become a part of will stay with me forever."

A PIECE OF THE RACIAL PIE

Gaye Lawrence

I was born in the city of Kingston on the beautiful island of Jamaica and I spent my childhood years there as well as a portion of my adult life. In 1995, I migrated to the United States of America to attend Broward Community College. I arrived in South Florida that April knowing exactly what I wanted to accomplish, a degree in Communication. While there, I had friends from several cultures and I was particularly fascinated with African Americans. They seemed obsessed with the color of their skin.

In my sociology class I was exposed through the voices of students to many issues that affected the African American community. Issues like institutionalized racism, affirmative action and just surviving as an African American on a daily basis. I recall feeling that these students felt that every misfortune they experienced was because they were Black. I thought they were too angry. However, this feeling would change.

African Americans and Jamaicans have many things in common. Our tradition of storytelling from generation to generation and the fact that we are descendants of slaves are just two of them. However, one of the major differences between both cultures is that Jamaica is a nation gov- erned by the descendants of slaves; the people of Jamaica are primarily Black, and Whites are in the minority. On the other hand, America is pri- marily governed by the descendants of slave masters; African Americans are a minority, and Whites control the majority of the wealth and power. I feel this difference in my social background is what made it hard for me to understand why African Americans were so concerned with the color of their skin and the impact it has on the quality of their lives.

In college I was very confident and never intimidated by White pro-
fessors or any person of another race that I had to deal with. Then one
day it happened: My first experience with racism. I was working in registration at one of the community college campuses and a professor came
to the window to register for a continuing education class. I heard whis-
pers about how much she discriminated against Blacks in her classes but
figured that if I ever came across her I could handle it. She could never
break my spirit. I was the only person at the window when she came. She
asked me to register her; however, she needed an override to do it and I
was not able to complete the registration for her. I informed her of the
problem and told her I would get my supervisor to assist her, but she proceeded to argue with me, informing me that she knew what she was
doing. I asked her to excuse me while I went for help but she continued
to argue saying that I was stupid. I was very annoyed but I still stayed
calm as I went to get my supervisor. She came, keyed in the code for the
override and gave the same explanation for the problem to the professor,
and then I registered her and printed her schedule. As I handed her the
paper my hand touched hers and she pulled away and wiped it on her
clothing as she looked at me with disgust as though I was "a piece of
dirty cloth," as they would say in Jamaica. Then she grabbed the schedule, which had fallen during the exchange, and stomped out. I was
shocked by her behavior. After all, I was well groomed. My hands were
clean. There should be no reason for her to be terrified of touching me.
Within a fraction of a second I remembered her reputation and figured
the problem was the color of my skin.

The tears rolled down my face. I surprised myself with my reaction
to her behavior. It was a feeling I had never experienced before. I actually
felt unclean and worthless, if only for a second or two. Excusing myself
from the registration window, I went to the bathroom and I cried and
cried, then regained my composure and went back to work. If someone
had told me the day before that I would react to such an incident the way
that I did, I would have asked them if they were crazy. There is no way
Gaye Lawrence would cry over such an incident. No. Instead, I would be
angry and probably ask her what was *her* problem. However, this was not
the case. I felt, firsthand, what I always heard my friends talk about, the
sense of being treated terribly or unfairly because of the color of my skin.
I can't say that I know why I reacted the way I did; I can only guess it was
embarrassment, coupled with anger. But that day was an eye opener for
me. It allowed me to be more empathetic and less judgmental about the
way African American students felt. But it never changed my perception
of self; it just made me more determined.

After graduating, I transferred to Florida State University (FSU) in
Tallahassee. There, people followed me in stores suspiciously when I
went shopping. My White employers constantly felt the need to tell their

clients as they introduced me, "This is Gaye our new employee. She is Jamaican, she goes to FSU and her husband is doing his Ph.D. at FSU." Was all this necessary for a brief introduction? Yes, for them it was. It told their clients that we hired her, but she's different. First of all, she is not African American — as though there was something wrong with that. And secondly, she goes to FSU rather than Florida A&M University (an historically Black school). And thirdly, her husband is well educated and also attends FSU, so she is okay, we can tolerate her. It's not that we are lowering our standards or anything. I found this to be very disturbing and, again, I realized the prejudice shown to African Americans. After being here for a couple of years I had to acknowledge how hard it must be to live with these prejudices and acts of discrimination every day of your life and the impact it can have on one's self esteem. However, the key is not to allow acts of discrimination to cheat you out of your piece of the pie. If it means you have to work twice as hard to get your slice, then do so. Think positively; do not dwell on the negative. It is this philosophy that attracted me to two narrators — Yvonne Odom and Harvey Stephens — while doing interviews for the Race and Change Oral History Project in Delray Beach, FL. This was the message they both gave.

Yvonne Odom, now a teacher in Palm Beach County, was the first African American girl to go to an all-White high school in Delray Beach in the mid-1960s. She had some bad experiences, but always managed to stay positive. She recalls some of her experiences:

"I remember the 'colored' fountain the 'white' fountain and as a child I remember going to the 'white' fountain, purposely drinking from it, thinking in my mind if somebody said anything to me I would pretend I couldn't read because the 'white' fountain water was cool and the 'colored' fountain was not. So, to me, I was just playing a prank I guess. . . . The restrooms, I remember all of that. Riding on the bus — I remember having to sit to the back. But it wasn't like it was unpleasant . . . because you knew that was the rule and nobody make a big deal of it. We accepted it and I think my father shielded us from a lot of it in the fact that we drove a lot.

"We moved [to South Palm Beach County] in 1959. At that time I was going into the eighth grade [and] very disappointed . . . as a child because you come into a little Boynton Beach town [and it] had nothing for Blacks, to speak of. . . . [A]t that time with segregation, the Black kids from Lake Worth and the Black kids from Boynton Beach, the Black kids from Delray Beach and the Black kids from Boca Raton all went to the [same] high school. . . . Notice now, the Board of Education law was passed in 1954. You talking now, 1959, when we came here and nothing had been done. It was still very segregated here. We were to go to Carver when you graduated from the eighth grade. So I graduated from the eighth grade, summer came, [and] we came to Carver [and] settled like everybody else. My classmates from Lake Worth from Boynton, Delray, Boca, did all the normal things kids did. I was on the basketball team — Coach

Pompey was my basketball coach — and I did well in school. I was gonna be Miss Carver attendant, so I had a very pleasant experience.

"[Then] one day after coming from a football game, . . . my father simply said, 'Bonnie,' — that's my nickname — 'I filled out this application for you to go to Seacrest' . . . I'm thinking, Seacrest? Why should I go to Seacrest? I don't wanna go to Seacrest, you know. So then I thought about it, and by the time . . . the news had gotten back to the school . . . it became a big deal. Everybody was all excited [saying], 'Oh yeah, you would be good' . . . and I'm thinking Seacrest? Now I'm gonna have to give up the basketball and all that stuff. But then I'm thinking, I'll just join the basketball team there, being this little naïve colored girl. Oh, I'll just be on the cheering squad over there. This will be good. . . . Now, what I found out later was that school was also being prepped for me. I learned that from . . . the young lady who had carried me around. [I] received a letter from the school district reassigning me to Seacrest High School.

"The day came they told me to arrive at about 10 o'clock. That was puzzling, but [as] I think back now, they didn't want me there to start the day. I learned later that they had blocked off the roads. That, I did not know. So I guess they did not want a mob mentality. My father brought me in the car. I also learned later that he had to have [a] private conversation with the principal about his concerns . . . gave his daddy speech, protecting his daughter. That I never knew until years later. So I was just going to school, never thinking anything about it. Then, when I get in there, I met the principal who I'm telling you was very, very, very nice. And this is one thing I counsel young teachers, or whoever [is] working with children. Children know when you are sincere. Initially they may look at your color or whatever, but children are the test of if you're fair. They know when you're fair. And I knew right away he was a warm person. His name was Mr. Fulton.

"[The] one thing that disturbed me on my schedule, they did not put me in a PE class. . . . I enjoyed PE. They gave me a study hall and in the Black school we had no study hall. We had all classes because our teachers expected us to do well. They demanded that we do better because they knew we had to compete better. This is what disturbs me, what is going on now in the school systems. This lackadaisical attitude. . . . Our Black teachers knew the obstacles that we had to face, that we could not just be equal to a candidate. We had to be much better in order to get the same job. So, those teachers knew that and they prepared us that way. When I went there I was not afraid, and my feeling was that I was going to get an education. People often asked me [why I was not afraid] . . . and I reflect back on that, 'cause I had high self-esteem already. And that's why I try so hard. In your students you have to build that confidence . . . it reverts all back to self-esteem. . . . And yes, I had incidents of name-calling, but it was, I guess, adults around these children [who] were able to minimize it so it never got out of hand.

"I was the only student [Black student] for a whole year, so I had no choice and then I had my mind made up that I was not going to avoid any situation. . . .

My dad just treated me like I was going to school ordinarily. I was very active in my other school, and I'm sure if you were not that way it probably would have turned out differently for somebody else. I ran for political office. I won my little primary but I lost the general election. PE was one which I sat out the first semester, which disappointed me. Then I went to the administration and told them to enroll me in PE class because I guess they thought I was gonna get beat up. Another thing they asked me to do on that very first day is use the faculty restrooms and I told them no. I told them I would use the same rest room everybody else used. That was one of the precautions they wanted me to take and I just wouldn't do that.

"[I] learned that, dang, I know a lot more than a lot of these kids, because we were told that all White kids were smarter than we were, that all White kids did everything right. And I'm thinking, these kids skipping school . . . they had a smoking area on the campus at Seacrest — unheard of on a Black campus. [So] what I learned more than anything is that bad is a balance. Bad is in every race. Good is a balance; it's in every race."

Harvey Stephens, also in his 50s, is an artist and landscaper among many other things, and he has lived in Delray Beach all his life. He shared his take on race relations, and on survival:

"Well, as a kid, it was terrible, horrifying and terrible, because if you was Black you had to lock yourself in like a cage in your own mind. I have a picture, a piece that I wrote, it's called Shackles. [If] you were a Black person you were required to — I don't know if you was required, but it was the ways you identify your own self as this person that has to confine themself from things. So you withdrew. You never really would allow your mind to think too positive. Might sound crazy, but you did. If you was out and about as a kid, you could definitely expect to hear someone call you a nigger. It just was a common thing, and everywhere you went it was just a part of being Black.

"We were going out with my dad, and we'd be on the back of a truck [with] my brother. This White girl coming out and she had her bikini on and we did it just for the heck of it because we just wanted to see what my dad was gonna do. We knew he was gonna have a fit so my brother whistled (laughs) and [my father] stopped that truck and he jumped out and he asked us what the hell was wrong. 'You gonna raise up hell and get me killed here? But that was . . . because, see, we was in our period. We was kinda coming out of this and was getting kinda rebellious to that period and what was good enough for my mom and dad was not acceptable to us. The thing that I really found out was it wasn't all White that was looking down on us. It was these people that was . . . that made such a mockery, that looked down on everybody that was Black, and it was years before we realized that it was.

"I have a brain and I have abilities and to tell you the truth I never finished school and done did everything I ever wanted to do. I worked as a carpen-

ter, did layout, did transit, was butcher, I'm an artist. I never went to school for nothing. I'm a handy man. I can do, I can make anything I want because God says so. So I'm not limited to anything. I'm capable of doing anything I want to do, and then, even now, if I want to go to school I still can go. I can be anything I want to be, anything I decide. If a man has any intelligence, anyway, he has the ability to get anywhere he want to. It's you, yourself, that hold you down.

"I have a picture. It's about . . . the worst part of being a slave was being transported across the ocean. Everything was totally new to the African people. The water was as frightening as anything and being locked down and chained and seeing all the people being so ill and when they brought them up to get exercise, all the dead ones they had to toss over and all the fish and everything was eating them. This is the way the Black person got shackled. That super fear, it was so dramatic until it became instilled in us. And it wasn't the idea of being a slave that was so bad; it was the idea of that fear, that transition, that you didn't understand anything. You don't know where you're gonna go. You don't know whether you're gonna die and the only thing that you have going for you is that inner being that's telling you to hold on. . . . When they did survive, they was shackled, they was locked in the trance of what happened, so their frame become a bit retarded and it's to [this]day. Some people are still locked and they lock up in themselves. They don't realize it. It's so simple. It's not about Black and White; it's about you opening the door, stepping out, doing what you have to do."

A few weeks ago an African American lady came into the office of the company where I work currently for an interview for a Certified Nurses Assistant position. I asked her to complete a form so we could conduct a criminal background check on her. She got very upset with me and wanted to know why it wasn't enough that she signed an affidavit stating that she had no criminal background. She said to me, "Bet if I was White you wouldn't ask me." I looked at her and smiled and said, "Yes, I would. It's a requirement of the State of Florida that we do a check on every employee. But, guess what. Even if it were not a requirement, my advice to you would be to do it. Do whatever it takes to help you get a job, as long as it's honest. Try not to worry too much about those who treat you unfairly. Get your foot in the door and prove yourself. I know it's hard, but we've got to do what we've got to do to get what we want. Right?"

As I drove home that evening I thought of the lady in my office that day and then I thought about my little six-year-old daughter, Melissa, born in the United States. I wondered what life in this country had in store for her as an African American. And I made a vow to myself to encourage her to take her piece of the pie, and know that she deserves it.

Stephen Luscher currently resides in Hollywood, adjacent to the Ft. Lauderdale area where some of the narrators in the Race and Change Project also resided at the time of the collection of oral his - tories. As a newcomer to the area, he was fascinated by the history of racial tension he uncovered through the interviews he conducted in Fort Lauderdale. A professor of Public Speaking and Business Communication at Florida International University's Biscayne Bay Campus in North Miami, he holds a B.A. from the University of Maryland and a Master of Arts in Linguistics from Florida International University. At the time of writing, he was pursuing a Master of Arts degree in Speech Communication at Florida Atlantic University.

RACE RELATIONS IN FORT LAUDERDALE: A DISCOVERY

Stephen Luscher

When I moved to Hollywood, FL, just south of the city of Ft. Lauderdale, I had no knowledge of the history of Black-White race relations in the area. In fact, it had never occurred to me that the Ft. Lauderdale area had ever experienced any tension between Blacks and Whites in the past.

I owe this in part to my experience living in Miami for 10 years prior to moving. In a city whose culture has become dominated by the Cuban influence, history and race for the non-Cuban in Miami only seem to have two eras — before the boatlifts and after. Since the after-era has pre-occupied the region only for the past few decades, racial tension in the city only seems to revolve around being Cuban or not being Cuban. I had become so accustomed to this view of my city, and thus, America as a whole — with all of the media attention these days focused on the pro b- lems brought on by immigrants — that I failed to realize there was a fairly recent history of racial tension going on between two groups of Americans that are not part of the Hispanic wave, two groups who have been living with one another for hundreds of years.

It never occurred to me that there was a recent history of racial hos- tility between Blacks and Whites in the Ft. Lauderdale area for another significant reason. I was born in the early '70s and therefore came to a social consciousness in the '80s, the era two decades after the Civil Rights Movement and just before the major wave of the Hispanic immigration movement that we are now experiencing. Racial tension didn't occupy much of the news in my formative years. The space shuttle, the Cold War and its ultimate demise, the invasion of Grenada, the bombing of Libya, the shooting of the Pope, the Iran-Contra scandal — I can remember the headlines but none about race. Plus, I grew up in an upper middle class neighborhood on the North Shore of Long Island where diversity consisted of the one Black, the two Orientals and the couple dozen Jews in my high school graduating class of 243. Even the small state college I attended in upstate New York had very little racial diversity: mostly White Christians with a substantial minority of Jewish students, all from nice homes in Long Island and other suburbs of New York City. Our differences were barely even religious; the Jews just went to a different type church and they did it on Saturdays. That racial tension existed in the world never occurred to us. We were too occupied with inconsequential controversies of our own small lives: who had new parachute pants, was Bon Jovi's latest hit as good as the last, how would we get beer on Friday night? Everyone spoke English; pretty much everyone had a White face; we all came from well-to-do families.

Thus, moving to Miami in 1994 was a culture shock to say the least. At first, I thought it was kind of comical that pretty much everyone I encountered in public spaces spoke a language other than English — this in a community in the continental United States! I, like everyone else, learned to function in Spanish, however. I got my haircut in Spanish; I banked in Spanish; I dated Spanish-speaking women. When in Rome, do as the Romans do. The Hispanic-Anglo divide that characterizes Miami is what came to shape my understanding of racial tension in the country. So, I couldn't conceive of the Fort Lauderdale area as ever having any racial tensions that would be different. To me, Ft. Lauderdale was basically the suburbs where all of the non-Hispanic White people fled after the boat lifts.

It was only through conducting oral history interviews for a graduate course at Florida Atlantic University that I became aware of the racial climate of Ft. Lauderdale and its past. Even when registering for the Communication course with the title "Race and Change," I hadn't a clue about what I would learn. I thought we would be studying the impact of racial integration on human communication or studying the differences in communication among races. As a trained linguist with a graduate degree in the field, I was aware that language is an all powerful force that transcends everything, even race — the ability to communicate in language is, in a linguist's mind, what makes us human, what differentiates us from the beasts. In fact, there are no races in Linguistics, only languages. I thought of the Ft. Lauderdale community as an environment where pretty much everyone spoke the same language. But in the course of conducting oral history interviews with Black and White residents, I found a divide: two people could speak English to one another and yet be speaking in a different language.

When I went to interview James Bradley at the Old Dillard Museum in Ft. Lauderdale, I spoke the fast language of an eager investigator and he spoke the slow language of almost unconscious passive resistance. The interview was a little strained, with me — a White, 34-year-old, educated male from the middle class northeast — trying to learn the history of racial tension in Ft. Lauderdale from my narrator — a 75-year-old Southern Black man whose entire childhood academic education was earned in the very building in which we were sitting.

"Old Dillard," as the Museum is known, is the location and the actual building of the high school that James Bradley attended and was graduated from in 1934. He helped to spearhead the movement in 1989 to save the building when the county's school board had decided to destroy it due to its dilapidation. Today, it is a beautifully remodeled two-story structure in an all-Black neighborhood, on the National Register of Historic Places, standing once again strong and proud as a testament to the community's survival. James Bradley exuded the same pride as his personal history with respect to Dillard High School and the Ft Lauderdale community dribbled out in small, yet precious pieces. With persistence on my part and patience with the eager interviewer on Bradley's part, together we conducted his oral history.

"[F]rom as long as I've been in the world, you know as long as I've been here, I remember the things that were going on at that time. You couldn't go to . . . there's only two schools in Ft. Lauderdale, Dillard High School and Ft. Lauderdale High School. If you couldn't go there, you had to come here. You couldn't go into the businesses, like the restaurants, places like that, movie theaters. You couldn't go in those type places. You see, on this side of Ft. Lauderdale, we had our own movie theater on Fifth Avenue. The picture theater. This way you didn't have to go to any other theater. . . . It was just the natural order of things. [Most social gatherings] would be like a picnic because a lot of meetings were held at the church. That was about the best place to have the meetings. You know, the 'getting together' with the community, they were held at the church.

"[A]s long as you stayed on your side and I stayed on my side. But there could be some problems if you allowed it to be. You know, like I said, the rail-road track up here, that's where the White community and the Black community met. We had our own businesses here — theaters, churches, things like that so therefore, you did not necessarily have to go to a White theater. You couldn't go, but you had your own facilities on this side.

"[Y]ou went to the stores to buy clothes and things like that. You know you had to go to the downtown area to purchase clothes and shoes and what have you.

"Well, once the salaries became compatible and there were better job openings, things like that, and you was able to go into places of your choice, any hotel, any bar or restaurant, nightclub or whatever, that's when things got to be . . . you could see a difference then . . . one thing that stands out in my memory

was when you could get a better job. You know, better pay for your better job qualifications."

I couldn't fully gather the import of Bradley's final words, "better pay for your better job qualifications" until I interviewed Alan Levy, a Jewish agriculturalist who moved as a young boy with his parents from Chicago to Ft Lauderdale. Contact between Blacks and Whites in the '40s and '50s, he points out, was almost exclusively in relation to commerce, nothing truly social: no gatherings, picnics or parties — just work. James Bradley's recollection that things got better as a result of better wages complements Alan Levy's observation about social interaction only being related to work. If work was the only connection of the two communities, then Blacks began to feel social progress when they experienced financial and political progress in the workforce.

I interviewed Alan Levy in the Tower Club in downtown Ft. Lauderdale, a penthouse restaurant in a bank building, replete with real estate and stock brokers powering deals over lunches. It's a private club, and Levy pointed out his picture on the wall as we walked into the restaurant's main dining room, which is pretty much three walls of windows looking north, west and south out of downtown Ft. Lauderdale. Befitting a successful businessman, Levy had insisted on treating me and my colleague interviewer to lunch.

His experience seems very much like my own. His story is the narrative of a boy who grew up almost oblivious to the existence of racial tension. He speaks fondly of his childhood growing up in the tropics engaged in water sports — fishing, swimming, spending lots of time at the beach. Indeed, the only thing negative he mentions about his younger days is the heat, which — as he explains — is what drove him to the water. It is only later in his story, when he reaches high school that Levy exhibits a consciousness of his experiences with the Afro-American community and its relationship with the White community:

"I remember the warm weather, the foliage. It was like living in the tropics. It was before air conditioning, so you would remember very hot, hot days, and those muggy nights and of course you would remember the winter days that turned cold and damp. The homes had fire places and you'd light a fire and that was your means of keeping your house warm other than a little space heater that you had. The summer was very, very warm here. You would look for a little breeze. You went to the beach a lot to feel those breezes because it did get very warm . . . the original schools had no air conditioning either. We would open the windows and live by the breeze. It wasn't bad. You just didn't know any better. That was what is was, and if it got too cold they'd close the schools. When it got 40 degrees, they'd close the schools.

"It was a pretty city, Ft. Lauderdale. I spent a lot of my youth here. You could ride a bicycle just about anywhere. You could walk. There was a lot of

freedom for the young people. It was a fairly safe, secure city, so that we enjoyed the outdoors a lot. It was a lot of things oriented towards the water, the river, the ocean. A lot of sports had to do with water, fishing and diving and such. . . . It was a good life. There was a little downtown Ft. Lauderdale. It was a very balanced town.

"For a little town with as few people here, we had five movie theaters, we had several restaurants, several hotels . . . you'd go downtown on the weekends. On Saturday all the kids would go to the movie theaters, you know pay nine cents to the Sunset theater to watch the movies. The Gateway theater opened 50 years ago, I think. That was the most modern thing in town. We all went there; every Saturday we went there to meet our little girlfriends there. Then we'd go to the Royal Castle and get a hamburger for nine cents, ten cents or whatever it was.

"There were two high schools. One was the Ft. Lauderdale High School and the other was the Afro-American high school, Dillard High School. In Pompano, there was Pompano High School — Pompano Beach High School, later called — there was the Afro-American School there. Hollywood had South Broward High School. The reason I mention these is these were the teams we played in sports, our competitors. To find others we'd venture. We would play teams in Miami, Coral Gables and Miami Beach. It was a very interesting, very sports-minded, very competitive environment — a good place to grow up.

"The Afro-American Community was pretty much restricted to their own community. I'm told by people who lived in that community that it was proba-bly the finest life that one could have had because it was a very caring group of people in that area. There were families that cared about other people's families, and they had camaraderie in that community. But as far as acceptance, in those days in the '40s and '50s, there was no relationship between the Black commu-nity and White community, other than working.

"The opportunities for a Black person in Ft. Lauderdale were certainly quite limited, although there [were] the jobs of maintenance, service-type work. We heavily depended on the Afro-American community. Agriculture depended on the Afro-American community, and [the interaction of White and Black per-sons] was established through the relationship of commerce. The Afro-American community shopped in the stores that were on Andrews Avenue. There was interplay but it was a patronizing type of relationship. It wasn't healthy. Afro-American people were not allowed in the White area after six o'clock at night, regardless. I think even the buses stopped running after that."

Both James Bradley and Alan Levy lived in Ft. Lauderdale during the time when the policies of segregation were seamlessly blended into this form of transportation. But for Betty Taylor, the concept of "busing" had a whole different meaning. She grew into her adulthood at a time when buses were used as a means of desegregation — to integrate Stranahan High School. She was one of those who was bused.

At one point during the recording of her oral history, referring to the integration and busing experience, Taylor was asked if it was traumatizing. She did not respond. But, from her story, the long lasting result of being a part of the desegregation movement were not so much trauma as it was a determination to move beyond her social circumstances through hard work. Indeed, she exudes the work ethic as much as James Bradley exudes pride, as proud of her accomplishment as a restaurant owner as Bradley is of the Old Dillard High School he was graduated from.

I was deeply impacted by the story Taylor told us in a study room of the African American Research Library and Cultural Center, just up the street from Betty's Soul Food Restaurant, the successful business that is the source of much of her pride. My accomplishments in life pale in comparison to hers. I thought about how easily I would have failed had I been in her shoes. In her interview she talks about how she decided to work when other youths her age partied. I was one of those other kids, but in a social environment where there was only one race. She had to overcome peer pressure and racism. Her story is testament to how, with hard work, one can overcome almost anything.

"Living with my parents, working hard toward schooling, striving to try to do something for my life for myself as I got older, and the person that really inspired me was . . . I used to always listen to Martin Luther King. That gave me a motivation to try to do something for myself.

"I remember when I first started going to high school. It was Stranahan High School. It was the first integrated school. That was when they bused us to Stranahan. That I do definitely remember. That was like being aware of what was really going on, because I had never been in school with a mixed group of people and that was my first time, Stranahan High School. I learned a lot from that experience.

"Mostly we used to live [in the apartments] in that area and we would mostly be in the community. We wasn't going out because we was like still young. When I got older, from high school on, is when I got aware of what was going on.

"It was hard, trying to survive. I saw the struggle my parents had to go through in order to provide for us. It was hard in those times and my goal was to make it better for myself, that I was gonna do what I had to do to make it better for my kids as well as myself and that's what made me strive to really get out there and try to see what I could do to make it. It was rough.

"I remember a teacher that I had at Stranahan High School, which was my English teacher. I remember how she just pushed to make and tell us that we could do better, that we could do whatever we wanted do. She was my English teacher that really impressed me to strive to do good.

"This guy, he was a White kid in class with us and we used to call him Jumpback because he would always tease with all the Black kids and we all just loved him and we used to call him Jumpback, which was his nickname, but I don't remember his real name. That was my first encounter with a White kid

*and that was great because he was a very nice guy. After I got in business —
we both finished the same year of school, which was like '71 — he was a representative for one of the companies I was buying from and I remember when he
walked in the restaurant. 'Betty! . . . Jump Back!' and he did the 'jump-back,'
so it was real fun. That was my first memory with a White guy. We really
enjoyed it. All the kids knew him, especially the Black race because he was so
friendly to us. He lives right here in Ft. Lauderdale still.*

"*I graduated in 1971 but my first year at Stranahan was ninth or 10th
grade, or something like that, and that's when they were busing us to Stranahan
High School, and that was my first time going to an integrated school. The kids
did the normal things. Every so often you would have fights and they were calling names and things, but I was like the little quiet one. I stayed out of all that.
I would just go to school. I was, like, neutral.*

"*[After high school] when other kids my age were going out and partying,
I decided I was going to work and did well for myself by working, spending time
just focusing on my work. I had the kids and used to pay babysitters. . . . It was
a lot of hours and a lot of hard work. . . . six in the morning 'til 11at night.*"

Taylor still works a lot of days, "six in the morning till eleven at
night." Her soul food restaurant is a popular meeting place for local
politicians. It's been a stopover for many national figures such as sports
promoter Don King and Florida Governor Jeb Bush, and it's a favorite
eating spot for Miami Heat players. Taylor is a success and enjoys quite
a bit of local fame.

And, she is not finished yet. She is looking forward. She ended her
interview discussing her "goals" for next year and the year after; where
she sees Betty's Soul Food Restaurant a few years from now; the developing business plan; a practical MBA earned while doing business the
old fashioned way, working hard at it.

My interviews with James Bradley, Alan Levy and Betty Taylor
have made me, too, ambitious about the future and the role I have to
play in my new community. I look forward to further examination of
what has happened with race relations in the area in the past and to
start, perhaps, a new examination of what is currently occurring.

Most significantly, I will be able to see the unfolding effects of the
massive Hispanic immigration wave from multiple perspectives: as a
Northerner carpetbagger in South Florida; as an Anglo living in a largely
Cuban-American Spanish speaking community of Miami; and as a resident of the Ft. Lauderdale area who is now also more racially aware.

Barbara Bell-Spence tells her story in Belle Glade

(left to right): Narrator Havery Poole, Sr. greeted by Oliver and interviewers, Glenn Malone and Craig Smith

Irene Clay and interviewer Clare Bornstein

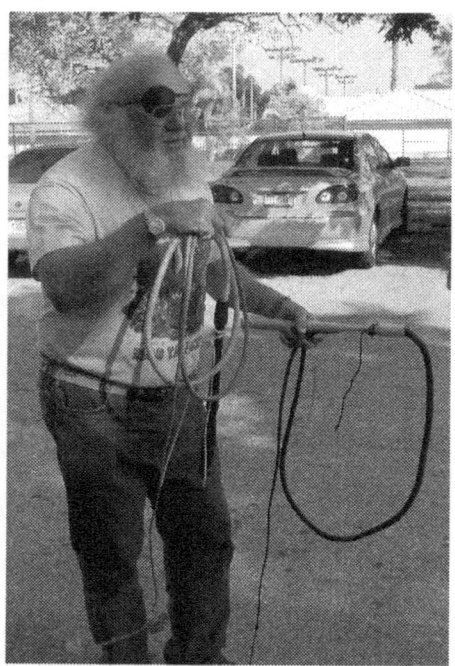

Florida native narrator Butch Harrison demonstrates whip tricks

Photos by Natasha Pierre-Louis and Ry Nielsen

RACIAL AWARENESS: WHITE LIVES/BLACK LIVES

INTRODUCTION

The following writers used the archival oral histories as the basis for their autobiographical look at issues of race and prejudice in their lives and the lives of people they met in classes on writing across cultures. They are native-born Americans from different generations, White and Black, born in Florida and other parts of the country, all exploring the impact of the experience of listening to Race and Change Project interviews on expanding their sense of racial awareness.

Narrator Sandy Eichner, seated right, at interracial gathering in the 1960s

Lise M. Steinhauer came to Palm Beach County from the Northeast and raised a family here. She is pursuing a master's degree in Liberal Studies at Florida Atlantic University, where she discovered oral history, which brings together her passions for research, history and writing. After decades of genealogical research, Lise heard dates and names come alive in these narrators' voices. She has conducted oral histories for the Historical Society of Palm Beach County, which led to presentation of a paper to the Florida Historical Society. She has an essay in a pending book on the Civil Rights Era in Florida, and is writing a multicultural account of an event in Florida history.

Women Crossing Racial Borders

Lise Steinhauer

I had little use for the word minority growing up during the 1950s and 1960s in my New Jersey suburb. Not only were there no African-Americans, Hispanics or Asians in my classes, but there was no awareness that they were missing. By the time I reached my teens, the United States thought so much of itself that world history and geography were not even taught in my top-rated high school. A peek at other cultures slipped in only through the subscription to *National Geographic* that my grandmother renewed every Christmas for our family. Even my more affluent classmates vacationed in Florida or Colorado — apparently non-American was considered un-American.

My ancestry is German on both sides. Although all my relatives since my great-grandparents have been born American, family stories and traditions sealed my cultural identity as a German-American early on. I didn't realize until later that I was in a comfortable position among the largest group of US immigrants; I escaped the cruel prejudice I heard about years later that others had endured. Someone once said to me, much as you try, you can never know how the world looks to a Black woman in America, nor even to the White man at the top of the heap. Don't assume that either can see things as you do.

I did struggle, however, with other cultural differences; my "other" was affluence. My friends wore Villager skirts while my mother sewed mine. We were not poor, but my mother worked while most others were June Cleavers who did not. In elementary school, I visited other girls after school, noted the differences in our homes, and never invited them to mine. Although I do not recall specific incidents of meanness, I felt embarrassed and inferior.

A girl from a private school joined my Brownie troop, and we became best friends from about age eight to twelve. I was practically a part of Gail's family, spending weekends at their home and at their house on Greenwood Lake a few hours away. From that propitious start, I fell comfortably into affluent circles where, in those days, chances were slim of meeting other races outside of domestic help. Gail's family had a series of live-in maids on six-month visas from Scandinavian countries so my exposure still didn't get out of Europe.

I never felt that I had been raised with negative prejudice — only with an awareness of differences. My mother might comment on our Catholic neighbors having more than the 2.5 children requisite of the times, but she was just as likely to attribute a neighbor's frugality to being from New England or another's manners to being southern. Stereotyping? Yes. Racism? Not by today's definition, but political correctness is constantly changing.

My engineer father was curious about everyone and everything. "The world is Black and White and every shade between, he would say. Wouldn't it be boring if everything were gray?" When a man grilled and shared Polish dishes with my friends and me at our swim club, my father grilled *me* with a million questions. What kind of sausage does he use? What spices do you taste? Ask him for the recipe. What part of Poland is his family from? Was he born here or there? The simple barbeque grew into a cultural foray. Youth made me impatient with this process of having to analyze everything in detail, but through genes or habits, I developed the same curiosity about people. But it would be years before I had a chance to use it much.

Although the Newark riots of 1967 were only an hour away, I have no recollection of witnessing segregation first-hand. Only once did color affect my life as a slice of white bread in a Wonder Bread culture. When my sister, Paula, was about 15 and I was about 12, I became aware that interest in other cultures had rules. A neighbor housed an exchange student who was attending Princeton for a year. Tunde was the son of a Nigerian tribal chief, dark-skinned, cheerful and eager to do what he could to fit in. He spent a lot of time in our living room playing Clue or chatting with our entire family, but Paula was his constant companion. No one showed concern about their being seen together at a movie or shopping — and this was in 1965. But apparently, either my sister had crossed a line, or my mother thought she had. One day I heard my mother's raised voice from downstairs and moved to the bottom of the stairs to catch part of the lecture. "What do you think your life would be like having his baby?" I never learned whether my mother's accusations were justified. My sister didn't confide in me. But they continued to spend time together until Tunde moved on. Forty years ago, a child out of wedlock would have been a serious concern even if the father had been White William from Wisconsin. Although I sensed that sex between Paula and a Black man would have been even more serious, I didn't know enough to be sure what the rules were.

At Bennett, a small girls' college in New York State, the crowd was more diverse but nearly everyone was Americanized and, like at home, affluent and light-skinned: White. From there I moved to a Euro-American neighborhood on the Upper East Side of Manhattan for a year while I worked on Wall Street. I worked with many Jews, and on their holidays the few other Gentiles were surprised to see me at work due to my German name. But I was still surrounded by money, and no color.

At 20, I slid into privileged Palm Beach with friends who moved there. But after a while, I experienced "real" Palm Beach County on the other side of the bridge and heard people use the "n" word for the first time. Controversy came a little closer. In my work, I comfortably hired and supervised Black maintenance employees or subcontractors. The handsome, sharp-dressed Black owner of a janitorial service felt vulnerable enough with me to relate this story: He had socialized with a White couple both in public and in each other's homes. One day he saw the wife in the parking lot at the Palm Beach Mall. He went over and hugged and kissed her in greeting as he always did when they were with their spouses or other friends. She pulled back. Don't ever do that again, she told him coldly. "I'm sorry. Excuse me," he said politely, and turned away, confused. Was she afraid of him? Was she afraid of someone seeing her embrace a Black man? Both possibilities were painful to him. The illusion that he had overcome racial barriers vaporized. Maybe some of my own illusions did, too, hearing his story, since I still had the idealism of youth. I tried to think about it from both sides as has always been my habit, but I hoped I could be more sincere in my own relationships than that White woman.

After I was married and while raising our two children, I hibernated in a sheltered world again, centered on our Presbyterian church and their Episcopal school. We were surrounded by affluent White Euro-American Gentiles and took plenty of criticism from family and friends for not exposing our children to the "real world." Yet recently, when I asked my daughter, now 22, about her own multicultural views, she said, "I saw you talk to all kinds of people so I learned that different people were interesting, and to be nice." This was only one of many things that led her to a habit of actively seeking cultural diversity. She is attending a Lebanese club, taking Turkish lessons from another student and designing an African-American public garden for her master's thesis. But Melissa's memory of my interactions with other races surprised me. She must have taken to heart chance encounters she witnessed that I don't even remember. Maybe I was more open than I thought in those days.

When my marriage ended, my children were in college and so was I again, free to explore the world with no one else to please. I made fast friends with a Jewish South African who delights me with her use of the English language and the knowledge and attitudes she gained outside the United States. It wasn't a big step for me racially or even intentional. But, it's progress, and we keep our differences an open subject as our friendship deepens. Like Melissa, although I hadn't been exposed to different races I had apparently learned to respect, enjoy and learn from them.

One of my classmates in a writing across cultures course at the university — I'll call her Janet — is my daughter's age. In a classroom exploration of how various people experience cultural awareness, we shared our early memories of race. Her hometown was similar to mine: a northern suburb with mostly white Anglo-Saxon Protestants (WASPs), some Caucasian Catholics, very few Jews and virtually no other ethnic representation. Although born of a Gentile mother, Janet's cultural identity originated from her father's Jewish surname. The family celebrated both Hanukkah and Christmas, but that was the extent of traditions passed on to the children. As she neared her teens, Janet's parents divorced and her father and his parents moved to Florida. With her Jewish parent and grandparents at a considerable distance and her mother practicing no religious faith, only the last name remained to proclaim her ethnicity. If, instead, her mother had been Jewish and her father had bequeathed her the name Salerno or Smith, Janet would have fitted right in. But, she recalls, in the Chicago suburb where she lived until sixth grade, "Being Jewish set you apart. Kids reacted to my name." In the alphabetizing of students typical in school, she was always grouped with the same kids and, she recalls, "They were mean. They would call me names and stuff."

Moving to suburban Atlanta at age 13 was a worse change. For instance, Chicago's drug culture had kept its distance from her but in Atlanta Janet had classmates who committed burglaries to support crack habits. During their first year, the family lived in an impoverished part of town. The Jewish name became less important, but now she was one of only two White students among the Black majority riding her school bus. She did what she could not to stand out, wearing the street style of the urban poor — white tee shirts and ultra-baggy blue jeans. The other White girl on the bus appeared to choose to ignore or defy the dominant culture, because she wore flannel and Doc Martins and dyed her hair red in the then-current 1990s grunge rage. One day on the bus, the Black teens grabbed her lipstick from her hands, broke pieces off and smeared the red cosmetic into her red hair. "She had to have felt it," Janet says. "Her scalp must have tingled. But she couldn't do anything about it." The girl froze. So did Janet. She wanted to intercede but she stayed silent in her seat, feeling helpless to risk a response. What if they turned on her as well?

Thirty years after Dr. Martin Luther King, Jr. was assassinated and my neighbors invited an African to live in their home, my fellow student's Black Atlanta classmates harassed a White girl who dared to dress differently from them. And while Janet was enduring anti-Semitism in elementary school, I don't think I even realized I had Jewish classmates at that age, 30 years before. Although America has become less segregated and more multicultural in the decades between my early life and Janet's, reactions of Americans to each other seem to be as varied as the cultures themselves.

Now I explore others' lives through oral histories. At last, I have an entrée into other cultures. The girl with no exposure to diversity can devote herself to meeting it face-to-face, shaking its hand, asking it a million questions, and even, eventually, getting paid to do so. Daddy would be proud.

The other day, I caught myself sounding like Mom, too, telling a friend about the men who keep my yard in shape. "The very tall ones are Haitians. The very short ones are Guatemalans, and none of them speaks English. But I understand when they inquire, '*perro*' to be sure my dog is not loose in the yard." And I try to convey with gestures what I want them to do. When that fails, we just laugh and they point me toward their bilingual supervisor.

The course where I met Janet also introduced me, in a different way, to three women who, like she and I, had experienced culture differently when they moved from one area to another. All three are narrators who had been interviewed for the Race and Change Project either in Delray Beach, FL, or the Lake Okeechobee area.

Sandra (Sandy) Eichner also started out in the North. And, like Janet, Eichner has a Jewish surname but says she did not receive much religious education. Born in the 1930s, 20 years before me, she was raised in the Bronx with two older sisters by her single father until she went "seeking adventure" in South Florida. There she observed very different attitudes towards Blacks and Jews in the pre-Civil Rights Era. She doesn't recall any discussion of racial issues at home.

> *"I lived a pretty sheltered life. I did not encounter personal prejudices when I was young but there was an awareness in elementary school, and an awareness of Black and White possibly in high school. There was a large Black — what we called 'colored' in those days — population in Jamaica, New York, and we mingled during the day but as the times indicated, we parted company after school. I never thought anything of it until I moved away, when things were different.*
>
> *"Miami Beach . . . [in 1953] was awesome. It was clean. The houses were yellow and pink. It was a Mecca for young people. But I was really taken back when I saw separate drinking fountains, separate public restrooms, I wasn't*

prepared for this. . . [T]here were curfews for Blacks to be off the streets by dark
— that was a shocker.

"*I met my husband and we got married down here . . . We moved to Port*
St. Lucie . . . for two years . . . We were one of two Jewish couples. The aware-
ness of being different was evident. At Christmastime our house didn't light up
like everyone else's house. In the '60s, when we were living in Hollywood, the
racial climate was definitely changing. They were developing Hollywood then. I
was conscious of the fact that it was a Jewish community. At that time there
was considerable prejudice. There was the Kenilworth Hotel and a couple of
places in Miami Beach where Jews were not welcome. And there were signs out:
'No Jews. No Dogs.' Jewish people could not even think about moving to Fort
Lauderdale. Even in Miami Beach, the north end — blatant prejudice. There
weren't a lot of choices because there were areas we couldn't go. There were no
personal incidents, [but] there were reports of the restlessness and ultimately the
riots in the streets and the assassination of Martin Luther King [in 1968].

"*My most significant memory [of that era] was the League of Women*
Voters. [One day when we met,] the recognition surfaced of how well we got
along. But generally at 5:00, we part[ed] company. That was just the reality of
the time. So we came up with the idea that wouldn't it be neat if we got together
on a social basis. This one incident impacted on my life because from that point
forward, friends emerged . . . The idea [was] to realize Dr. King's dream of
Blacks and Whites intermingling. . .[T]hat night, two Black couples and four
White couples [gathered]. It was dynamite! It was a challenge . . . for the other
Black couple. I sensed, understandably, a great wariness, like, 'What are your
motives?' We discussed our similarities as well as our differences . . . We had
picnics with the children. We met in each other's homes. We had potluck sup-
pers . . . We grew to 35 couples.

"*So I went into the northwest region [of Hollywood], a big step for a*
White woman . . . into this perfectly beautiful, elegant home with a lot of inter-
esting, well-educated people. I learned what, otherwise, I would have had to
read about in the newspapers, the painful experiences. I learned about the dark
side of our country's history . . .[and] the limitations our culture had put on
[Blacks] early on . . . It's quite one thing when you read about it and you think
you're empathizing, but it's another when you come into personal contact, espe-
cially on each other's turf.

"*[In the early '70s], the group tapered off . . . but a few of us remained*
friends and got together. Circumstances in our culture were beginning to change.
I saw people accepting challenges and [saw] their careers flourish; many of them
return[ed] to school. Confidence soared and things appeared less polarized. I had
hoped that we could resuscitate the group at one time . . .It limited my opportu-
nities for crossings, not having the group . . . [T]hings had changed."

Eichner, at least, had early exposure to Blacks, unlike me, growing
up one state and two decades away. When she later met "blatant prejudice" in Florida, she accepted it matter-of-factly when it was directed

towards her, and took it on proactively when it was directed toward Blacks. That impressed me.

Shortly before Sandra Eichner arrived in Miami, Carmen Canales came to a very different part of South Florida. Born in a housing project in Puerto Rico, Canales was in the second grade when she moved to Belle Glade, south of Lake Okeechobee, in 1950. Her father had come to Florida in the Forties to help build a sugar mill and stayed, so he brought over his wife, Carmen and her two siblings. Canales described the prejudice and segregation they encountered in both Belle Glade and nearby South Bay.

"When I was in Puerto Rico, there was always a mixture. There was Black, White, and I know racism exists every place, but we didn't see it . . . There weren't many Hispanics in Belle Glade then. When we came over here, the neighborhood where we found a house didn't want any Hispanics; they just wanted all White. One of the residents was a good friend of my daddy's from work, and he spoke to the landlord . . . Once they got to know us, we never had any problems. When we moved, the landlady even cried because she'd fallen in love with us. [W]e were a family of five living in a one-bedroom house.

"[I]n 1952 [my father] bought a house in South Bay, [which] was all White; we were the only Puerto Rican, the only Hispanic family. [T]he neighbors didn't want Puerto Ricans living beside 'em. It was not so much the younger families, but the senior citizens . . . [Eventually] there was very few that didn't accept us. In school . . . it was, like, accepted. We had more problems with the adults than with the children . . . [N]ow there's a mixture. There's White, African-Americans, Jamaicans, Mexicans, Puerto Ricans.

"There's a dish Puerto Ricans make called pastelas. [One day] Mom . . . gave a neighbor some and one of them fell on the road. I had seen one of my American friends look at it and say 'Ooooh, what is that?' and I said, 'Ooooh, I don't know.' I was embarrassed. [O]ur coffee would have like a cheesecloth strainer that we'd pour the coffee through, and one of my friends wanted to know why my mother was making coffee in a sock. [But] I think our friends learned from us and we learned from them.

"In South Bay, if somebody came over to see my daddy, and some of the Puerto Ricans were Black, or if some Black families from the sugar mill came over, they weren't allowed inside the house. This was not something that was allowed in the Glades. Daddy always had chairs outside. Mother would always bring food and coffee because this was our custom, that nobody was ever turned away, nobody was ever mistreated. We were taught it wasn't a color issue . . . It was either American, Puerto Rican, Mexican, Cuban . . . The color issue was made here in the Glades because that's 'the facts of life,' I guess is what I have to call it . . . There were and there are issues and there always will be.

"My worst experience was when I was a teenager and I was working at a department store. I went to a drugstore . . . to eat, and there were some friends of mine from school. The waitress told me I couldn't eat there because I was

*Puerto Rican. It was embarrassing. I guess you kinda take it in stride, but you're angry. It's just part of life. It **was** a part of life back then."*

Canales's calm acceptance of such a life shocked me — her time and place were far from mine and I was grateful to learn about them in such a personal way. The third story I heard was also far from mine and different from the other two — a window on history. I became even more aware of my former — and even present — seclusion and ignorance of racial differences.

Like Sandra Eichner, Yvonne "Bonnie" Lee Odom was raised by a single father, along with seven siblings. She was born in 1946 in Daytona Beach and remembers equal rights activist and educator Mary McLeod Bethune of Bethune-Cookman College. Odom's father graduated from Bethune-Cookman College when she was two years old and taught high school. He was also a minister like his father, who began the Odom legacy of education; he was one of the first graduates of Florida Memorial College when it was a two-year college in St. Augustine. Odom would continue the legacy in a very memorable way. She talked about her life in Central and South Florida and how racial prejudice changed with the place and the times:

"[Daytona Beach] had such a large minority population, we had our own movie theater . . . [and] municipal pool . . . [and] all my teachers were Black, all my classmates — Sunday School, church, everything . . . My father had a car and took us to a lot of things . . . Silver Springs had the 'colored' entrance . . . but everyone else there was colored so . . . nobody made a big deal over it. My only experience with whites was if you went downtown to Daytona. I remember the 'colored' fountain and 'white' fountain. And as a child, I remember going to the 'white' fountain, purposely drinking from it, thinking if somebody said anything to me, I would pretend I couldn't read . . . [R]iding on the bus, I remember having to sit to the back. My father shielded us from a lot of it . . . [W]e drove a lot in the early Fifties. He knew the spots where we could stop and eat rather than be denied service. He was not confrontational. This was all a preparation.

"We moved [to Boynton Beach near Delray Beach] in '59; I was going into the eighth grade. . . . [Later] I was finishing up my freshman year, a very successful year [and] learned . . . there was a movement to integrate the school system. . . . One of those on the committee came to my father's house and asked if he would consider allowing me to integrate [Seacrest High School in Delray]. . . . They were looking for . . . the Jackie Robinson-type.

"The day came, they told me to arrive about 10 o 'clock. . . . I learned later they had blocked off the roads . . . and [Daddy] had had a private conversation with the principal about . . . protecting his daughter . . . I found out the photographer who took the picture . . . in the paper . . . [was] restricted from even being near me . . . I give credit to the Black and White leaders in Delray. . . They have

a history of working together. . . .Each race will have that extreme element, but for some reason Delray has always been able from both races to have those with minds of common sense to do what is reasonable.

"I was the only [Black] student on the campus for a full year . . . . And I had my mind made up that I was not going to avoid any situation . . . [N]obody told me this. My dad treated me just like I was going to school ordinarily . . . [I] went down to the Boca Raton Hotel and Club, where the prom was, when it was not even integrated . . . [B]y the time I was a senior, there were four [Black] girls who graduated in that class . . . [Y]ou don't see yourself . . . as anything but just a student going to school.

"I had the tools to survive what I encountered. I was called 'nigger,' but I just said, 'That's their problem. They don't know me' . . . There was an incident one time in high school where . . . I rode with three White girls and we decided to stop off at the Royal Castle in Boynton . . . I could see the expression on the little waitress' face when I walked in. It was like, 'Oh my God.' She took orders from everybody but me . . . Then . . . this White man came out, very nice smile, and he goes, 'I'm very sorry but we just can't serve you here. We'll be so happy to serve you at the take-out window.' I just looked at him and said, 'Never mind. Forget it' . . . The White girls were so apologetic. I said, 'Look, just take me home.'

"The first year I taught in 1968 at Delray Elementary, one of my White students — and I didn't have that many — apparently had been going home and telling mother about me . . . The first Open House, you could see her pulling her mom up . . . I could see it on her face. . . . The very next day she asked her daughter to be taken out of my class. The [assistant principal] told me, 'Don't even fight it. It's her loss.' And that's the way I look at it . . . .The young girl insisted that her grandmother make me this quilt. I still have it. It's all tattered and torn. I use it a lot.

"The more we talk to each other, we will see that we are more alike than we are different and that it's our views, our values that will bring us together. Race becomes secondary. We're not there yet, but we're on our way."

Yvonne Odom's story brought to mind the first integration I remember of my junior-senior high school in New Jersey. It must have been about 1968–1970 because I was close to graduation when a Black boy entered seventh or eighth grade. Since I knew which town he lived in, there must have been some discussion at home or at school. I can even picture him — small, clean-cut and conservatively dressed — but I had no personal contact due to our age difference. Even so, I wondered how he felt. What was it like to be so different from everyone else? Why did his parents choose to live in an all-White area? How did his neighbors feel about it? There was no thought of asking anyone back then. From now on, however, my curiosity will be fed.

Monica Melton describes herself as a "re-entry student." She graduated from Michigan State University in 1984 with a Bachelor of Arts degree in Business and returned to school in 2000 at Florida Atlantic University for a Master of Arts degree in Women's Studies with a concentration in Intersections: Women, Race, Ethnicity and Nationality. She explored the situation of women from a global perspective, with an emphasis on how gender, race, ethnicity, and nationality inform conditions of oppression and lib - eration. She is enrolled in the Ph.D. Comparative Studies program at FAU and her research interests are Black women, HIV/AIDS and the prevention perspectives of HIV-positive Black women.

BLACK WOMEN, PROGRESS AND CHANGE

Monica Melton

I grew up in Detroit, during the mid '60s in a middle-class, upwardly mobile, progressive community during the Coleman Young political era, which started in the '60s and culminated in his becoming Detroit's first Black mayor in 1974. Mayor Young, Detroit's longest serving mayor, reigned for 20 years and he created a city where large numbers of average Black folks had the opportunity to flourish and prosper. The city was a mecca of Black power, from business ownership — small shops to major fast food and automobile franchises — to political power — city council, judges, and police force. Today, things are different because much of the Black economic base has moved to the suburbs leaving the city bereft. But I grew up during Detroit's heyday and much of who I am and the way I think was shaped by the strong, affirming Black culture of that time.

Yet, even within my nurturing environment, encounters with difference occurred. I was vaguely aware of dissimilarity, but ironically, my experience of being deemed different first came from the variation in my family's personality and mine. My mother and grandmother, Nana, were very strong influences in my life and as the oldest daughter, I was encouraged to be just like the matriarchs in my family. Both women are entrepreneurs — innovative and forward thinking women with a high regard for fashion and style. They also championed the rights of women and the disenfranchised. So being anything less than a combination of Madame C.J. Walker, the administrator, the quintessential womanist Shirley

Chisholm, with model Beverly Johnson's class and sass was strongly dis-couraged. Difference was not accepted, or appreciated.

For instance Nana, the fashion icon was distraught about my size 11 junior physique, especially my butt. So at their urging at around 13, I could be found standing and bumping my hips against the wall in an exercise that was supposed to reduce the size of my derriere. Today, I envy this generation's worship of big butts and I wish that I could have loved the body that I was taught to look at as flawed. In addition, my mother, the consummate entrepreneur, encouraged me and my younger sister to go into business even though I was interested in a career in law. So I took her advice, got my undergraduate degree in business manage-ment and eventually ran my own lady's consignment boutique for five years. Yet, I felt a void in my life and after 16 years returned to college in search of my own niche, and followed the beat of a different drum, a transition that my family didn't understand, or necessarily approve. But I had finally reached a point in my life where I was strong enough to live my life on my own terms. I accepted the fact that I was different, and now, so does my family.

My other experience with difference was when we moved to pre-dominately White Lansing, MI, in the early '70s when I was around 11 or 12. There were no Blacks in political power and no prominent Black business owners. In fact, the elementary school I attended had about three or four Black students in the entire student body, including my sister and me. We moved into an apartment complex with few children in my age group and no Black families that I can recall, so seeing Black people was a different experience for some children. I became "the brown girl." That's what other kids called my sister, too. This was a new experience for me, because I was part of the politically affirming era of "Say it loud, I'm Black and I'm proud." But after hearing it over and over, I realized that my skin *was* brown, even if it felt strange to be referred to in that manner.

I didn't want to be different, though. I wanted to be accepted by other kids, and I found myself behaving in ways that were not typical for me. For instance, my White classmate and neighbor Andrea and I would play after school and one day we went to a Kmart store close to our home and stole a couple of fountain pens. I don't recall how one pen ended up at Andrea's house, but to my surprise a few days later Andrea's mother called me at home to inquire about its origins. Andrea had told her mom that she got the pen from me, and although per-plexed by the question and the call, I confirmed Andrea's lie and said yes, the pen belonged to me. She was my only friend in Lansing and I didn't want to lose her companionship because there was no one else my age to play with and playing with my baby sister and her friends was out of the question.

Young girls are a capricious lot who frequently break up and make up, and Andrea and I were no different. However, lying for Andrea was so traumatic that when she gave me the cold shoulder I felt like it was our final break up. So, deeply hurt, I lashed out by calling her mom and telling her the truth about our escapade at Kmart. Well, as you can imagine, we both got in trouble and my parents were very upset that I had lied. All this happened close to the holidays, so when December rolled around that year my birthday and Christmas were ruined when my mother returned my presents to the store. To this day I rarely lie to my mom. Living in Lansing and learning that I was racially different from other girls was not a pleasant experience for me, but it would end up shaping much of my life, as much as my time in Detroit.

Years later, my first housing experience in South Florida would echo that childhood revelation. In March 1994, I marched off the Norway, owned by Norwegian Cruise Lines, a company where I had worked for the last year and a half. The cruise industry is not subject to American labor laws because they register their ships in countries that have no labor laws. Thus, my supervisor was within her rights to tell me that I had to go after hours and look for a man who had stolen merchandise from the ship's gift shop where I worked when we were at sea. However, being the brass American that I am, I politely told her "no." How could she expect me to go and look for a criminal like Inspector Clueso? I was fit to be tied: the nerve of the woman. At that time she advised me that she would take the amount of the stolen goods from my paycheck — $700.00. And since there were no US labor laws, what recourse did I have? Well, I conferred with my (now ex-) husband, and he told me it was okay to quit and get off the ship when we reached Miami and find a place for us to live and a job and he'd get off later.

I had some trepidation but, after all, I'd traveled the world myself. What harm could come to me in the "small town," which was to my way of thinking? I'd stayed on A1A in Fort Lauderdale on prior vacations from the cruise line so I headed back to familiar territory and moved into a motel with a weekly rate and began my search for our new home. How hard could it be? Little did I know that it would take me much longer than I expected to find an apartment — about a month. Since I was unfamiliar with the city I went to several rental agencies and asked to see places in an integrated neighborhood that was in a nice area. They showed me apartment complexes next to trailer parks. After several attempts with the agencies I decided I might have better luck on my own.

In the meantime, the owner of the motel where I was residing refused to take my gold MasterCard for my second week's stay, although he had previously accepted it with no problem. I was a quiet tenant. I didn't know anyone in town. And, my husband was on the ship and I wasn't having rowdy parties with the other guests. So what was the problem? The problem was me. The owner, who was from India, asked me after refusing to take my credit card, "Do you think I'm Black?" I'm sure my face was scrunched up in a perplexed look because he had a beautiful complexion, just like dark chocolate. I thought he was referring to his race but his skin was just as brown as mine. I couldn't decide if he was on drugs or if he thought I was, but I decided he must be crazy. My attitude was that my money was just as good as anyone else's. Besides, it was dark and I wasn't going anywhere. But he called the police, and I was politely escorted to my room to pack, and then to my car. I was astounded. This couldn't be happening to me, could it? Maybe it was a dream. But when I woke up the next day in the motel next door, I knew it was real.

Eventually I found an apartment in a suitable neighborhood. But my experience is not quite what I had imagined moving to sunny Florida would be. Coming from the Midwest, I had only experienced racial tension between African Americans and White folks. I had not experienced prejudice of this kind before so blatantly from someone who's skin tone was the same as my own.

Sometimes it seems like the more we change, the more we stay the same. Some would argue that we live in an inclusive society. But I wanted to listen to some other stories in the archival oral history Race and Change Project before deciding if Americans have progressed in our aversion to difference. I decided the best way to do this would be to take a journey back in time to revisit the past. What are some other women's perceptions? How have they responded to difference in their lives? The three women's stories span over eighty decades of perspectives on progress and change. They are narrators from the Hollywood, Florida and Lake Okeechobee areas: Helena Ash, from the Bahamas; Cathleen Anderson, a native Floridian; and Lexie May Childs from Georgia.

Helena Ash is a native Bahamian born in the '40s who came to Florida with her family as a child during Jim Crow segregation. Her story chronicles her encounters with difference and change in what she considers to be the most unlikely place:

> *"Nassau was more rural. We had outside toilets. We did have running water on the inside, though we had a pump on the outside. My brothers went to Catholic school. The nuns were in charge of the system. I remember the nuns were the teachers. I remember having a good time as a child. My brothers were involved in the Boys Brigade, which was equivalent to the Boy Scouts. My mom owned a store. She used to sell candy and goodies. I have beautiful memories of Nassau. . . . She lost her mom, that's one thing. The other was that the economy in Nassau still wasn't making enough for her. She knew if she got to America she could make a better life for her children. We came to America and settled in Dania for a short period of time. We stayed with relatives. Then, we moved to an apartment and finally we moved into Hollywood where we lived all our life.*

"[I remember] going to school and being picked at. That was my first recollection of being discriminated against. I still had the Nassau accent. Most Americans, when it came to the island people, were a bit jealous because they were hard working people. They stressed education and work ethics. We lived in an apartment for a very short period of time. My parents bought a home where we lived ever since. I think that was one of the things that they still use today. Foreigners come over and take their jobs and buy homes versus staying in apartments.

"As a child I didn't understand why I was being picked on. I know I talked different from them. But later on, I realized that it wasn't just me, but most of the people from the islands who still had the language difference or spoke with an accent. But also, that their parents, they always thought that we thought we were better than anybody else.

"I used to run home everyday from school until my eldest brother or my mom said, 'Until you stand up, you're going to have this problem.' Of course, one day I finally decided that I wasn't going to run anymore. The problem stopped. [I] had to fight. They always put up the biggest bully, the one that everybody was afraid of in school. But once they saw that I was able to stand my ground it was understood. Once you made your place and let people know you're not going to take it, then the camaraderie came. But that was a real opener for me because I really didn't expect that, all of us being the same color — it was a shock to me."

Ash's narrative highlights her unexpected skirmish with difference. She migrates to America with the expectation of being embraced by African Americans, a socially outcast community, and she is disappointed by their initial rejection. Next, I thought it would be good to get the perspective of a White Floridian and that's when I encountered Cathleen Anderson, also from the Hollywood project. She was born in Pompano Beach, FL, in the '30s and she has a rich history because several generations of her family have left their mark on South Florida. In her story she reminisces about her grandmother, a woman who loved children, and the stance her grandmother took on difference in the segregated South at the beginning of the twentieth century:

"My grandmother was elderly and she was helping to raise my [mother and her] sister Clara, [and] my cousins; my uncle was drafted into the Army, and she was helping raise his children, William Hines and Terrance Hines. Well, his wife died in 1910 and there was nobody. See, it was very sparsely settled; there was no one to take care of the children because most of the African Americans worked on the farms, especially in the wintertime.

"[My grandmother and others] used to teach them how to read. [T]his . . . little [Black] girl . . . was in [their] home school. My mother had not started in the first grade, but she did. She went to Pompano Elementary School. My grandmother used to teach, or had taught, [or] was teaching her children how to *read before they went. There was no such thing as kindergarten. Nobody ever heard of it back then because my mother, on the 16th of October, will be 86 years old.*

"This little Black girl lived west. See, in Pompano most of the Black residences were west of Dixie Highway. And, as I said, my grandmother lived on Dixie Highway and SE Sixth Street. NE Sixth Street was when you crossed the railroad track. And she was so cute, in fact, my grandmother used to make a couple of dresses for her when she made dresses for my mother. She was my mother's best friend when they were children. She spent a lot of time with my grandmother. In fact, she stayed there because her mother and father worked on the farms and she loved to come over and my grandmother was a magnificent cook, wonderful cook. She would come over early in the morning and sometimes she would spend the night.

"The superintendent of instruction came because she knew how to read when she went to school and he said to my grandmother, 'You shouldn't be teaching the little Black girl.' And well, my grandmother said, 'You know, she lives here, she stays here.' And he said, 'Well, does she live there?' 'No.' But you know, if her parents didn't get back from the fields or if they had to do something and the little girl was there. And my grandmother said, 'Well you know, we'd feed. . .I fed my children, I fed her,' and she said, 'I'd get 'em baths and make 'em go to bed' . . . But he said, "You ought not to do it," and 'Don't teach anymore Black children how to read.'

"I think they moved away. I think they moved to Fort Lauderdale or someplace and I guess my mother was about 10 or 11 years old when they moved away. The father got a job as a — I don't know what you would call them, sort of like a foreman on a farm."

Anderson's grandmother, a woman who loved all children regardless of societal constraints, points to a broader perspective on history than mainstream accounts of that time. She took an unpopular stand against Jim Crow policies due to her love of education and children.

Finally, I encountered the story of Lexie May Childs from the Lake Okeechobee project. She is southern like Anderson, but Childs is a Black woman who migrated to Florida from a smalltown in Georgia. Childs was born in the '20s, and shares her experience of gender difference, and rebellion:

"[F]or 15 years I . . . never was a mile out of the little town [where I was born] and I married when I was 15 years old. I went through the seventh grade at that time. My mama would have to pay for me to go to school. But then that's where I dropped out. I was out of school in April, somewhere around the 1st of April, and I married around the 30th day of April 1938.

"My mother was a widow woman and she had six kids. My daddy died when I was 13. My mother provided a pretty good life for us. I got three brothers and two sisters. When my daddy dies my mama was only like 31 years old

and I was 13. But the oldest one had to take care and I was the oldest, so that made me be more or less like their, I guess, the lady of the house. My mama had to work.

"In 1939, I was 17 when I got [to South Bay, FL] . . . You know the type [of work] that's here — bean picking, cane cutting, cabbage — so that was the type I was in. I picked beans, then for years I wasn't picking them — I cooked for the people in the field. I did that most of the time — I was running a selling wagon. Well, I was always there selling something, selling sandwiches and drinks and candies and cookies and when I wasn't doing that I was in domestic work. I worked for everybody, Miss Everybody around here.

"I was treated fine [racially] cause when you pick your beans they pick up yours, and carry it, and checked it out just like they did everybody else's. When you was cutting cabbage when you cut it, throwed it to the pot, it was just the same as anybody else's. Only thing about it, I can remember . . . we was cutting cabbage and we went to the field once and the men, just because they were men, they were going to get one dollar more than me. But I was in the same hole he was in and I wouldn't work. I remember that so clearly. I had two bosses. Went to one and asked him a question — never went to nobody to talk about money, with nobody, that's not me. So, I went to him to talk about what he was paying. He hadn't told us. Went to one and he told me to 'ask the other one.' Got to the other one and he said 'ask the other one.' Wait a minute now. I asked him and he told me to ask you; now I ask you and you tell me to ask him. No, I want to know what you gonna give me? So then he say, 'We pay the men seven dollars, and the women six,' and I say well, I don't want the job. If I'm gonna pack cabbages right there besides him if he get seven, I want seven.

"So that's all I ever knowed, and I gathered up my apron to go home and he said, 'Wait a minute, Lexie. You go back in there and get back in that hole and I give you what I give them.' No problems. I haven't had any 'cause everywhere I went, when I went to the job, I wanted to know how much you gonna give me. And if I was satisfied with what you say, I took it and went to work, and if I wasn't satisfied, then I gathered up my . . . boots and apron and I start walking. Cause it was his job and I was doing the work and if I didn't like his pay I didn't do it.

"People didn't have the same attitude as I had. Because I can't remember nobody going in there — now they might of went, but I'm not sure. But I can say that they didn't go with me. And I'll tell you something else, too. I didn't have children . . . So you have to take a good look sometimes. [T]hat man that got six children in the house can't do what that man do that ain't got none. You see, if me and my husband made five dollars a day we could have a big time. But if you had six children in the house, five dollar, you had to be careful. And most time they didn't pay you according to what your family was. They paid you according to what they were paying you. So that give me more opportunity to walk away from a lot of things that some people couldn't — because they had a family."

Childs's stand on equal pay for equal work, as an uneducated Black woman in the segregated south working for White men is significant in predating the E.R.A. struggle and the women's movement. Childs's story also gives us another version besides mainstream reports, because women supposedly had no occupational agency during this era. Likewise, many women's voices throughout US history have been erased, but the reclamation of their narratives offers a fuller perspective on American life, progress, race and change.

I, too, had to change perspectives at a certain point in my life. When I finished undergrad work at Michigan State University in 1984, I vowed that I would never go back to college again. I had been in business, gotten married and divorced, and traveled the world in the years after college. But something was wrong; I wasn't happy. I needed to follow my heart's desires instead of the desires of my family. But I thought — college, exams, and poverty? Oh, no. Couldn't my heart lead me somewhere else? Today, I'm working on my Ph.D. in Comparative Studies and I am passionate about my studies and my work. Life has meaning. The colors are sharper, the images clearer and much more textured. Like the kaleidoscope's whirl of shapes and colors as it shifts and rotates in different directions.

Todd McFliker has an M.A. in Mass Communication from Lynn University. His thesis, "All You Need Is Love to Dismantle an Atomic Bomb," which compares U2 to the Beatles as the music industry's cultural icons of their times, will be published as a book in 2006. He edits travel magazines and is also a writer and photog - rapher for RAG magazine where his music reporting has taken him on the road with talent such as Jane's Addiction and Pearl Jam. He spent the fall of 2005 covering the "Ultimate Rock Stars," Sir Paul McCartney, the Rolling Stones and U2. In the works: a text book on reporting live music, a doctorate in Mass Communication and work as a journalist for a British music magazine. Meanwhile, he lives with his two labs in Coconut Creek, Florida.

BLACK AND WHITE VERSUS COLOR TELEVISION

Todd McFliker

I'll never forget the first time I met my Black college girlfriend's anti-Semitic parents. It was during my first year at Florida State University, and I was dropping her off for Thanksgiving break in Miami. At the time I was ignorant to anti-Semitism and I thought my interracial interests would impress her folks. I foresaw myself being accepted as an equal, the same way I was on the high school football field. However, nothing could have prepared me for the negative reaction I received merely for being their daughter's white-skinned and Jewish boyfriend. Plopped in front of a color TV, I sat on a blue velvet couch holding Jackie's hand. "So you are Jewish, huh? You know, the Jews are responsible for getting Jesus killed," her mother informed me with a malicious stare. This was the first time I had ever experienced discrimination directed towards me, and I felt two feet small.

Why were my girlfriend's parents prejudiced towards me? Why did my parents, and grandparents, experience hardships almost every day in the 1940s merely for being Jewish? A generation gap seems to exist when it comes to interpersonal relationships between our generations. Why are our views on minorities — and interracial relationships in particular — so drastically different?

Interracial dating and marriage between two people of dissimilar races, including Asian, Afro-American, Caucasian, Hispanic and Native American, are more of a common occurrence in certain other parts of the world than in the States. However, such relationships have been on the rise since 1967 when the US Supreme Court overturned laws in the southern states prohibiting interracial marriages. An American's freedom to date or marry whomever he or she chooses is one of the "vital personal rights" protected under the Fourteenth Amendment. Yet, attitudes change slower than laws. Even today, people who have chosen an integrated way of life still often face harsh criticism from those who feel it is better to stick to their own kind.

During my early childhood in Kansas City I was sheltered, never exposed to other races, religions or cultures. The doors were shut to the real world going on outside of my private school full of Jewish American Princes and Princesses. But personally, I never appreciated my Jewish religion, and I wanted to engage in new experiences. When I moved to Florida for high school during the late 1980s, it was the first time I had any interaction with people of color. Before my big transition, the only Black folks I knew of were celebrities such as Michael Jackson and Walter Payton, people I'd seen on my color television. Still, I've grown up in a time when interracial relationships have become more and more popular, and Black-Jewish relationships are also improving. People are attempting to break down society's color barriers. In James L. Robinson's book from 1995, *Racism or Attitude? The Ongoing Struggle for Black Liberation and Self-Esteem*, he claims, "Blacks and Jews have a love-hate relationship but are drawn together by their mutual interest in fighting racism and anti-Semitism."

Susan Abrams Heyder is similar to me, another Jew with interracial experiences, although she is a generation older. She shared her story in the Race and Change oral history project in Hollywood, FL where she was born in the late 1940s. After attending the University of Florida in Gainesville, the mother of three worked as a first-grade teacher as well as a housewife in her hometown. Like my background in Kansas City, Heyder feels that she also led a sheltered childhood in the South Florida she grew up in. Despite her lack of prejudice, she felt separated from Black kids 40 years ago.

> *"You would never see Black people anywhere except working in [White] people's homes. I never saw African-Americans downtown . . . Certainly, I never saw them at the beach. It all sounds so bizarre to me when I look back," claimed Heyder. "There were separate venues in Hollywood . . . where . . . Blacks would be, where Whites would be, it was just very separate . . . I didn't see it as a negative. Now I look back on it and I see it as a negative."*

Heyder grew up with a Black woman who worked as a maid for her family five days a week. As a child, Heyder considered Artie Gregory a second mother. She remembers how thrilling it was to go to events in Gregory's Black neighborhood. "I loved it," said Heyder. "I thrived on it. It was so exciting."

One of my buddies opened the first interracial door for me in high school where I encountered integration. Playing ball, no one could miss watching Billy. He was the good-looking White Anglo Saxon Protestant with all the right moves, both on and off of the football field. Billy and I became buddies right away, and he was quite influential. He introduced me to all of the Black kids, showing me that there was literally nothing to be afraid of. The kids bussed into Boca Raton from Delray Beach were just like me, only their skin was darker. One guy, Jermain, became my first African-American friend. At first my family was somewhat intimidated by Jermain's rough and tough appearance, not knowing what to expect. He was a giant linebacker who bulged with muscles and looked mean. But I knew in my heart there was nothing for them to be afraid of, as they are not racist people. As it turns out, he played an extremely significant role in my teenage years. Sure, he didn't have the same opportunities that I had growing up, but Jermain was just another fun-loving kid on the inside, a giant teddy bear despite his "hard" appearance. He was no different than any average teenager.

In contrast, the generation just before mine rarely intermingled on a social level with other races. For example, Armando "Mandy" Perez, Jr. is a 49-year-old high school principal who shared his experiences in the Race and Change Project in the Lake Okeechobee area. The Cuban-born teacher also coaches the high school softball team. Throughout his childhood, Perez kept to his own ethnic group.

> *"Growing up [in the 1950s and '60s], you were made to feel that you kind of kept to your own grouping in essence. Outside the school setting . . . you pretty much kept to your own ethnic community . . . All of the Hispanic families were together. All the Anglo families were together . . . Once in a while you would have a friend that would cross over, but that was just not typical. People react differently based on their experiences with other races [and] this causes them to be frustrated at the entire race and not at individuals. I . . . remember hearing the 'n-' word a lot more in those days than I do today. It hasn't gone away, but it was very prevalent. Perhaps prejudiced acts were from children's upbringings. Whatever the case may be, there is certainly more of a racial balance and less anti-Semitism in today's society."*

Perez explains another aspect of interracial relationships in the 1960s.

> *"You crossed over racially during the school hours, but after school you didn't have interaction. As a junior, I did ask a girl to the prom. She was White, and the dad wouldn't let her go to the prom with me because I was Cuban. That kind of hurt my feelings for a long time."*

He eventually befriended a Black man at work who changed his life. Joseph was the first Black guy with whom Perez had a lot of contact. He had a talent for vocational duties and served as a role model on a construction site for Perez. Joseph taught him to look beyond the person's skin to see what is inside.

Perez also grew up in the era seeing changes in attitudes towards females as well. He attended the University of Florida where they were seen then as mere ornaments and rarely had organized sports. According to Perez, if you were a woman and also a minority, you faced "a double whammy" in discrimination.

> *"[Now], my wife works in a school setting . . . in a public school system in Royal Palm Beach . . . She has friends that are of all make-ups . . . [People need to] look beyond the person. . . . What they are worth is what's inside, not what they look like. When we go out, you don't ask whether [the couple is] Hispanic or Anglos or Black. . . . I think that type of social interaction that exists today didn't exist 35 years ago."*

Robert Gossett, a 53-year-old attorney from Hollywood, Florida, is a White Anglo Saxon protestant who relates his experiences growing up in Hollywood in the same oral history project as Heyder. At a young age, Gossett was ignorant of Black people, even being afraid to drink after a "colored" student from a water fountain. He never experienced interpersonal relationships with Black students growing up, merely because there were so few on his school campus in the 1960s. However, Gossett played high school basketball, opening the door to his first interracial experience.

Playing ball, Gossett recalls feeling that there was unfair treatment from the coaches, and accusing them of bending over backwards for the Black kids. "Because they . . . [were] Black, they . . . [were] getting to play and we . . . [were] not." Gossett obviously felt reverse discrimination. In his eyes, the White kids were being skipped in the football line-up for no good reason, and his coaches were making an overexerted effort to give the black athletes more playing time.

In contrast, when I played high school football in the early '90s, the kids from Delray Beach didn't receive any special treatment. The coach always allowed the most talented athletes to play, with no regard to skin color. In fact, I remember when I replaced a Black kid in the wide receiver position by beating him in a 50-yard dash. The coach's decision to place my opponent on the bench was merely professional.

Gossett's first Black friend was another basketball player at his school nicknamed Foots. Just like Jermain in my childhood, Foots and his wild sense of humor left a life-long impression on Gossett. Jermain would often take me back to his home turf to hang out. But unlike my escapades in Delray, Gossett remembers being careful to get out of Foots' Black neighborhood as quickly as possible. In fact, he was often cautioned not even to drive through "colored town," due to ongoing race riots in the 1960s.

Growing up, Gossett did meet a Black man for whom he developed a great deal of respect. Buster worked as a construction laborer for Gossett's father, and often took care of the youngster. Buster taught him many extraneous things, he said, from professional wrestling statistics to information related to America's space program.

> *"Buster was probably the least educated man . . . but the smartest man I've ever known. [He] knew more about common sense things, and how to treat people . . . and how to be a good human being than most anybody who had a Ph. D. behind their name. Sometimes you just want to grab [bigots] by the collar and shake them, and you just want to scream at them sometimes, 'Your ignorance is really, really dangerous.'"*

Fortunately, neither Gossett nor I ever faced ridicule for our interracial experiences. Following high school, I moved to college in Tallahassee in 1994, and my years at Florida State University were the time to experiment. I often wondered what it would be like to be with a person of another race, and when I met Jackie, an African-American female rugby star, I embarked upon uncharted territory. I introduced her to everyone, including my folks, as my serious girlfriend. I was certainly the first in my family to start an intimate cross-cultural relationship. Susan Heyder relates some of her own personal experiences with the interracial dating issue.

> *"I am certain that if I were to have dated anyone of another color as my kids do, things would've [been] halted [by her parents]. In fact, when our oldest daughter . . . has been dating a black young man for five years, easily . . . One of the first things . . . that my mom said was 'Oh, maybe you better talk to her about that' . . . And I said 'Why? We've welcomed everyone in our home all these years.'"*

Granted, my parents feel the same way as Heyder's folks. The fact that I didn't bring home a "nice Jewish girl" from college one vacation didn't exactly please them, but at least they treated my partner with respect. Meanwhile, Jackie's Christian parents crucified me in their living room during that Thanksgiving break.

Author Robinson writes, "It is not surprising that today's Blacks and Jews find themselves in conflict. What is surprising is that the so-called coalition between Blacks and Jews, which started around 1910 and lasted until the late 1960's, lasted as long as it did." I know that some of my Jewish relatives resent Blacks because of competition for jobs and university positions, merely for the sake of affirmative action. But still, I had trouble understanding why I was personally being discriminated against due to my religion. After all, organized racist groups in America have hated not only innocent Blacks, but Jewish people as well. According to Robinson, "These racist groups have tended to lump both groups together. Many Blacks have a hard time seeing Jews, who are White, as a legitimately oppressed group. So when Jews speak about anti-Semitism and racial hatred, many Blacks do not take them seriously. Certainly [because] Blacks see themselves as chief victims, there is little room for others to take on this role." Personally, I believe Blacks and Jews have a reason for a mutual bond. Jews must be the only Whites who really understand what it is like to be hated for reasons beyond one's control.

Soon after the unpleasant encounter at Jackie's house, we split up. We began to quarrel a bit too often, and I couldn't see a future for us following the distasteful meeting with her parents. I did go back to dating White girls, but with a better appreciation for the diversity of races and religions and the conflicts that can emerge.

Kami Barrett *is a South Florida native who graduated with honors from Florida State University with a B.S. in International Affairs and Creative Writing. She has an M.A. in Communication from Florida Atlantic University and works in public relations for a non-profit organization. The oral history experience has had an immense impact on her life, she says. "In principle, the United States has outlawed racial discrimination but, in practice, little has changed. Social, economic and political institutions still discriminate, although some institutions have modified their behavior by eliminating obvi -ous discriminatory practices and choosing their language carefully. Family, educational institutions and religious associations should foster the idea that awareness and education are needed to inform individuals that this is not a problem of the past, but a problem for the future."*

A LONG BUS RIDE FOR ME

Kami Barrett

My mother often refers to me as the child who came into the world sleeping. While most babies scream and wail within the first few moments of birth, I was content to stay asleep. I assume that is why I have such a calm disposition. You have the rest of your life to scream and wail at life's indignities. Why start a few seconds after you are born?

I am the only member of my family to be born in the South, and the youngest daughter of three girls. My father's side of the family is Italian, and my mother's side is Irish; both of them were born in Manhattan, New York where they were exposed to numerous cultures while living in the city. But, growing up in a middle class suburban area of South Florida prevented me from seeing what the "real world" was composed of in terms of race and culture.

I lived in an all-White neighborhood and the public school I attended is where I encountered people that were unlike me. In kindergarten, I was assigned to sit next to boy named Mario. If I did not have a class picture of him, then I would probably not remember that he was Black. As a child, it did not matter that the color of my friend's skin was different from my own. However, as I got older the majority of my friends were White. I realized years later, after interviewing a classmate in a cultural diversity course, how being racially different could affect a person's life in a major way.

Darla moved to the United States from Jamaica during the early 1980s at the age of 12. She recounted an incident that occurred on a public bus between her and a young White man. Soon afterwards, she discovered how rude people acted towards her because of the color of her skin. I found myself sympathizing with her feelings and I understood her actions that day. It was as if I was actually there witnessing the scene she so vividly recalled.

I imagined that day in 1983 as if I was there, sweat sliding down my back clinging to my white cotton blouse. I can see myself pulling my bag closer to my chest as I settled into the seat of that city bus. Jerking forward, the bus rambled down the busy streets of Liberty City, Miami. People squeezed by each other grasping the metal bars dangling above. The air became stifling and the scent of jasmine invaded my nostrils as the woman sitting next to me fidgeted for more room. Her oversized purse practically pushed me out the window and with every jolt of the bus her straw hat scratched the side of my head. To find a little relief I stared out the window watching the people walk back and forth along the sidewalk.

The bus came to a halt and people began to file out. As the jasmine lady rose to leave, an old man with snow white hair to match his Santa Claus beard sat down next to me. He unfolded his newspaper and began to read. I looked up, watching the people move past me. Two of them stood out among the sea of White faces as their dark visages glanced around the bus for a vacant seat. The older, whom I assumed was the mother, lightly held onto her daughter's shoulder.

"Oh this is my stop," a woman in a dark suit cried across the aisle from me as she gathered up her briefcase and hurriedly pushed her way towards the back door.

"Darla, go ahead and sit in that seat," the woman told her daughter who looked to be about12, my age then, too. She slid into the seat and almost collided with a young man who wanted to sit there as well. Sliding her legs around to the front of the seat, the young girl settled in, staring ahead, while the man was forced to grab onto the handle above her head as the bus began to move forward. The mother stood directly in front of him facing the back of the bus. A colorful wrap secured on her head hid her hair and gold bracelets, which jangled when the bus hit a bump, encased her long arms. Her daughter sat quietly twirling a braid through her fingers. Every time the bus jerked she would accidentally bump into the man who was standing close beside her.

"Sorry," the young girl said.

Glaring down at her, the blond man jerked back his torso and stared down at her with a look of loathing. I strained my neck to look around the newspaper that the old man had placed in front of me. By the third jostle, the young man let out a low grumble as the young girl knocked into him. Annoyance could be seen in the eyes of her mother. By now her fists clenched as she stared back at the man.

"Do you have a problem?" she asked.

Her Jamaican accent was thick as honey. The words rolled off her tongue as she spread her legs apart and placed her hands on her hips. The man ran his fingers through his hair and cocked his head to the side looking out the window. He ignored her onslaught of accusations. A smirk crept across his face as he shook his head. She began pelting the man with words in her island tongue. People surrounding the front of the bus began to turn around to see what all of the commotion was about. The man next to me lowered the paper and I caught a glimpse of the young girl as she tried to figure out why her mother was yelling. She nervously glanced around watching the people watching her.

The bus came to the next stop. The mother stopped yelling at the man. None of the passengers moved as she leaned over, grabbed her daughter's arm, and pushed her way to the front, with her daughter lagging behind.

"What did I do that was wrong?" the young girl pleaded. Her mother shook her head as they got off the bus.

I scrambled past the old man and followed them off the bus, wanting to follow them, wondering why the mother was angry. The mother leaned close to her daughter, speaking calmly, but anger still lingered in her eyes.

Confused, the young girl looked at up at her. "Because I'm Black?" she questioned. She looked stunned.

So was I, as I listened to Darla's story.

It was hard for me to understand why racial prejudice existed on that bus ride. Perhaps it's too idealistic to think that, as a society, we can overcome prejudice. Throughout my life I had been aware of racial discrimination from a distance. Through Darla, I got a close look.

I am grateful that the attitude I had as a child has never left me, because it is amazing how quickly and completely a culture's values and norms are integrated into a person's identity. According to Richard H. Ropers and Dan J. Pence, authors of *American Prejudice: With Liberty and Justice for Some,* "socialization is a lifelong process, though it is most crucial and powerful in an individual's early years." The family and the educational system are two of the most important outlets when passing on social knowledge from one generation to the next. But what if the family and education fail to properly instruct a child on the ideas and norms of society, such as prejudice? As I listened to a series of archival oral histories of South Florida residents in the Race and Change oral history project, I encountered a variety of people discussing their first cultural and racial awareness.

Cyril Pinder Sr. was born in Nassau, Bahamas, and moved to Miami in 1943. His Bahamian heritage wasn't an issue until he moved to Miami.

In an oral history interview conducted in Hollywood, Florida, Pinder discussed those first disturbing encounters with racism.

> *"I remember taking the bus to go to Flagler Street to buy a watch. I paid my 10 cents, and sat down behind the driver. A White man came on and stood in front of me. I didn't know why because there were empty seats throughout the bus. The driver then spoke up and said, 'Boy get up and let this White man sit down.' I didn't know why I had to stand up. 'There are plenty of seats,' I told the driver. 'I paid my 10 cents just like him. Why do I have to get up?' At that moment, a lady in the back told me to go to the back of the bus and not cause any trouble. I refused, and the White man took a seat. All of a sudden, the driver pulled out a gun and repeatedly told me to get up and I kept saying, 'Not a damn thing like it.' I remember the driver's finger trembling on the trigger. I got off the bus and walked home crying. I did not know that White folks treated Black people that way."*

If you look back in history, ideas of race and ethnicity hold a central place in prejudice. Ropers and Pence found that these prejudices lead to inequality, hostility, and violence. They affirm that, "while the treatment of Native and African Americans often offers the most powerful examples, the history of our republic is littered with gross examples of racial and ethnic prejudice and discrimination."

According to Ropers and Pence, issues of color have dominated American society since the 1954 Supreme Court ruling *Brown vs Board of Education,* and since Rosa Parks refused to give her seat to a White man. Race consciousness has emerged as a global phenomenon and nowhere is it more prominent than in the United States. The authors believe, "from the landing of Europeans in what became Virginia and New England until today, race has remained the cruelest, most divisive, and most prejudiced way of grouping peoples." But when does this divisive grouping happen? Does it occur during childhood or adulthood?

Susan Abrams Heyder, a native of Hollywood, Florida, cannot pinpoint the exact moment that she became aware of racial prejudice. Born in 1948, she was the daughter of a White Jewish family who moved down to South Florida from North Florida. Her father was an attorney and owned an airport park.

> *"I never saw Blacks downtown or at the beach, which sounds so bizarre now. During the segregation period, I remember seeing pictures of the signs that read 'whites only' and 'coloreds only.' My parents were fair-minded. When I was a young girl my parents hired a Black woman as a housekeeper. She was like a second mother to me. The first time that I became consciously aware of racial differences was when the maid took me to Attucks High School to see her nephew in a play. I realized that I was the only White face in the crowd. At the time I was a student at South Broward High School, and all I can remember is not ever*

seeing Black people. As I look back at my yearbook from 1967, I see some Black faces, but I do not recall them. I never communicated with them.

"I became aware of racial integration when I went off to the University of Florida. By the time I went to college, I felt pretty sheltered. The hippie movement was taking place, so everyone was entitled to their own opinion regarding social issues. I did not get involved in that world. Instead, I pledged a sorority and experienced prejudice firsthand. "As I went to each sorority on campus, I was asked my religion. I had no problem saying that I was Jewish. However, only Jewish sororities asked me back. I later found that there were two Jewish sorority houses and one non-Jewish sorority house that accepted Jewish girls.

"At that time, I did not have a problem with it. I grew up with the idea that Jewish communities tend to stick together and there is a comfort level. My mother grew up in Live Oak, Florida and her family was one of two or three Jewish families in the city. They were ostracized and were not included in parties that neighbors hosted. The Jewish families just stuck together. One thing that sticks out in mind is that when I would tell people that I was Jewish, they would reply, 'You don't look Jewish.' I always wanted to know what they meant by that. What does Jewish look like?"

Physical anthropologists have described and divided human beings into races since the 1800s. "There are physical, genetic differences between people today," Ropers and Pence claim, "but here race describes the physical appearances of people based on their external traits." The color of the skin is a major dividing characteristic used in describing races in the United States.

The problem with this stereotypical categorization is that what one group may consider beautiful, another group does not. "The problems concerning race are not the concept itself," the authors argue, "[or] the way different peoples appear, or the number of different races into which humans can be divided. They are, rather, what individuals of a particular race consider themselves, and the way they view their neighbors or peoples of a different race."

Some people suffer a lifetime of prejudice and hostility simply because their skin color is different and they are considered inferior. Prejudices are rooted in the fundamental ways American society is structured. Socialization is necessary for a society to survive and grow because it reflects and carries on social institutions, such as the family, education, and religion and, "too frequently," states Ropers and Pence, "these institutions teach rules and values that reflect underlying cultural values of prejudice, fear, and hate."

The family is one of the most important social institutions. Because children are unable to compare or evaluate what they learn with what other children learn, or with what other adults teach, they are often left vulnerable to whatever messages are taught by their parents.

For example, Robert Gossett, an attorney in Broward County, Florida, recalls his first memory of the racial climate in South Florida during the 1960s. In an archival oral history interview conducted in his hometown of Hollywood, Fla., Gossett describes his first experience with segregation.

> *"My mother and grandmother would go food shopping every Friday afternoon on Tyler Street. I remember seeing the signs for 'white' water fountains and 'colored' water fountains. I also remember there being separate bathrooms. My parents never discussed with me the differences between Whites and Blacks. I remember them referring to a certain part of town called 'colored town.' Looking back on it now, there was a distinction from my mother's northern attitude compared to my father's southern attitude. At that time, it was just known that Black people were different.*
>
> *"Since my father was a general contractor there were a lot of Black laborers that worked for him. One man, Buster, worked for my father and he kind of took me under his wing. He was the least educated man I knew, but Buster knew more about common sense then I would ever know. Buster took care of me and he made sure that I didn't goof off. He was a hardworking good guy.*
>
> *"When I entered high school, I was not aware of the changes that the Civil Rights Act would bring. I remember Black students entering South Broward High School when I was junior or senior. I first encountered the Black students while playing basketball. Two students, Greg Samuel and Foots Warner, played on the basketball team with me. I can remember feeling some resentment that Foots had taken my place on the team, and I blamed the coach. "I thought that because they were Black they got to play more in a game. But, that was the extent of the resentment. I don't remember any problems. There didn't seem to be any racial problems, such as jeering or name calling.*
>
> *"The awareness of things changing at this time was apparent in the news. I would watch the news and see reports on George Wallace and Martin Luther King. I then had a sense that things were changing. I began to acknowledge that I once had a fear of drinking from a water fountain after a Black person and that I would change somehow because I shared the fountain. But, I had positive experiences with Buster, Samuel, and Warner. As I look back, I wonder how we could have had a society with these attitudes."*

Even as a young adult going away to college, I did not realize that our society was still plagued with prejudice. My first real personal encounter occurred during my first year as an undergraduate student. I lived across the hall from two girls, Kristen and Tracey. At the beginning of the year, all seemed well as the girls in my hall got to know one another. We would chat and roam from room to room. Everyone's door was always open.

As I look back on the situation now, the majority of my dorm floor was White. Most of us were native Floridians and everyone *seemed* really nice. Kristen was a quiet girl who kept to herself, spending most of her time in her room. Occasionally, I would see her in the hall and say hello. She would respond with a smile and continue on her way.

Her roommate Tracey, however, was the complete opposite. She had a bubbly, cheerful personality. She was a year older than the other girls on the floor and she always gave us advice about school. Tracey was always friendly and would go out of her way to help people. But, towards the middle of the year Kristen and Tracey began to have arguments. I would often see the Resident Dorm adviser coming out of their room. Late one night Tracey came knocking on my door in tears.

"I just got into a huge argument with Kristen, and she started calling me names. She started referring to Black people as troublemakers and saying how she hated living with me," Tracey said.

I tried to calm her down, and she explained that this was not the first time that Kristen had made a derogatory comment about her race. I was shocked to learn that even in the late 1990s prejudice frequented the halls of my dorm. The fact that Tracey was Black and Kristen was White played into a stupid argument over the tidiness of their room.

That night, Tracey did not want to stay in her room. It was the weekend and the Resident Dorm Advisor was not there, so I asked Tracey if she would like to stay with me in my room. But since my roommate was there, Tracey did not have a place to sleep. Fortunately, one of the girls in the room next to mine was out of town. Her roommate, Melissa, however, who had always been nice to Tracey in the hallway, was very reluctant to have her stay in the extra bed.

"I just think it would be rude if you stayed in Amanda's bed without her knowing," Melissa said.

Tracey and I called Amanda, who was at her parent's home, and she had no problem with it.

"Well, I don't plan on going to bed for a long time, so the lights will be on," Melissa claimed.

At that point in the night Tracey was so exhausted by the argument that she just wanted to go to bed.

"I don't care, I am just really tired," Tracey said.

"Fine," Melissa replied, "Whatever."

I knew that Tracey was too distracted to see the prejudice that Melissa was showing towards her. I, however, saw right through Melissa. How can a person be nice and seemingly sincere, and then become harsh and indifferent in a matter of minutes? In the end, Tracey stayed in the room next to mine, but only after Melissa went down the hall to sleep in a friend's room.

According to the Harvard Project on School Desegregation study, racial segregation in the 1990s is spreading in public schools to an extent not seen since the 1960s," claims Ropers and Pence. It seems that while the United States should be leaping forward into an open minded progressive future, in some ways it is slowly taking steps backwards.

It may be naïve to think that American society will transform overnight into an equally diverse and accepting community. Some signs of tolerance and acceptance are also emerging, however. It is hard to determine which path American society will ultimately embrace. Without trying to sound too positive, I foresee a gradual expansion of acceptance and diversity. The more people become aware of the racial climate in their community, the more power they will gain to make positive changes.

Narrator Sandy Eichner and husband in 1955 in Florida

Carmen Canales recalls a past event.
Photo by Natasha Pierre-Louis

Narrator Lexie May Childs.
Photo by Natasha Pierre-Louis

Narrator Cyril Pinder, Sr.

RACIAL INCOUNTERS ACROSS CULTURAL LINES

INTRODUCTION

These writers engaged in a unique dialogue experience across races and cultures within the classroom that, blended with archival Race and Change "encounters," produced some interesting reflections on their lives and attitudes as well as the lives of others. Their essays are paired here to create a mirror-look at how we perceive others and, at the same time, how we are being perceived.

Writers and Interviewers Claudina Souther, left, and Shelly Weiss.
Photo by Ry Nielsen

Shelly Weiss is currently the Director of Marketing, Planning and Communications for a medical center. Previously, she worked as a television news reporter in the South. She holds a bachelor's degree in Telecommunications News from the University of Florida and is currently enrolled in Florida Atlantic University's Master's program in Communication. She says that her experience in the oral history class has impacted the way she views other people, as it serves as a reminder that everyone has a story.

♋

FAMILY VALUES ACROSS CULTURES

Shelly Weiss

It's incredible how a smell can take you back to another time in your life. A walk past the perfume counter at a department store where someone has just sprayed Chanel reminds you a lot of what your grandmother used to wear, or the aroma of an apple pie fresh from the oven can make you feel like it's the holidays in the middle of July. Other smells can remind you of things you wish you could forget. For instance, my nose knows the smell of vanilla body spray. Even if I get a small whiff of it now, I am back in my college dormitory with my freshman year Norwegian roommate at The University of Florida, Ingrid, who never left our room without bathing herself in it. Unfortunately, this was the extent of her personal hygiene, and because the sickly sweet smell was mixed with body odor, it is still one that I find offensive today. I had no idea that living with someone of a different ethnic background would be so difficult. I would learn a lot about this during that year. My suite mates had no leniency on this girl when it came to making their point about how unpleasant they, too, thought it was to have to deal with this.

We had made it to the Christmas holiday and before we went home our vacation the two other girls I lived with suggested a gift exchange. They knew exactly what they wanted to get for Ingrid. Upon the insistence of the girls — and I am sad to admit, in retrospect, that I agreed — we all gave her soap-related products as a gift. Part of me felt terrible, but another part was saying that we had the right to do this. I mean, she probably could have changed her sheets at least once since the beginning of the school year four months earlier. One of the girls was so bold as to suggest that Ingrid try one of the soaps right then and let us all know if she liked it. She had a very strange look on her face after all of this took place, but didn't really say much. Looking back, I realize now that things must have been pretty difficult for her. She was overweight and quiet, living with three loud freshmen sorority pledges. The other girls and I bonded and went out together, but she never came with us. In reality, we never invited her. She must have felt very alone. The other girls and I moved into our sorority houses the following year but stayed friends. I would see Ingrid on campus during the rest of my time in Gainesville, and we would exchange pleasantries, but it never went beyond that. Perhaps she wanted to get away from the three of us just as much as we wanted to get away from her.

I think kids in school learn to be cruel to their classmates who are different at an early age. It is a trait that is difficult to overcome, and sometimes even as an adult, I find myself slipping back into the pattern of gossiping around the water cooler about co-workers. I think it is all in how you handle this very ugly part of human nature. No one knows this better than my friend and co-worker Claudina Souther, who remembers starting school in America as the scariest time in her life. We had the chance to share experiences in a deeper way as classmates in a course on writing across cultures. Both the United States and school were much different than anything else Souther had ever known, she said. In her home country of Colombia, all of the kids at her private Catholic school had looked just like her with dark eyes and dark hair, but when she started public high school in New York things were different. In broken English, she would try to communicate with the other kids, but they did not want or try to understand her. Instead, they treated her like an outsider. It was at school that she had her first taste of ethnic diversity. The first Black kids she met were involved in a gang, and she became the target of their teasing. "They would teach me bad words and get me to repeat these to other students to get me in trouble," she said. "I just wanted to fit in and understand how to communicate and make friends with these kids." Throughout the rest of high school, things did not get much better. She tried to avoid the lunchroom all together because some of the gang members told her they would be there waiting for her and that they had plans to rearrange her "pretty face." "I barely survived high school, and I was willing to do whatever it would take to make sure things would be different for my kids."

This experience is so much different from the way I remember things when I grew up. Even during sorority rush, the feelings were of inclusion rather than exclusion. "Did you hear? A Black girl is coming through Rush this year," said the chair of the event for Chi Omega Sorority at The University of Florida. "I wonder which house she will choose?" one of my sisters asked. "Wouldn't it be great if she came here!" another said. As I looked around at the group of White faces of the largest sorority on campus, I breathed a sigh of relief. I felt so lucky. This house had really become my home away from home, and for what seemed like the first time, a Black girl was choosing to rush the traditionally "White" houses, and it was okay with us. Even before this, the winds of change were already blowing strong through our house. I was one of a few Jewish girls to have chosen and been accepted amongst these blond haired, blue eyed girls, and it seemed they were ready to open the doors a little further. While this girl did not become a Chi Omega, she reminded all of us that we were ready to learn from and about people from other cultures.

For Souther, culture and difference presented an everyday battle, but at the age of 16, things changed dramatically. Queens College was a sort of rebirth for the young Colombian girl who had struggled for most of her teenage years to stay on the right track and away from those who tried to prevent her from succeeding. While waiting for one of her first classes to start, a young Black man walked into the room and took the seat next to her. She remembers feeling fear shoot through her. In an instant, she was back in the lunchroom where she had known so much pain. But as she got to know him, she relaxed and realized that he was much different from the kids at her high school who had roughhoused her. Here in college she grew as a person and began to gain a new appreciation for her Colombian heritage. Later, she met and married an American man and started a family. Today, she spends a lot of time with her two kids to make sure they understand their roots. They attend a private Catholic school like she did as a child. She worries that there is little ethnic diversity in their classes compared to what they would experience in a public school, however. So she tries to tell them about her experiences. She hopes that by transferring her values and beliefs to her own children it will help prepare them to stand on their own in the world and to never make others feel like an outsider as she did. This was the same thing my parents advocated all of my life, preparing me for the world.

I was born in Detroit, but right before that they hired a nanny. She was a woman of compassion and honesty who moved in with us when my mom became bed-ridden during her pregnancy with me to help my dad take care of my older sister. My mom was back on her feet shortly after I was born, but the nanny, Bernadette, loved us, and we loved her, and she ended up staying for close to 10 years. Bernadette became a large part of my early life. After spending several of her teenage years as a nun, 15 years later she became a teacher. During that time my folks met her and she seemed to blend right in with our family despite the religious differences. I think it must have been because my parents allowed us to learn about her and her traditions while including her in our family gatherings and celebrations as well. Sitting at midnight mass with her one Christmas Eve, she taught my sister and me about Mary, the baby Jesus, and the meaning of His birth. It all seemed a little strange, but we knew we should respect something that affected her so deeply. With no children of her own, we were her family, and it meant the world to her to share such an important part of her life with us.

This definitely was not the typical nanny situation in families where the caretaker is more like a salaried employee than a beloved grandmother. Susie Mae Brown, who is in her 80's, knows all too well. As a Black woman caring for White families in the 1930s and '40s, she knew real pain and prejudice. In the archival oral history Race and Change Project, she discusses how things were in the Belle Glade/South Bay area around Florida's Lake Okeechobee. I listened to her recorded interview and found myself picturing what it must have been like to walk in her shoes for a day, to experience her life:

> *"All this was bean fields. I picked bean shells. There was a second-hand store over there. The water we drunk was from Hoover Dike. We washed our clothes in the canal. It smelled so bad. We lived in shanties. I spent my life mostly around family. My life was all right; there wasn't much to do. When they built the highway 27 highway, my husband worked on it. I raised five sons. My husband had an accident — he was workin' on the railroad at the time [so] I had to work, I worked in a motel, [a] restaurant. I worked in the fields, but they took me out of the fields and into their houses. I worked with the peoples in the houses keepin' the children, cookin' for them, cleanin' for them. I was a nanny this time.*
>
> *"[I]t's been a long time since I worked in them fields. I had some good friends; they kept my chil'ren for me while I was workin' and they wouldn't charge me or nothing. I always try to be nice to everybody. Never had no complaints. [One place] I had to go in the back, I would be sittin' up in the car with the lady and we'd come up to the house and she'd go in the front, and I had to go in the back. I started doin' that, but I quit. I said, if I'm in there cookin' and cleanin' her childrens, takin' care of her childrens and doing everything, I told her, I can go there to the front? She said, 'Yeah, come on.' I told her, when they gone, if the children got hurt, they gonna be listenin' to the maid. They was all nice to me 'cause I'm the nanny here.*
>
> *"I got polices and teachers and everything, all the people, in fact. I felt all right. It was something I said I would do in those days. They was calling us 'niggers,' but they never did call me that. I done fed them and everything. If they didn't listen, the lady of the house, she would go in the house and get me a belt and the rest of them [kids] would go and break me a switch and I used them. And I raised their children — their children still call me, I have pictures of them now . . . I have special children in my pocketbook, I said that's right, this is your Black granny. They just come and throw their arms around me. They really treated me nice . . . I tell them all, nobody did it but Jesus."*

As my sister and I got older, I think Bernadette felt less needed and realized it was time for her to move on. She moved into a home of her own but still lived close to us. She would cook a big Christmas dinner and our family would exchange gifts. We got presents that "Santa" had brought us. I knew they were really from her even though she would never admit it. That was part of what made her so special. It was really remarkable to think a retired nun would find her place with a Jewish family, but our lives fit together perfectly. My sister, Stephanie, and I always felt close to her, like a grandmother figure. Writer Patrick Moss suggests in his *New York Times* article about the 1990s families that this could have been because of, "distaste for the middleman" — the middlemen, of course, being the parents. "The cynical observation is that the middle generation may be supporting both the young and the older generations, so they have to be more materialistic. They also have to routinely exercise power, particularly over their children. And this is something growing children often resent. Grandparents, however, often offer a kind of sanctuary for the grandchild, an environment in which the exercise of power and the existence of a pecking order have no place." I think, for me, this was certainly the case. Bernadette, to her credit, had an undying patience for children.

Some kids are with nannies so much they often become a "second mother." That was Susan Abrams Heyder's relationship with her own former caregiver, who is Black, despite the limitations that society had placed on interracial relationships of any kind when she was growing up in the late '50s and early '60s. Heyder, who is also Jewish, discusses the cross-cultural experience in the Race and Change oral history project conducted in the Hollywood, FL area:

> *"We've always had, in fact to this day we always had, when I was a very young girl, we had a woman, Artie Gregory, that worked for us five days a week. She's still my second mother. We see her all the time. [But growing up] it was a very separate existence. She came, she worked, she went home. I really have to say, my parents were very fair-minded. There was never a verbal attitude to me [but] if I was to have dated anyone of another color, as my kids, things would have been halted much sooner. My daughter has been dating a Black guy for five years. My dad's been gone all this time, but my mom said, 'Maybe you'd better talk to her about that.' I said, 'well, we've welcomed everyone in our home all these years.'*
>
> *"[Still] the Jewish population tends to stick together. There's strength in numbers, a comfort level. People are more comfortable with someone that shares your own values and background. Just making someone Jewish, or African American, doesn't mean they're friends for life, or meant to be. But it certainly is a starting point, a little more of a foundation."*

Heyder thinks her parents would have tried to discourage an interracial relationship, but it was her relationship with her "second mother" that helped Heyder open up her own mind and progress a little bit further than the previous generation had been able to.

Being so close with my family and always having a huge support system made it hard for me to go away to school, and hard to move even further away for my career. Eventually, however, I found my way back home to South Florida. But soon after graduation from college, my perspective on life and people, in general, changed even more. I became a television news reporter and started my career in Abilene, TX, which was much different from any place I had ever known. It looked like an old, one-horse town you might see in the movies with a group of people that was hard to break into, and I am sure I did not stay long enough to have any real impact. It was also like going back in time, and I never really felt comfortable. Jewish organizations were nowhere to be found, and it was clear that my co-workers did not understand my background. The station I worked at was unpleasant, to say the least. The main anchor was a small-minded bigot who made it clear that he did not like me, or any other Jewish people, and would never like me, no matter what I did. It made me more homesick than any other time in my life.

Many cities started off small and provincial like this, but most have managed to progress well beyond this point. I now live in Hollywood, FL, close to where I grew up. In the Race and Change oral history project in Hollywood, Cathleen Anderson, a city commissioner whose family has been in Broward County forever, remembers what it was like before the community grew up, a time when racism was rampant:

> *"My racial identity is White. I was always aware of it. In my family we always had a Black lady to help my grandmother since I was a child. My grandmother was elderly and was helping to raise my [mother's] sister Clara [and] my cousins. My uncle was drafted into the Army and she was helping to raise his children. I was always aware of it. I remember Genie, she used to come to our house about two days a week to wash on Monday, iron on Tuesday, and sometimes she would come other days to help my grandmother clean. My grandmother had a stroke and she was unable to do everything herself, so Genie was a part of our family and we had a big time when Genie came. We'd wait for Genie in the morning because in the cold weather Genie would bring a special kind of sweet potato. She'd cook it, and I never knew how she cooked it and she'd never tell us, but when she got there she'd peel the potato and then bake or boil it, and then she'd put in a special kind of sauce and fry it in the frying pan and we would have it for breakfast. It was out of this world.*
>
> *"Genie had to be home by dark. Unless a Black lived in Blounts Quarters [housing for laborers], they had to be across the railroad by dark. . . . Most of the African Americans worked on the farms in the winter time. Dixie Highway was a dirt road that had been cut out of a palmetto patch. Most of the residences for Blacks [were] west of Dixie Highway . . . I still remember today in 1950, my grandmother was so sick, and you had to tell the police department if a Black person was staying at your house overnight. My grandmother had another stroke — and [eventually] died. Genie would stay with us. Her children were grown and her husband could take care of himself, and she stayed with us and would sleep in our house. My mother and aunt would take care of my grandmother at night and Genie would take care of her during the day. It went back then, and*

I know they forgot to do it, and the police came by and said that they under-stand Genie is staying here, and he came in and saw my grandmother, who was in a coma — don't know if that was the law or what [but] I was always aware.

My grandmother tried to teach all of her kids to read before they started school, including a cute little Black girl who was my mother's best friend. In fact, my grandmother used to make a couple of dresses for her when she made dresses for my mother. This little girl was smaller. She spent a lot of time with my grandmother; in fact, she stayed there because her mother and father worked on the farms. She was smart. My grandmother said she was the cutest, sweetest little girl. There was segregation. The superintendent came to my mother's house because the little girl knew how to read and my grandmother said, 'You know, she stays here.' He said that she ought not to do it, and she better not teach any other Black children to read."

My school experiences have always included people of other races — teachers as well as students. I think for those in the younger generations, it is hard to imagine what segregation was even like because it seems so far from the norm. While segregation has been outlawed for decades, there are many people who still feel like it should be legal. I found that out when I saw the hatred of differences in Abilene, and to an even greater degree, when I moved to Dothan, AL. Dothan was a nice town that made me feel safe. The small number or Jewish congregants who lived there welcomed me at the temple. It was a racism rally that I covered well outside the city limits for the television station I worked for, however, that made me realize that hate was still alive among those who weren't educated about other cultures. The group was denouncing Blacks, Muslims, Jews and others who were not like them.

I began to feel panicky, even though I was supposed to be impartial — simply there to tell the story. Bonfires were burning and it seemed like there were hundreds of people dressed in white, their faces covered. It was hot, and loud. Our television crew was pushed through the crowd to a man who was in charge. He did a quick interview without telling us his name, and then disappeared back into the night. Once again we were get-ting jostled among these extremists. It was hard to stay focused on the job at hand, the job of getting our camera and microphone into the faces of the right people. I think my photographer sensed my feelings. It must have been because I was stiff as a board, staring into this sea of anger. "Let's get this over with," he said. His discomfort was evident as well. We finished the interviews and got out of there as fast as we could. I was scared and angry at the same time. We never saw their faces. Since they were engaging in this sort of activity, I thought they should let the world see what the faces of racism look like, what fools look like.

It seems, then, that the burden of change lies with future genera-tions. Perhaps the best thing that can happen to us is being exposed to racial situations that we find disturbing. Today, people who have had trouble racially, like my friend and classmate Claudina Souther when she was young, have a responsibility to make sure that they overcome these feelings. Souther works at it on a regular basis with her children. She is open to them and speaks to them about what happened to her. But instead of letting them be afraid of differences, she encourages them to explore.

Claudina M. Souther's family migrated to the United States in 1978. The journey has been painful and joyous, she says. "The thorny road has led me to a beautiful garden of red roses. I have a master's degree in Communication and an undergraduate degree in Spanish and I have also been blessed with a beautiful family. Oral history is an integral part of human nature. Just when you think you are all alone in this world going through character-building times, you hear about other people in another region going through the same trying times as you once did. History links us all together and there is no racial divide — we are all in this together. Oral history is the glue that holds us together as one."

AN INTERCULTURAL JOURNEY: TWO CULTURES, ONE WORLD

Claudina Souther

The journey of my life changed at the age of 11 when, on December 11, 1978, my mother, brother and I arrived in New York City from Colombia, South America. My mother, a single parent, wanted a better future for her children. Her life in the States was not easy, however. She was a factory employee working 12-hour days six days a week for minimum wage but after five long agonizing years of working hard and not having her children with her, she successfully brought us to this foreign land. When my mother first left for the United States I was only six years old, and my brother was 14. My mother's dream was for her two children to be successful, to achieve the "American Dream." She wanted to make sure that we had a place to live and to not be dependent on others for our survival. Unfortunately, she was not successful in achieving her goal of finding us a place to live. After we arrived, we stayed at her friend's apartment for one month. After that, we moved to a cousin's apartment, and finally, three months after arriving, we moved to our own one bedroom residence.

Growing up in New York City was not easy, and I encountered many drastic changes in my life. For one thing, the climate was different. I was used to nice warm weather. In Colombia, the mornings were cool, the afternoons were warm, usually with sun showers, and occasionally there were some thunderstorms and minor earthquakes. I arrived in the thick of winter the wind was cold, and it felt like ice was always between my toes. I never got used to the winters in the Northeast. Fortunately, after living in New York for five years, we decided to move to Florida where it felt more like home.

Another big change was the food. After 25 years, I still remember the first meal my mom cooked for us in the United States — soup. The ingredients were something like this: you put yucca, potatoes, chicken or meat, corn, onions and some unfamiliar spices in a big pot and you let it cook for a couple of hours. When I tasted the food it had a different flavor, however. It was not the same soup I was used to, but I ate it anyway. I was used to my grandmother's version, and I was expecting to eat the same thing, but it was not. It took some time for me to acquire a new palate and enjoy different kinds of meals. It is amazing that after so many years of being in the United States, there are still some foods that don't quite taste the same as they did back home.

School was another big adjustment. In Colombia I went to Catholic School, an all-girls school. The teachers were mostly nuns, and some were lay teachers. In NYC, I was enrolled in a public school just four weeks after arriving from South America, and that was a culture shock. I did not speak a word of English. On the first day of school my mom walked me to school but did not go inside with me. I was on my own. Being all alone in a strange environment is the scariest feeling a person could ever have. The wind did not only feel cold on the outside — my soul was also frozen with fear. Somehow, though, you pull yourself together and realize you have to become a warrior.

Just when you think you are the only one who has gone through a difficult situation, however, you encounter people in your path who have experienced somewhat similar circumstances. That school experience was not uniquely mine; I discovered Pedro (Peter) Hernandez in his interview in the Race and Change oral history project conducted in Hollywood, FL. He talks about his experiences when he was enrolled in school. Along with his parents, Hernandez migrated from Cuba to Spain, and then moved to the United States to South Florida at the age of 11. Like me, he was dropped off at school by a parent — his father — who drove away. He remembers that very first day well:

> "The first day of school. I will never forget that. My dad dropped me off in school. So, here I am outside in school with the kids, and I did not know where to go. I saw the kids outside, the doors were locked, and all of a sudden the bell rang and everyone went in, and I am standing outside, and I say, where do I go? I did not speak any English at the time . . . The language was a major barrier. I could not understand what people were saying to me, and I couldn't relate anything that I wanted to say to anybody. So, it was different . . . The school was the big monster — it seemed like at the time."

The story is so familiar; you are all alone, no one to turn to, but somehow you manage to overcome obstacles and find your place in a new environment. Slowly, you start making friends, and those friends help you heal those first traumatic experiences that happened in the schoolyard. I remember that my fifth grade teacher, Ms. Carrey, assigned a translator to me. I do not recall her name, but if I remember correctly she started introducing me to kids who also spoke Spanish, and I started making my own group of friends. Hernandez also had a translator.

"He was of Mexican descent . . . Warren was a piece of work. Like any other kids I learned — kids are cruel. Warren was very helpful, very instrumental in me trying to go to the classes . . . But it did not work. . . . I would sit in the classes and I could not figure out what they were saying . . . But within three months I was speaking English . . . One day I dreamed in English, and ever since that I never had to translate anything from English to Spanish. So I would say for the language barrier that was the day I did no longer had to have dual minds as to the input being in one language and the output being in another; it would just flow."

The school year for me was not rosy, however. Before coming to the United States, I never had any racial experiences. In fact, I had never met a Black person in my entire life until I went to public school. I did not think one way or another about it; they were just Black people who were different from me, and I was different from them. I was always taught by the nuns to value people. No matter how rich or poor a person is, or what color he or she is, that person is created in God's image, they said. "Everyone should be treated with love and dignity." To this day, I try following that "Golden Rule," but it is not always easy.

In school, some of the Black girls would harass me during lunch hour and threaten me. I told no one, but I would ignore them and go a different way to avoid crossing their path. The year finally ended and none of the girls ever did anything to me. Later on, I found that one of them, a mulatto — she and I had become acquainted — had asked those girls to leave me alone, and thank God they did. The mulatto girl was one of the gang leaders. Peter Hernandez had a similar situation happen to him in middle school. "There was a Black kid, Anthony, which I don't remember his last name because everyone always called him Anthony. Whenever I had problems with the Blacks, Anthony would step in and say, no, he is my friend . . . When you become friends race doesn't become an issue. It is just a person to person."

Being singled out and harassed in a place that is supposed to be a safe haven can toughen you and make you a survivor. In my own case, I became street smart, suspicious, and afraid of people different from me. I learned discrimination by being threatened. It took some time for me to learn to trust Black people again.

Barbara Bell-Spence, who was interviewed for the Race and Change Project in the Lake Okeechobee area, talks about her experiences with people different from her during her school years from the perspective of a Black person. She was born in the Belle Glade, FL, and went to school during racial segregation. Spence and 10 of her classmates decided to go to a new high school were desegregation was beginning to be implemented. As she recalls it:

"I was always, I guess, an adventuress and that was one of the reasons a group of us decided to venture over. Once we decided to go to another school, we were really considered traitors, an outcast. So, we were like, we had to depend on each other . . . the others at the high school really didn't start accepting us or having much dealings with us until our senior year. So, it was a trying time, but then you learn how deal with and go on and accept what you have and try to do the best you can . . . When I first started going to school [it] was the first time I saw a White person with a sunburn peel. I thought they were snakes because she just peeled a big layer of skin of her back — weird people . . . It was just something totally unusual and unpredicted because I could not understand, and I still can't today, why they sit in the sun, and go through all that pain to get dark like people they supposedly hate, and then to have to pull layers of skin off in order to obtain that [dark color]. It was just boggling at that time."

As time goes by, though, you learn to accept people and their differences, and hopefully any sort of enmity becomes a thing of the past. Once we become adults, encountering differences across cultures can still cause problems, I have found. But it is important to appreciate the benefits from individuals who are culturally and racially different from one another.

At 17, I moved to Florida, or better yet I ran away to Florida and fell in love with the Sunshine State — it reminded me of Colombia. Four years later I met my husband, an Anglo-Saxon Protestant. When our relationship got serious and he proposed, I made it very clear to him that our kids needed to be raised Catholic and to go to Catholic School as well and he was okay with that. Intercultural marriages have their challenges in today's society although they are becoming more common and acceptable than ever. Marriage, regardless of cultural and background diversity, is in itself an institution that brings forth a vast range of conflict that the couple has to learn to cope with and work out, such differences as lifestyle choices, friends, problem solving, religion, parenting style, extended family, and sexuality. Now add to the equation different cultures with different worldviews and value systems. Such marriages can work, but communication is paramount for success. Learning to compromise has become one of our marriage's strongholds. One example is Christmas time. In the North American culture, Christmas is celebrated on the 25th of December; in the Hispanic culture the 24th is our big day. So, in our household, we celebrate Christmas on the 24th and we go to Mass at 6:00 p.m. with the kids, and have celebrations with my family members. On the 25th we go to my husband's family and have another celebration there.

In an article by Bernardo Attias in the book, *Intercultural Relation - ships,* he states that, "Anxiety accompanies intercultural relationships. Anxiety is probably stronger in intercultural relationships than in intra-cultural relationships." In an intercultural relationship two cultures are emerging, and each person may have preconceived negative as well as positive notions of each other's culture. The challenge is, however, to reduce the negative and build on the positive. But both must realize that issues of differences will come up sooner rather than later, and that is okay.

In my intercultural marriage I had to learn and adapt to some of the traditions that were foreign to me — like Halloween. This festivity has brought much conflict into our marriage. When I was growing up in Colombia, we did not celebrate Halloween — we celebrated All Souls Day. This was an all-day event in my household. My grandmother would get up early in the morning, gather her family and would drag us all to church to attend Mass and pray for the deceased. Then we would go to the cemetery and pay our respects to all the deceased members of our families and close friends. On the other hand, Halloween was the night that witches and warlocks celebrated their new year, I learned. So to celebrate this day was very troubling to me. It was inconceivable to have my kids dress up and "beg" for candy. My husband would argue that it was just a night to have fun and it was a kid's adventure. I could not see his point. But how could I deny our kids this American tradition? It took me four years to give in to this holiday and his pleading. I finally decided to speak with our priest who explained to me that Halloween was actually a Catholic tradition that went back centuries ago. He also explained the pagan gods and how all of this got incorporated into society. I was not totally convinced, but I decided to let my children have fun on that day with one condition; their costumes needed to be of a saint or heroic figure. None of that "witchie" stuff.

Another tradition new to me was the Easter egg hunt. Again, Easter was a time of solemnity and much prayer not about a bunny laying eggs. How idiotic was that. It just did not make any sense. Now in our household, we compromise, emphasizing the true meaning of Easter and still having the Easter egg hunt, but it's very much downplayed. We go for our Easter Mass and then have brunch with my in-laws, creating a new tradition for me and my family, and one that I have learned to cherish.

Traditions, customs, and principles are not only passed down from family members to their children, but also from other people who care for the well being of children. In a personal interview with Shelly Weiss in our cultural diversity course, she candidly talked to me about her life as a child. Weiss was born in the United States and raised by both parents. When she was growing up, one of the many principles her parents taught her was to "always tell the truth." Weiss's mom instilled in her daughters the message that, despite their differences, they needed to "stick together" and to "learn to appreciate one another."

While growing up, the Weiss's had a nanny, an ex-nun who, later on, also became their teacher. The Weiss family is Jewish, but during Christmas time the nanny taught Weiss and her sibling the significance of Christmas and what this festivity meant to the Christian population. So, from the nanny Weiss learned about Christianity. In my household, Christmas is the biggest event of the year, but I also make it a point to teach my kids that other festivities are celebrated as well during the month of December such as Kwanza for the African Americans and Hanukkah for Jewish people.

After graduating from the University of Florida, Weiss took a job as a reporter in Texas. "I was very excited at first to land a job where my dreams were going to be fulfilled. I had always wanted to be a journalist and Texas was going to be the place where my dream was going to become a reality," she said. "Even though I was employed for a small market, reporting, I was thrilled. Unfortunately, the news director did not favor me in the least, and made my job experience very unpleasant — so much so that I became homesick and eventually moved back to Florida."

Weiss is now Director of Marketing and Public Relations in a company that has brought her much joy and challenges along the way. Working for a big corporation exposes you to people of different cultures and backgrounds. Some cultural customs are hard to comprehend, Weiss conceded. There was a memorable conversation Weiss had with a co-worker regarding marriage.

> *"I have had the opportunity to work with a variety of people from different ethnic backgrounds, and cultures. Although quite a few have become 'Americanized' there was one person whose culture I will respect but never understand. I was talking to one of my male co-workers about women who choose to have a career over marriage and his view on marriage is different than mine. He was born in Bombay, India, but came to America when he was five years old. Although, he has grown accustomed to our culture, his heart embraces and prefers the Indian culture. Misha believes in arranged marriages and that the woman's place is at home. He proudly told me that he and his wife of 14 years were arranged to be married by both parents and that he did not get to know his wife until way after marriage. I explained to him that it was inconceivable for me to marry someone that I was set up with, without a say in anything. Just the thought of my parents picking my husband-to-be was just too nerve-wracking, especially since my parents' tastes and mine were completely different."*

Learning from others can be an enriching, broadening experience, however. In this cultural journey, I continue to learn and appreciate other cultures and customs. There is still so much to learn. In fact, I need to learn about football. As much as I want to understand the game and to have tail gate parties, there is still that mental block. How in the world do you have a bunch of grown up men getting pulverized in a field just for a ball? And on top of that, they get big money. Maybe one day I'll get the logic of this American game.

Jamonica Rolle has a master's degree in Communication and is currently working as a high school English teacher in Pompano Beach, FL. She resides in Lauderhill, Florida with her daughter. She says, "South Florida has a history that is rich and constantly evolv - ing. This project has helped me understand the impact that past leaders have had on our lives. Maintaining oral history is so impor - tant for future generations to hear firsthand accounts of what life was like. This is so much better than textbooks because it gives life to history."

♋

THE LABELLING INFLUENCE: AN AFRICAN AMERICAN PERSPECTIVE

Jamonica Rolle

As the knife pierced my flesh, the tears froze on my cheeks and the cold air rushed inside. The pain was intense. The fear was even greater. I lay there on the hospital bed so close to death that I could feel it breathing down my neck. It smelled of defeat. Death whispered in my ear, "Not yet. You have work to do."

I closed my eyes and I could see my grandfather's face, but the smile usually bright, had disappeared because of me. I could see him marching to Washington D.C. fighting for civil rights and serving as a leader in the city of Pompano Beach, FL. I could see him as he stood in front of his science class at Boca Raton Middle School telling his students about the importance of making good decisions. He was a pillar in his community. A God-fearing, Bahamian native who believed in hard work and doing the right thing.

There were certain things that my brother and I weren't supposed to do and I could feel my family's disappointment as I lay in that hospital bed, still a teenager, unmarried and giving birth. I could imagine the people whispering as my grandfather walked down the aisle of his church where he served as a head deacon. They'd say, "Did you hear that Deacon Rolle's oldest grand-daughter had a baby and she ain't even married? What a shame."

The weight of several generations of hard work and expectations lay heavy on my soul. People saw me as "someone different" — Black, but not really. I spoke correct English and was know as the "smart girl"; voted most likely to succeed; graduated in the top 10% of my class. For many, this was unusual for someone growing up in Pompano's poorest area. There seemed to be an agreement about most of the people that came from the town's Northwest side. Only a few would "make it out." The rest would "just make it." I was expected to be the former, not the latter. I was thought of as unusual because I caught a bus to go to a private school on the other side of town instead of being educated at the underprivileged schools in my neighborhood. I was unusual because, when the other black children were out at the Friday night football game, I was home reading and studying.

I was unusual because I grew up on a street that bore my family's last name, honoring my great aunt, the late actress, Esther Rolle. Nowhere in Pompano could I go and not be recognized. Being a Rolle seemed to carry a lot of weight. I got extra candy when I went to the local candy store because the owner said he admired my grandfather's initiative to organize a march to Pompano's city hall to fight some injustice done in the African-American community. I got extra popcorn in my bag at the movie theater because the worker liked my great-aunt's character, Florida, in the television show "Good Times."

But being a Rolle also meant I felt pressured to be perfect, a statue for my people, holding a torch, expected to run all the way to the finish line without tripping or falling along the way. The pressure was greater than the suction machines used by my doctor as she performed my daughter's delivery. I lay on the hospital bed, unsure of who I was and where the pressure would eventually propel me.

It wasn't until I spoke to "Katherine Hall" (not her real name), during an interview in a Communication course at Florida Atlantic University that I realized that no matter what view a person has of their position within their family and community, their self-image is nearly always impacted. Unlike me, her struggles with identity came from *not* feeling accepted. She grew up in a small town in Florida where she felt extreme pressure to change herself so that she would blend in with those around her. "Lighter skinned Blacks always called me names," she said. "And I was the last one chosen to be on teams and to go to sleepovers. I really didn't like myself because I thought that my skin was too dark. So, to make friends, I do whatever my classmates told me to do, including their homework."

Hall also talked about how her sense of self worth was further shattered. When she was five, her father left their family and became involved with a White woman. "This hurt me real bad because I felt like it was my fault," she said. "Visits to their house seemed to be the total opposite of what I was used to. I noticed that their house was real nice compared to the hostile situation I lived in. It was a happy environment, with mellow music always playing. [My stepmother] was real nice, too, and she let me play in her straight hair that I wished that I could have. They seemed to be happy and I thought their happiness revolved around her being White and having money. This made me not like myself even more.

"I really didn't know a lot about money, but I knew that I didn't have some of the same things that others had. My mother taught us to be grateful for what we did have and to be proud of ourselves, never allowing anyone to belittle us. She even got upset one time when a White couple gave us money to buy snacks at the movie theater. She said that she didn't want anyone to think that we were begging."

Slowly crumbling under the pressure of not feeling accepted, and the need to hide her "poorness," Hall dropped out of high school in tenth grade.

It was difficult to understand her position, because my parents had gone out of their way to hide the harsh realities of life from me. Growing up, I was told that African-Americans had abundant opportunities, and by the 1980's when Hall and I grew up, we could be pushed into any path imaginable. I was told about people like Dorothy McIntyre, who grew up in the 1950's, and even then, still had opportunities to go to college.

In the archival Race and Change oral history project in Hollywood, FL, McIntyre talks about the opportunities available to her and how her position within her family and community impacted her decisions. "I had the opportunity to go to college," she said. "In fact, I had registered for Grady's Nursing School . . . Even after I got married, [her husband] wanted me to go back to school, but I didn't. Being the oldest daughter, I stayed home to take care of mother and father."

McIntyre grew up in Liberia, a close-knit Black and Bahamian community located within the city. She boasts about what her family was able to accomplish and their position within the community. "[My father] had the bicycle shop and he was in construction," she said. He had people to work for him . . . I think I have been very blessed with the kind of life my mother and father provided for us.

"I wasn't afraid because I have a father who didn't play around, and he knew everybody in the city of Hollywood, so we were treated with respect. We were treated with respect because if I come home and didn't like anything they would report it to Professor [Joseph] Ely [Principal at Attucks Senior High School], and that would be it."

It was easier to relate to McIntyre because I received similar respect, but I was unsure of how things would change once I had had my daughter. I was almost sure that I'd be viewed as an outcast, no longer good enough to be a Rolle. But by the time I finished my interview with Hall, I began to see success in a different light. I began to understand that success was created by something greater than a person's last name and their family position in a community. I thought of how I'd use my new insight to influence the remedial reading students that I was teaching at a school in Pompano Beach, north of Fort Lauderdale, at the opposite end of the county from McIntyre's home.

My students had seemingly come to a consensus that they were inferior and were incapable of being successful. In a ninth grade class of nearly 30 African Americans, who were reading on the fourth or fifth grade level, most agreed that their community position as poor, under-privileged students rendered them helpless when it came to passing Florida's state required competency test, FCAT. They came to a consensus that one female student was correct when she said, "[Students] pass the FCAT out west because they're White and White people are smarter than Blacks. Plus, their parents put more into their education. They read to their children every night and can afford to get them tutors when they can't learn."

They also blamed their family for their problems with their education. "I know I can't read well because my mama can't read that good. I never saw her pick up a book or magazine to read. Not even the newspaper. And I can't remember a time when she actually sat down to read to my brother and me. She was working all the time and this probably caused me to not like reading," another female said.

As they went on with stories about why they would not be successful, I told them about Harma Mims Miller and how she was able to triumph over obstacles much larger than they had. Miller had grown up in a poor migrant farm neighborhood in Belle Glade, Florida. Being a migrant meant traveling to do farm work in the summer and even missing several months of school because of it.

Miller's voice is sharp as she speaks during her recorded oral history interview in the Race and Change Project in the Lake Okeechobee area. *"Schools in the area were built to produce domestics and mechanics. So all the things that were done for Black people at the time were done so they could service the sugar cane industry and the vegetable growing industry. My father was a crew leader and he had to learn more or less from other Black people about how to manage everything. He only had a sixth grade education.*

"Fifty to 20 years ago, there was a quadrant of this town where all Black people lived and [in] the other three quarters, Whites were spread out in luxury . . . There was no intention to produce educated people. That was not part of the plan even though that was the exact result. They did produce highly educated people and from those groups of camp classes came doctors and lawyers, physicists and chemists . . . Many of the students who did exceedingly well didn't even have microscopes or any chemicals to work with and they still turned out to be okay and enjoyed very high paying jobs and jobs with high education status."

Although Miller didn't consider herself to be one of the most successful people from her community, her successes were distant dreams for many of my students. With a bachelor's degree in Spanish Education and a master's in General Linguistics, I told them about how she became Belle Glade's first Black female commissioner and how she worked in education for more than 25 years.

"I would be somewhere in the middle," she said. "There are people who have done some outstanding jobs. The phenomenon is that people who lived here had a special kind of drive that was born of them, working in this extremist culture."

My students listened as I told them of Miller's accomplishments. They listened, but it was a future they didn't see for themselves. They were unable to separate themselves from the label that had been placed on them. Yet, they were empty and in pain, no longer wanting to be "poor," "Black," and "uneducated."

This was the same pain I felt as I struggled with being a "Rolle." For me, the pain was so overwhelming that I could not carry my daughter to full term. I remembered seeing my two-pound baby girl barley breathing and growing angry. Her body was limp and shivering as the machines pumped air into her lungs. A tube dangled from her skull to give her blood. She'd have to have surgery to see if she would ever be able to breathe on her own.

I could relate to the spectacle that my students felt they had become. Because they were poor readers, they were labeled and analyzed by many different people and organizations within the educational system. Some of my friends and family called to ask how my baby and I were doing after the delivery, but most flocked by to see it with their own eyes. I felt like we were on stage at a slave auction block — proud that we had survived the Middle Passage, healthy enough to be looked at, yet ashamed for the reason we were being viewed.

Continuing with Miller's story, I explained that one's community could play a positive role in their success. As Miller says, *"The migrant culture was very nurturing and very supportive. People would make extreme sacrifices so others could go to school. That was part of the Black culture at that time, particularly the migrant stream . . . It was very close knit and nurturing. I remember, I never had to worry about going hungry because if we didn't have food, somebody else would and would share it. So it was a close knit community where everybody nurtured everybody else and families were close."*

I explained this because I knew that my students were growing up in the same community in which I grew up. I told them what it was like living in Pompano and some of the stories that my mother told me. She said that people in Pompano stuck together so much so that if one mom was working late, the other would see to it that her kids were fed, did their homework and were put to bed. Once, she and her siblings got into trouble because they didn't listen to a neighbor and go inside when the street lights came on. She said that when my grandmother came home and found out, she lined them up and whipped them for being disobedient.

One of my young male students said, "In my neighborhood, everybody basically stay to themselves. Nobody don't bother us and we don't bother nobody. Sometimes we play with the other kids on the street, but we don't borrow from each other and our parents don't get together, like they do on television." He was right. Things had changed in Pompano and all around. There was a sense of loss of community.

I asked my students questions about their role models and I found that there were very few. I also found that the role models they had were not like the ones in the '50s and '60s. Theirs were the local drug dealer who had been able to "come up" and make a business out of it. Or, they admired the sports figure or rap star from their community. Gone were the figures like Dorothy McIntyre's father and my grandfather.

By the end of the week, I sat in my classroom, looking out of the window at all of the seemingly unconcerned teachers hustle to make it off campus before the busses. I thought about how education had become so technical with teachers rarely finding the time to teach anything other than test-taking strategies. I wondered if I would have been reprimanded for introducing my students to Harma Mims Miller while the FCAT (state achievement test) was still approaching. I thought about whether they would ever get a sense of purpose and dignity if their "community" was gone and their parents were often not available.

My conversation with Hall in our university class reminded me of the reason that I sat in that classroom often well after most other teachers had gone home. She told me that, sometimes, all it takes is one person to show that they care to help a person move onto a path towards success. "There was only really one person who influenced me to finish school and go to college," she said. "As my mom lay on her death bed I promised her that I'd complete my education and be successful one day."

Although I wanted to go home, and be able to leave thoughts of my students at school, I knew that without people like me they'd remain lost and empty. I wanted to have an impact on some of them, to be able to influence them to take the path of greatness, to stand out in the minds of many as Professor Joseph Ely did with Black students 60 years ago in Hollywood. The voice of Helen Saunders Franks, another Race and Change narrator and a neighbor of Dorothy McIntyre, echoed in my mind as she talked about the influence that Ely had on her.

"[I credit] Professor [Joseph] Ely with instilling a lot of self-esteem in all the students and really teaching us what's important. He suffered a lot because we wasn't given the opportunity with new books and the tools he needed to make it a better school. He endured a lot . . . I wasn't really going on to 12th [grade], but he insisted that I come, and he told me that he would get a bus to take me to Dillard [High School]. He helped more students go and finish high school before Attucks

*became a senior high school. He never neglected the students there. He knew every-
body. He knew my whole family. And he could call — even after we finished high
school and we met him, he knew exactly who we were.*

*"He endured a lot to make it easier for people today. [He was called] Uncle
Tom because he would seem to give the superintendents such good respect when
they wasn't doing anything for the school. He still highly respected them, you
know. But, I guess that's the way of showing the students that, regardless of
whatever people do to you don't let it stop you from making it big. And most of
the students left there and went on to college and, you know, did well."*

Professor Ely was mentioned by many narrators as they spoke
about their experiences. As Dorothy McIntyre said:

*"I think he knew there were changes coming, the way he taught us to speak to
people . . . He showed us how to do things . . . Professor Ely always taught us,
look them in the eye, anyone, and you wouldn't go wrong. You may be Black,
you may be poor, but you have pride, which is very good. And that's what I
instilled in mine . . . He was the head, but we had several good teachers who
cared about you."*

My thoughts were interrupted by a knock on the door. Barging in
unaware of the fight that I was having with myself, my colleague said,
"Rolle, I saw your car still out there in the lot and I was wondering what
was going on."

"Just thinking about our future. You know, these kids feel hopeless
and like they don't have anyone to turn to. I'm getting tired of the
bureaucracy and I'm not sure I want to play a part anymore," I said.

"Yeah girl, I know what you mean. But you can think about that
later. It's Friday. Let's go."

I gathered my briefcase and walked toward the door, making sure
that most of the trash had been picked up off the floor. Turning off the
three of five lights that remained lit, I noticed the gaping holes in the
wall didn't seem as enormous with the room darkened. I walked
toward my car, not listening to my fellow English teacher babble about
all the paperwork that she was tired of doing. I was preoccupied with
how I'd have to work to remove those labels from my students, to break
their poor self-images and propel them in the right direction. I knew it
would be a difficult road and I wasn't sure how I'd travel it without
people like Professor Ely — and like my grandfather.

As I got into my car, I saw the incubator laying on the backseat. I was
taking it to a hospital charity auction to give to another who needed it.
My daughter, Janay, was doing well. She was breathing on her own and
could sustain her own body temperature. I spotted the label taped across
the front of the little clear box : "Premature," it read. As I pulled out of the
lot I wondered who Janay's influences would be one day.

"Katherine Hall" is a pen name chosen by the writer; her story is true. She earned a B.A. in English at Florida Atlantic University and wants to continue writing.

A Closer Look at Class, Blacks and Change

Katherine Hall

"Let our posterity know that we their ancestors, uncultured and unlearned, amid all trials and temptations, were persons of integrity." —Alexander Crummell

Although I do not pretend to be unaware of the greater misfortunes of persons born in Third World countries, my story is about the misfortunes of poverty and hardships African Americans experienced growing up in the South after segregation. For four generations my family's economic and class status remained unchanged. As a child I often felt less privileged than most other people who were born on American soil. Throughout much of my childhood, the only thing I ever remember my parents saying about our dire situation was that it reflected on the circumstances created by slavery.

For a number of reasons, the elements of preparation, hard work and opportunity will always make a big difference, but when you are on the bottom of the economic and social ladder it may seem very difficult to see your way up and out. Yet, however slow it may be, there is proof that our family's Wheel of Fortune is spinning because today I am receiving a university education. The first college student of my generation, I am aware there is a chance for me to become successful, and maybe move up into the middle class.

For my maternal grandparents, however, America did not live up the popular theme, "a land of milk and honey." Their lives were very difficult due to too many overwhelming responsibilities. For one thing, because they were both illiterate domestic workers with seven children, there wasn't much opportunity for them to create a change. Because neither could afford to get an education, they were forced to go to work at an early age just to help support their parents. After leaving their respective hometowns in Georgia, they met in 1945 while working for a wealthy White planter in Sarasota. Although they were happily married for 50 years, they barely made enough to support their family with the necessities of food, clothes and shelter. After working for more than half his life for the planter, my grandfather was forced to retire due to old age without receiving a pension because he was always paid by personal checks. However, they did inherit $500, a car and a television when the last member of the White family passed away.

From what I was told, they continued all their lives in this same position because there were no other choices at the time. My paternal grandfather was illiterate also, but he had more advantages economically by comparison. He worked as a janitor at a bank and was able to retire with a pension. When asked why he never advanced, he said his lack of education and the necessity to remain employed prevented him from going any further. But he made sure that he raised his children well by encouraging them that, once educated, they would have a better opportunity than he did.

Even though my grandfather was poor, he was full of integrity. Once, while cleaning up after work, he found $20,000 in a bag in the garbage dumpster outside the bank. The next day, he immediately returned the money to the supervisor on duty; still, he was never rewarded for his loyalty. My father has always resented his father for turning that money in. He seems to think that the money belonged to our family since no one else had claimed it. Considering the family's hardships that he endured while growing up, he thought that the money would have helped them create a better lifestyle. He concluded that they would never gain financial wealth working for minimum wage. My paternal grandparents were very strict, determined to ensure that all their children were educated. Most of their seven children are now in the middle class; my father is the exception.

As for my parents, both were teenagers when the schools were integrated, and they should have been able to benefit from some of America's changes. But unfortunately, they did not see America as the "land of opportunity." Instead, they both were radicals who believed White Americans were trying to include African Americans in their society only as a strategic plot to spy on and hinder them. On many occasions my parents led to me believe that they were doing far better in their segregated schools because more students graduated. My father would always rephrase Dr. Martin Luther King, Jr.'s popular quote. Instead of agreeing to "I have a dream . . ." he would say King's dream was a nightmare.

My parents both graduated high school but, financially, they didn't reach very far. When they married in 1974, three years before I was born, they were financially unstable. Can you imagine growing up in a wealthy country, surrounded by people who appear to have benefited from America's ample opportunity, but never having a share of it for yourself? They would work really hard to support a family that grew very quickly to seven, but we barely made ends meet. I remember things being even more difficult during the holidays. My mother would have to decide which was the most important: paying the rent or buying the appropriate gifts. Almost always she would pay the bills and tell us kids that the holidays were just ways for retailers to make extra money. If one of us was ever upset about not getting a birthday gift, she would give us a big hug, tell us how much she loved us, and fix a special meal of whatever we wanted to try and cheer us up. Christmas time was especially hard for everyone.

Before going to school and hearing a different viewpoint, I had pretty much accepted what my parents told me. One day at school, just before Christmas break, the teacher asked everyone to make a list of whatever we wanted for Christmas and turn in the list at the end of the day. She said that if we had been good for the entire year, we should be able to receive whatever gifts we had put on the piece of paper. If not, we wouldn't get anything at all. After turning in the list, I remember going home that day very upset at the fact that my family didn't even have a Christmas tree yet. My mother had told me that there was no such thing as Santa Claus. Yet, all the other children at school talked about the toys they expected from him. They knew that there were presents already underneath their trees. All I had was a bunch of empty promises from the last few Christmases that I could think of.

At that age, I didn't really know whose fault it was, or if there was anybody to blame for my misfortune. At the time, I blamed myself. I believed that I didn't get any presents because I was a bad person. Even my parents forgot that there was no Santa Claus and suggested that my bad behavior — such as forgetting to complete chores — was the reason for no presents at Christmas time. I decided I wanted to know desperately if there really was a Santa Claus and if he would come to our house, so I went and asked my mother. She proceeded to give me what she called the "big people's talk." I was right, she said. There was no real Santa Claus, and Christmas was a holiday reserved for rich people. Although I loved my mother very much, those fantastical stories I learned at school were fresh in my mind and I couldn't help but start crying, mainly because I knew that we just couldn't afford to buy anything. The following day, my mother went to a non-profit agency and got a voucher for a Christmas tree and some small toys. Although the toys were neither expensive nor what I asked for, playing with them on Christmas Day sure eased the pain of poverty that I felt so early in my life. The joy was only temporary, however. When I returned to school after the break, I learned that many of my White classmates had received everything they had asked for.

Throughout my teenage years, and up until the time I dropped out of school in the tenth grade, I had to either hide my economic misfortunes or explain them and risk being made a spectacle of, especially to those who were more financially secure than I. I used to believe that life was just harder for people who were born Black and in poverty. So when I first met Jamonica Rolle, I thought we would have a lot in common. Both of us were African American females studying at the same university, and we met in a cultural diversity course where we shared our stories. But that was pretty much the end as far as our commonalities went. In fact, our upbringings couldn't have been more different — as different as an old penny and a shiny new one.

I was from Arcadia, a small town in Central Florida where everyone had pretty much kept to themselves. Ours was one of only two Rastafarian families there. So, while I was anxious to get away from my hometown, there wasn't much zeal in me to meet new people. As a result, I hardly knew anyone outside of my family and a few friends from high school, and I lost contact with most of them many years ago. On the other hand, Rolle was very popular in her hometown of Pompano Beach, just north of Fort Lauderdale. At the university, she seemed to be very comfortable in her surroundings as well. Her earliest memories of growing up in Pompano Beach brought back immense pride and joy as she recalled an environment that was primarily Black. She lived in a small house that was passed down to her grandfather. "Though small," she said, "it still had an enormous amount of value since it was already purchased and given to my grandfather as a sort of inheritance."

Now, when I heard this I began to feel a little bit uncomfortable because I had never met another Black person who had any family members who were so fortunate. As far as I could remember, just about everyone I knew grew up living from one shabby apartment to the next. Suddenly, I felt like we were coming to a place on the road that had been a dead end for me and a one-way street for her. Somehow she had crossed over some imaginary line that I just couldn't quite understand, although I could see it. Still, I decided to show some of the good manners my mother always said would get me respect, even if we didn't have any money. So I sat patiently, quietly, and waited for her to continue.

She said that even though she does not remember being very rich, she thought she had a rich heritage; and I agreed. The house that she was raised up in was located on Esther Rolle Avenue, named after her famous maternal grandfather's sister. The same African American actress who played the mother, Florida Evans, on the television show "Good Times" that I watched in reruns as a child. Her grandfather was recognized as a community leader. People would go out of their way to satisfy the Rolle family. The Rolle children were always invited to birthday and holiday parties in the neighborhood, whether they knew the hosts or not.

You could see that she felt really proud of have such a good heritage and even I forgot about my shameful upbringing and secretly enjoyed a sense of pride just even knowing Rolle, however momentarily. On the surface we seemed pretty much alike, but after comparing our histories, there was an obvious difference between us. My family's history showed an inability to overcome class qualifications and Rolle's family showed positive advancements, socially and economically. The economic plight of Blacks coming out of segregation and class differences within the Black community are issues that seem to cut across generations. I wanted to learn more about what others experienced.

In the oral history archives of the Race and Change Project conducted in the Hollywood, FL area, I found an interview with Reeta Mills. The Florida native, 55 at the time, recalls vividly the social and economic conditions surrounding the African American communities before and after integration in her hometown of Hallandale, just south of Hollywood: *"Because we couldn't buy things we needed from White stores, many Blacks had their own business selling just about anything you can think of. But after integration, many of the Blacks had to close up their shops because people quit buying from them and started patronizing the White businesses . . . The only people who survived were those who owned their own property. Others were forced to live in very small rentals owned by Whites . . . People who were once independent business owners had to become domestic workers for White homeowners since there wasn't much else to do back then."*

Deotha Roby is older than Mills, and survived hardships during her upbringing and after integration. Before I listened to her oral history interview, I had taken for granted that societal changes were prevalent in the South, even if certain areas like where I grew up were stagnant. Roby grew up in Georgia and moved to Hollywood in 1958. She had a vision that she could do better financially in Florida because its labor economy was growing at the time. But before that, in the 1940s, when she was just 10 years old, life was very hard for Roby and her family, she says. "In order for me to get to school, I had to walk three miles and three miles back everyday . . . I had only two dresses that I wore to school. Each day after school, I would hand wash a dress in order to wear it on the alternating days. With 11 children, my father could not find enough work to care for such a large family. So, my siblings and I had to do piece work on cotton farms and tobacco farms just to help feed the family. At age 11, I was taught to cook and began working inside the homes of White people." While working for these White families she recalls, "I was never able to go to the front of the house unless I was sweeping the front porch . . . In many homes I couldn't even eat the same food that I prepared for White people."

Whenever she heard of any prospects for earning more money, she took advantage of the possibilities. For instance, she recollects:

"I was earning $1.75 a week when I went to work after school at a nearby White community. I left that job and walked another two miles away to a location that paid $5.00 a week for the exact same position. I recognized the times were changing and even took a chance and relocated to Florida where the opportunity for making economical advancements would be higher. As soon as I got here, I went to work for an agency and was making $6.50 a day . . . Gradually, domestic workers were being paid more and more because a few years later I made $9.50 a day. The pay rate was going up because the economy was rising at

the time . . . Before I stopped working for that particular agency I had been making $12.50 a day."

Afterwards, she went to work permanently in the home of a wealthy doctor for over 25 years. When looking back on her life she says, "It was very hard for my parents to keep a job and take care of a large number of children at the same time. I didn't think I would be witness to the type of changes that I made." Unlike her parents, Roby had a positive outlook on life. As a result, she concludes, "I feel like I *am* a person. I am proud of what I learned at a later date. Now I feel like I can accomplish anything I put my mind to."

Although I didn't grow up with many luxuries and aspirations, today I'm a proud, ambitious African American woman in her 30's who is aware of the wealth of opportunity present in America. Looking back on my life I can honestly say that the one person who influenced me the most was my mother. Times were hard, but she did her best to make us happy. She told me that, because she learned the hard way, she wanted to spare her children. My six siblings would say she loved me best, but she always said she loved each one of us equally. When I dropped out of high school, she recognized my intellectual capability and made sure that I got my G.E.D. as an alternative shortly afterwards. Later on, she convinced me to go to college so that I could earn more money.

She passed away in 1999. I felt an obligation to finish college, not only for myself, but to keep the last promise I made to her as well.

Anne Bennett-Ciaglia, *born Anne Wendell Grimley, in 1957, lived most of the first half of her life in Ridgewood, New Jersey, a small town in the Northeast. Raised with four brothers and sisters during the tumultuous '60s and '70s in relatively homogenized surround - ings, she was not personally affected by racial tensions, she says. But, "the Race and Change Project enabled me to achieve my per - sonal goal of acquiring a realistic, multi-faceted cross-cultural per - spective in my daily life." She has a B.A. in English from Florida Atlantic University in Boca Raton, Florida and is now working on a master's degree in Communication. She resides in North Palm Beach, Florida where she is a freelance writer.*

A LONG WALK TOWARDS DIVERSITY

Anne Bennett-Ciaglia

My mother raised my brothers and sisters and me while my father negotiated corporate-mandated geographical moves that took us first to the Deep South, then to the Midwest and eventually settled us into a suburb in the greater metropolitan area of New York City. Competition among northern-born housewives in my mother's social circles was reserved for those who set out to have the most children. I am number two in the race she didn't win, but placed nicely in, with a total of five.

Fortunately, I have no memories of New Orleans, Louisiana, my birthplace, or of the incidents my parents encountered there. But at about age seven, I remember asking them about their experiences there. One night I overheard a guest at our home question them about our pre- vious life in the South during the burgeoning civil rights movement. The rapt expression on the guest's face and the whispered tone of the exchange stirred my curiosity as I peered around the darkly lit staircase unnoticed by my parents. I wanted to know more. They told me tales of "colored" and "white" drinking fountains and "Whites only" signs that were commonplace in daily life. My mother, alone on the street with small children in tow, had happened on an ugly scene at a lunch count- er where a Black patron was refused service and was ejected onto the front walk in front of us. Not a month later, riding on a town bus with my sister, she witnessed a young Black woman and her child ridiculed to tears by two rednecks and heckled as she walked to the back of the bus. My father said we lived in "foreign territory" as he and my moth- er had had no first-hand experience with intense racial discord and hatred before their experiences in New Orleans. They had grown up in White suburbs and had heard of racial bigotry, but neither had experienced it at home. I remember how proud I was to hear my parents speak of their disgust over the climate of pervasive hatred in which we lived for three years. But I think the detection of fear in their voices is what I recall most clearly, fear of the ugliness they witnessed for the first time and the memories of having to try to shelter their children for three long years from this "sub-culture."

My first personal experience with different cultures came during that same year when we were transferred to Highland Park, Illinois, a small suburb of Chicago. There we became somewhat of a minority, as we were one of only two Gentile families on our block. As we would eventually discover, those old enough to go to school would be part of a tiny classroom skeleton crew on Jewish holidays. On those days, my best friend, Amy Lieberstein would sit quietly in her bedroom window watching me walk to the school bus. I always wondered what she did on those days, but we never discussed it. I don't recall how I knew it at the time, but I was aware that there were significant fundamental issues between Christians and Jews, far beyond different school holidays and worship days of the week. I do remember feeling like the "other" in our neighborhood — like we were not in the "in" crowd — but I would not be able to articulate that until I was much older. Thinking back now, I realize how different my life would have been if my parents had taught us about Judaism while we had the rare opportunity to live among so many Jewish families.

Amy and I kept in touch for years after we moved, and she even paid us a visit once where we recalled old memories. We laughed over our identical memory of a holiday dinner where I was thrilled to be included. The main dish was tongue, a meal, thankfully, I have never endured since. My ashen expression when dinner was presented apparently became legend in their household for many years. I remember my discomfort during Amy's visit those many years later, that somehow I was still living in some kind of multicultural isolation with no clue of how to escape it while living in our predominantly homogeneous surroundings.

Another personal cross-cultural experience came at the end of a cycle that was set in motion by my mother. She began hiring live-in help, or "summer girls," a classification that had no particular significance to anyone outside our family — my mother simply made it up. First, there was Jody. I have only a benign memory of her heavy, squat appearance and stringy blond hair. She was caught shoplifting in a local store, I learned later, resulting in my first memory of unrest between my parents. For my father, in those days, there was no gray area in the words of the Bible's Ten Commandments; you simply followed them to the letter. My mother was, and still is, the more tolerant and sympathetic of the two — one who, for better or worse, might have given her a second chance. The day Jody left, my sister and I climbed up on the bay window in the living room and watched my father walk her out to a waiting car, talking quietly and sternly until he slammed the door behind her and the car sped off. There was someone else after her who was thin and pimply, with not much to say and I vaguely remember a discussion between a neighbor and my mother that she may have been slightly retarded, and no match for our brood of five.

Jeanette was our last try and turned out to be our collective favorite. She was Black, not significant in our household other than that this was our first introduction to a person of color. She introduced me to hours of "My Boyfriend's Back" played on her portable record player and gave me a safe haven from the confusion of a large family. I rarely had the undivided attention of either of my parents. This was not so with Jeanette. Her made-over basement bedroom was alive when she was in it, eyes as bright as the pink foam curlers she always wore to bed. She taught me how to dance in that room, something I was never good at, but that didn't seem to matter to her.

One day, Jeanette came to my mother and announced that she was "in the family way" by her boyfriend Walter. My mother told me years later that it never occurred to her to send Jeanette away, although she was afraid for her in light of the social restrictions of that era. She never shared with me what transpired between her and my father regarding Jeanette's condition. One night Jeanette simply served dinner in her maternity uniform, an occurrence my parents often laugh about now; however, we kids never noticed anything else out of the ordinary. It was the first time my father had heard or seen of the impending new member in the family, yet nothing was said around us until my sister overheard some whispered words between my parents later that night. Those words resulted in Jeanette taking care of us right up until she delivered her little boy. She had found her way into all our hearts, even my Dad's. Walter fared much worse. He wound up still smitten, but alone, after she announced that she was much too young to settle down. Little baby Rodney went to live with his grandmother in South Carolina. I still wonder what became of him and if he ever got to know his mother the way I did.

My limited encounters with other cultures came to an abrupt end after I went to college, however, attending a small school in Massachusetts just outside of Boston. At eighteen, I had somehow escaped making the acquaintance of anyone from a divorced home, for instance, but before my first week was over I had met several. Soon after arriving at school, a few of my new friends and I took the train into Boston where we found ourselves embroiled in the subway system which, for me, was a terrifying experience. As the doors slid shut, and I reached out for a handle to steady myself, I remember feeling dizzy with this sudden exposure to different colors, unfamiliar languages. I looked around at my friends expecting some sign that they, too, felt uncomfortable, but their faces gave away nothing. This would happen several times. I was embarrassed at my naiveté, anxious to make up for lost time in the one-dimensional world of sameness in which I had been raised.

When I complained later to my parents that I felt I didn't fit in, my mom, always the introspective one of the two, assured me I was in the right place. "You'll find your place in the world with what we taught you at home." I think that was a kind way of telling me to get used to it, and I was not entirely happy with that answer, but I became more determined to seek out difference and not to shy away from it.

In my late 30's, after raising kids of my own, I returned to school to seek a master's degree in Communication and to further my multicultural experiences. In a writing across cultures class I met Sophie Mazanek, a fellow student, from Geneva, Switzerland. While we talked, I soon discovered, surprisingly, that our profoundly different upbringings had virtually no similarities despite the fact that that we were both White and of European decent. At the same time her reaction to me was equally as surprised, and this brought back a familiar feeling of naiveté. Once again, I felt like "the other." As we each spoke, we traded wide-eyed looks and sideways smiles. This experience, though, unlike some of my others where I encountered profoundly disturbing differences, intrigued me and drew me forward, making me want to hear more about Mazanek's day-to-day life in the multicultural world that I was continuing to discover.

She was raised by her single mother in their two-person home after her parents divorced when she was three. They lived in a sprawling suburb of Geneva, Switzerland, where they shared an 84-block complex of apartments with hundreds of families representing different nationalities. Her childhood environment was rich with people of multiple cultural backgrounds such as Swiss, Italian, Portuguese, Spanish, German and Arab. The common language spoken among her friends was French; however, they all each spoke their own native languages as well. Adjustment in her neighborhood consisted of becoming accustomed to neighbor's different mealtimes and religious customs; whereas, her own Swiss traditions called for meals to be served promptly at 6 p.m., in a quiet, efficient and structured environment, and a high emphasis was placed on education within her home.

Mazanek dined in the evenings with her mother after she returned home from work, and she almost always had the floor, not having to share with any siblings. One or two children per Swiss home represented the norm and the economic system was largely based on small families. Some nights, her mother would invite guests in for dinner so that

Sophie would be exposed to those from different cultures practicing different customs from their own. I envied her enthusiasm while I watched her recount her childhood experiences.

She and her mom attended Catholic Church on Sundays and were in the minority by doing so, as her myriad of friends and neighbors of other nationalities were attending conservative synagogues and mosques. "We never thought we were better than anyone — just different," she said. I wondered about this, remembering my parents' experiences in the South where being racially different had caused riots and chaos. She added, "The more southern European cultures ate very late and tended to play loud music, but we learned to adjust. I consider myself very international."

The most important aspect of our conversation was when she told me that she planned to raise her own children exactly the same as she had been raised — in a multicultural environment. She planned first, however, to be educated and well established before having children, which is very much in keeping with what she explained were deeply engrained Swiss values. She didn't wish to change anything about her childhood, and she says she was taught to be tolerant and open-minded, traits that have stayed with her.

Mazanek's remarks made me think of my daughter, Kaitlin, who now lives in a suburb of New York known for its superior school system with liberal curriculum and clubs and that boasts a multicultural population — 60% White and 40% African American, Asian and Hispanic. One of the biggest reasons she tells me that she thrives there is, in her own words, "Because Mom, it's not so lily-White — it's the world I'll be working and living in." Her comment is one of the reasons I let her go — it was so ironic that she was given an opportunity to fulfill a wish I may have wanted for myself at some point. Her father and step-mother, a successful Asian American woman, chose the community specifically because they had heard it referred to as one of the most successfully integrated areas in the US. Kaitlin's eyes, at 17, don't see difference quite the way I do at 46 because, for her, the real world is rich in other languages, cultures and skin colors — much like I gather Sophie's must have been. I continue on my quest to change, however, through courses, travel and new experiences.

On a recent visit, my daughter and I sat in the trendy town coffee shop, *The Blue Stone Café,* in the center of Montclair. This is the "it" spot with her and all her high school senior friends this year and was to be her first place of employment in the coming week. As I sipped coffee and she slurped hot chocolate out of our large ceramic mugs, she chatted about the latest win record of the boy's lacrosse team, her varsity soccer team ratings and stats entering the upcoming state tournament. The front door "whooshed" open three or four times, ringing the bell and letting in the cool air, and my eyes wandered as my ears picked up a few different languages — first Spanish and English within one group of kids and Japanese and English in a family of four. Kaitlin waved at a boy in a third group, who wore a black, red and green knit cap and threw up a peace sign. I smiled appropriately, stifling the urge to ask his name, rank and serial number, knowing full well that she would think it was because he was Black. It would simply be because he was male, enough reason for concern. "Wow, this place is like a little slice of the U.N.," I said. Kaitlin smiled at me — that knowing, smug teenage smile — so I added, "I just meant that it's unusual for me to see young families and teenagers of so many different nationalities all comfortably together — and it's really refreshing." Kaitlin laughed out loud. "Yup, Mom. You are growing up!" "Very funny," I said. But in my heart, I thought, it's about time.

That day was still resonating with me when I started working on the next phase of my project for the writing across cultures class. But the idyllic-looking setting of Montclair, New Jersey circa 2004 was far from many of the tales I encountered from the narrators of different cultures interviewed in the Race and Change oral history project conducted in Delray Beach. I close my eyes and I can still remember Salusa Basquin's voice, a young, hopeful man who emigrated to the US from Haiti at 13 in the 1980s and whose integration into the Belle Glade/Lake Okeechobee area when he first arrived was not easy.

"When I got there, math being universal, I didn't have to prove what the teacher was saying to prove my knowledge of the class. This was in the eighth grade. I understood very little English. There were two other Haitian students that had gone through the wave prior to my coming, so much so that one of the girls who was Bahamian-Haitian was approached by the teacher to help me. But she said, 'I am not Haitian. I don't speak that language,' and the other young man followed suit when the teacher asked him, even though he didn't speak English properly. I was shocked and I looked at the other students and they also turned their heads. No one was accepting me except the teacher. My ESOL teacher, Mr. Taylor, was accepting.

"The racial make-up of the class was 50% African American; Mexican, about 30%; Cubans, about 10%; White Anglo, 10%. But I felt alone. But it was a lack of cultural understanding that caused that, not a feeling of racial tension. It was like the food chain and there was oppression of different groups with cultural tension as different groups came into the school. They didn't understand the way we dressed, the way we acted, the way we danced, or even the way we sucked our teeth! Culturally! And with a Haitian, we can just give you a look and tell you with the look that you are worthless and mean nothing to us; whereas, with an American boy, he has to use words to do that.

"Haitians and Cubans at that time, we had boats coming in with a lot of people coming in. You know the term 'boat people.' I minded the term at the time. We were somewhat attacked because of that term. And for the five of us Haitians who went through high school together, we became proud of being

Haitian so we could work our way through school. Some of us went through sports or through music so we could get more accepted into the American culture. A lot of us have learned now that we have to turn the statement 'boat people' into a positive statement for us. Like, you have recognized my being here by calling us 'boat people,' and I admired you for that."

Basquin's words about his cultural pride struck me more than any other passage in the taped interview where he recited his story of assimilation into the American culture. His life's work now is to perpetuate Haitian cultural pride through music festivals in the Delray Beach community. I can only speculate about the difficulty of his struggle to keep his culture alive in places other than in his own heart. As I continue on my own personal journey to welcome different cultural experiences into my life, I'll remember this bittersweet aspect of the émigrés' reality. So much of his/her cultural heritage has to be lived from memory, since they have had to leave their homeland behind.

By contrast, Paula Adams, who was also interviewed in the Delray Beach project, reminds me a lot of myself. She was raised in the 1950s at a time when she would have had little chance of understanding Basquin's struggle in the area 30 years later. She had to face racial integration at its very first baby steps during the civil rights movement and her reaction to it was much wide-eyed dismay at leaving her self-described "perfect life" behind. My reaction would most likely have been identical to Adams's had I lived in the South before desegregation in that race was simply not an issue I contended with daily, as my exposure was so very limited. I hope I would have embraced the changes, but faced with the turmoil of the times I fear that it would have taken me many years to adjust.

As Paula Adams remembers:

"My family moved here in October, 1956. I came from a country setting in Michigan and we came in to Delray. All the children were White . . . and life was just one big bowl of beach and sunshine . . . The old fashioned perfect time in history when Daddy came home from work and Mommy cooked and we played . . . I was an only child, so I do realize now that I lived a sheltered life.

"We called it Dullrey Beach . . . extremely dull. There was nothing going on around town. You could walk all around town, anywhere. I lived at the beach. There was a movie theater at Northeast 5th Avenue. It was just a great time in life.

"None of us really thought about race . . . There were no Black children in the schools . . . Carver was the Black school and Seacrest was the White school and there was never any interaction that I was aware of. I believe my first awareness of anyone of a different race was back in Michigan. We went out about 50 miles to town and I first noticed some people who weren't white-

skinned and then when we got to Delray there was a Black and White school. One day I was at the beach — probably at the beach six out of seven days — and there was all this hullabaloo and activity and mass of humanity up Atlantic Avenue and it was the beginning of integrating the beach. Suddenly there were a lot of Black people coming to the beach. I never realized before that they were not allowed to or that they couldn't come to the beach. If I had thought about it I probably would have thought, why would they want to get a tan? I think I was 15 at the time.

"There was a shoe store in town, Carr's Bootery. He was Jewish. It didn't mean a thing to me. There were several Jewish families in town and it was never brought up. I looked it up in the phone book and it was never brought up that there were many Jewish names in there.

"In my senior year, in 1961, by that time I had blossomed a bit and become active a bit and was on the Student Council and Yearbook Committee and met with . . . the principal of our school and we were told that our school was going to be integrated. It must be that day or the next day, but we were told not to talk about it. I was asked or chosen or told to be the person to show our first Black student around the school. That was fine with me. So, she arrived. Her name was Yvonne Lee. I never gave it a thought how she must have been feeling. So we had a tour of Seacrest High School and you could just hear either silence or just hubbub because people just stopped . . . and stared. They just stared. And we spent, I don't remember how long, over an hour to the gym, the cafeteria, and then we went to my locker and it was to become our locker and that was the beginning of integration at Seacrest High School. I remember a lot of kids after school asking me, 'What were you doing?' And my reaction was, 'Why shouldn't I?' . . . So I went home and told my parents about it and they were surprised, but not upset or anything.

"In the summer of 1962, my friend Yvonne wrote me . . . and I just pray that I wrote her back. But when I came home again once . . . and was at a basketball game I saw her and she ran down from the stands and we embraced. But sadly to say, I don't believe we ever had any contact after that."

Adams's last sentiment sounds like a woman who may have been anxious for more contact, not only with her friend Yvonne, but with a less homogeneous environment. I can relate to that feeling of frustration, of wanting contact with different cultures, yet never living in an environment where the opportunity existed for interaction.

My last narrator's voice reached out to me and spoke in volumes about differences in our upbringing, similar to those of Mazanek and myself. What attracted me to her the most, though, was the level of self-esteem that seemed to resonate from her as she recited her childhood experiences and how she grew up. She was raised, as I was, in a large family, and also in a home where education was stressed as a prerequisite to all other endeavors. Yet, that is where our similarities ended. Her secure personality drew her attention at a young age, making her the perfect choice for a very important task.

Yvonne "Bonnie" Lee Odom told her side of the story for the historical archives. She grew up in northern Florida with her Baptist minister father in a large family until they relocated to Boynton Beach in 1958. She eventually became the first Black student to desegregate Seacrest High School in Delray Beach in 1961 — the same student that Paula Adams considered her first Black friend back in the newly integrated South Florida climate. Odom's life was quite the opposite of Adams's. She was raised in a single-parent household, unusual for the early 1960s; but she describes her life as rich in experience, family and education. Her audio-taped interview opened my eyes and eliminated a stereotypical response that Adams and I may have had regarding how one might fare being raised by only one parent. In fact, Odom's northern Florida hometown had quite advanced cultural and educational programs during that racially repressed time in history. As Odom tells it:

"It was a pleasant time. I remember my father, never mentioning anything about race, but you knew he was adamant about education. My grandfather also graduated from college. . . . He was one of the oldest students in his class. We were around church a lot . . . because we had such a large minority population, we had our own pool — we actually had two pools and a movie theatre every Saturday. . . . We took lessons and we had beauticians. Our school teachers were supported. Then, in 1959 . . . I went to a private boarding school in Jacksonville and I had a couple White instructors. . . . Prior to that, my only experience with White[s] was as a child. I remember purposefully drinking from the 'white' fountain because the 'white' fountain['s] water was cooler. I had to be in elementary school . . . but it wasn't like it was unpleasant. It was like you knew it was the rule and I think my father shielded us from a lot of it because we had a car and we would drive to a lot of places.

"I was very disappointed coming to Boynton Beach [just north of Delray Beach] at that time because they had nothing for Blacks here at that time. We were bused to Carver [in Delray] when you graduated from the eighth grade. I was on the basketball team and I did well in school and I was going to be 'Miss Carver' and I had a very pleasant experience. One day I learned there was a movement to integrate the schools and they wanted to draft kids that they thought would do well [at Seacrest]. . . . They were looking for the 'Jackie Robinson' type. This is something I became privy to later . . . I give credit to the White leaders and the Black leaders in Delray for being so progressive because they have a huge history of working together with both races who are reasonable.

"[Our] Black teachers knew the obstacles that we had to face, that we could not just be equal to a candidate, we had to much better in order to get the same job and they prepared us that way. I was not afraid. People often asked me that now and you have to build that in students to build their self esteem. . . . My

father just treated me like I was just going to any ordinary school. . . . W]hat I learned more than anything was that bad is in every race. Good is a balance and it's in every race. [And] students tend to hang based on their likeness. It's more your qualities that bring you together than your race. It's a battle. We've been fighting this [forever] and it's not won yet."

Odom's last words about 'bad being in every race' remind me of a conversation I had with my father recently on a visit up North.

Chilly New Jersey afternoons in October don't change much from year to year, at least not for me. A simple cold breeze and a pile of blowing multi-colored leaves can bring back the first half of my life as quickly as a dream. But those memories are very tough to shake off by merely awakening. My father and I sat watching Kaitlin run the field hurtling her hard body and six-pack abs up and down the field in hopes of a soccer goal, and talking about diversity. I sat real close, trying to steal some of his warmth. "My Dad was a racist, you know. His dad was a longshore man — not a nice guy — and a real womanizer, too," he said without looking at me. I knew all this, as my mom had told me about my great-grandfather years ago. "Yeah, I know, Dad. He looked me in the eye and told me a little story. "I had a friend at Newark Academy — another guy on scholarship like me, and he was Jewish. I brought him home for dinner one night over a weekend. My dad walked me out when we were ready to leave and told me not to bring him home again. He didn't want his 'kind' in the house." I waited a few minutes for him to finish his thoughts, but he didn't. So I said, "Dad, I'm so sorry — how embarrassing for you. But at least we have you to thank for not accepting that behavior and passing it on to us." He gave me a squinty, blue-eyed smile, and went back to following Kaitlin up the field.

Sophie Mazanek says her life is based on one simple philosophy: helping others. "A major aspect of my personality is my ability to communicate and influence others. As a result, I have developed an interest in pursuing a bachelor's degree in Public Communication with a minor in sociology. In the future, I intend to work for a world organization such as the United Nations because I feel that it will offer me a chance to give back to others what I was once privileged to receive. The oral history project helped me to realize that racial inequalities are still very prevalent in our society, and afforded me the opportunity to express my concern about the issue."

MANY MILES BETWEEN NORTH AND SOUTH

Sophie Mazanek

It was 6:45 a.m. and we were rushing out the door because we were already late. My mother usually dropped me at one of the neighbor's houses by 6:30 every morning before leaving for work. Our neighbors were from various other southern European countries, and my mother and I were one of a few Swiss families residing in the apartment complex. On the third floor, a "happy Italian family" was living with no major problems, or so it seemed. Marco and Sabrina, the children, were my friends. Marco and I were both 11, and Sabrina was 12. The parents were hard workers. The mother worked for a bakery and also baby-sat children on Saturdays to bring in an extra income; the father worked for an insurance company. We played together everyday and they would teach me how to count in Italian. We had lunch together, made our homework together, and also practiced judo once a week at a club. We went to catechism and church together and on Thursdays we did not have school so we hung out at a place called the Thursday Club and made collages and activities. We were close, and my mother was very grateful that I had such friends. She was glad, as well, that Maria, the mother, agreed to watch me before and after school while she worked.

After running down the stairs, we started to knock on the door when suddenly we heard a woman sobbing and speaking loudly in Italian. We were wondering what was going on because they normally were quiet in the morning, so we knocked gently. Maria opened the door and she looked devastated. She seemed to have been crying the entire night and her left eye was all black and teary. Sabrina and Marco were standing right behind her. They appeared to be shaken and scared. My mother and I were stunned and very concerned. When my mom asked Maria what happened, she collapsed into a tearful fit, her hands trembling, her nose flaring, as she told us what had transpired. Her husband had been fired from his job the day before, had came home drunk, beaten her up, and then left without telling her where he was going. We could see on their faces that the family was worried and afraid of what was going to happen next.

In the three years that I had been going over to their house nothing of this magnitude and severity had ever occurred. The parents seemed to communicate well, even when they were speaking loudly to each other; I knew that it was their way of expressing themselves in their culture. Sometimes I even felt envious of their close relationship since my parents were divorced. Nevertheless, I will never forget that morning. I felt so sorry for them. What were they going to do? What was going to happen to them? Would the parents divorce or separate? Where was the father? As far as I remember, I did not really understand the reason for the father's act. I did not question the fact that they were foreigners or wonder, then — if it was a cultural thing. I was more concerned about Marco and Sabrina. But I sometimes heard stories that it was more common in the southern European cultures to get animated during a dispute and that it could lead to alcoholism, abuse, or physical violence in the household. Nonetheless, those were just rumors from people, and I never thought that could happen to my friend's family. Among Swiss families, I did not know anyone who experienced such a tragic situation. However, I might have never known about it because Swiss people are very reserved about their problems. They do not like to share their sorrows with others, while southern cultures tend to be more open and do not mind doing that with outsiders. If this happened in my household, I know for a fact that my mother would have probably left the house with me without telling anyone to avoid being seen by the neighbors or anyone who would come and knock on our door. Even our own family would have never found out about it.

After the incident, my mother called her boss and told him that she was going to be in late. She spent some time at my friend's house trying to comfort Maria and gave her some advice about her options. Maria said that she did not know what she was going to do, but it seemed that she was not yet ready to let her husband go. She was willing to forgive him because it was the first time that "such a thing" had happened in her marriage. She was very religious, and even though she and her husband were acculturated to the Swiss life they remained Italians from the south. There was no question of separation or divorce.

After that morning, things dramatically changed because my mother hired another lady to take care of me before and after school. I saw Sabrina and Marco less than I used to because the parents got back together and the father distanced the family from others. I will never know if it was because they were ashamed of what had happened or if it was because they wanted to protect their family from rumors and people's curiosity, but it was not the same. In school, they would not speak much. It seemed like they had lost their enthusiasm. After a year of unemployment, the father decided to move back to Sicily with his family and that was the last I ever saw of them.

I thought about that experience recently after a conversation with my classmate Anne Bennett-Ciaglia whose background could not have been further from mine. She was sitting next to me in my writing across cultures class, but I had never spoken to her before. She was a Caucasian, probably in her early 40's, with blond hair and blue eyes. She looked like a classic American. I had heard her speak prior to the interview and she had struck me as a pleasant person, so that day when she approached me and asked me if I would like to be her partner for the class project assigned by the professor, I accepted the invitation and was enthusiastic to share my experiences with a Caucasian-American. We were both fair-skinned, but from two different countries and continents, which made it even more interesting. When we started the interview she volunteered to speak about her family and the community where she grew up, Ridgewood, NJ; however, surprisingly, her story reminded me of the movie, *The Stepford Wives*. It seemed like everyone in her family and community looked and acted the same. They were all rich and White living in a quiet neighborhood where there was no crime and where not much happened. On the other hand, for someone like me who grew up in such a diverse setting, and traveled a lot, I had expected more of an American. I was disappointed to hear that her only encounter with diversity was related to religion.

She briefly referred to her younger sister who formed a friendship with a girl who had a different religious belief. Her family is Episcopalian; the friend was Jewish. But their friendship did not create a problem in the community and their dissimilarities actually strengthened their friendship. Still, Episcopalian and Jewish beliefs are as disparate as day and night. Episcopalians believe in Jesus Christ — they are more conservative and closer to Catholics beliefs — while Jewish people do not. As the interview progressed, I realized that Bennett-Ciaglia had not encountered any cultural diversity in her early life and I wondered how she felt the first time she met with the "outside world."

How amazing it must have been for her and her sister to meet people of different colors and different ethnicities? I do not know at what age she moved to Florida but it must have been a shock for her to see the diversity in ethnicities, races and religions in this part of the country. Her experience was new to me and I definitely considered it interesting because of that. She brought to my attention the fact that places in America were only reserved for the privileged White class 30 years ago. I am not even sure that the restrictions are totally banished today.

I remember the first time I really understood the meaning of racism. It happened last winter in Miami when my best friend, Fitzgerald, came to visit me from Switzerland. He is originally from Ghana, Africa, but moved to Switzerland at the age of 13 with his parents, and they relocated to Geneva. Fitzgerald lived half of his life in Switzerland and became a citizen in 2003. He paid me a visit during an eight-day vacation spree he was spending in South Florida.

One day while giving him a tour of downtown Miami, we were walking towards Bayfront Park, talking and laughing, when I noticed a police car slow down about three feet away from us. As I watched the car, my initial assumption was that the driver was slowing down to let us cross the street, so we continued on our original course still talking and laughing. As we proceeded, however, the cop pulled up next to us and asked me in a concerned tone, "Is everything all right?" I was stunned by his actions, which I considered blatantly prejudicial and racist. I could not help wondering what made him doubt the fact that we were fine. I responded, "Yes, everything is fine," and Fitzgerald and I continued walking. Still, the interaction angered me and made me realize, for the first time, what African Americans had to endure in this country.

While I took the incident seriously and considered it as a racist encounter, it was not an issue for Fitzgerald, however; his self-esteem is strong. Additionally, having been raised in Switzerland, he had not been exposed to this type of attitude before, since racial relations are different over there compared to America. Blacks, Whites and other nationalities all live harmoniously together. Racism, like anywhere on earth, does exist, but it is not openly expressed.

After the incident, Fitzgerald and I resumed walking and did not discuss the event any further, but I recall thinking how insulted I would have felt if I had been in his shoes. I still don't understand why people display prejudiced behavior, but I see that at some point clashes over racial issues, cultural differences or social class issues arise in relationships. The human instinct to mark a territory takes over and insecurity and fear replaces fairness.

I had the opportunity to learn more about racial issues from two narrators in the Delray Beach, FL, Race and Change oral history project. I could relate to their experiences and empathized with the Black people living in prejudiced America.

Alberta Perry McCarthy, for example, was born in Newport News, Virginia, but grew up in Providence, Rhode Island. She lived a nomadic life with her parents, moving to various places in the United States. After experiencing several years of prejudice, McCarthy was asked to run for City Commissioner of Delray Beach. She had planned to work behind the scenes and did not expect to run for office, but nevertheless, in 2000, destiny worked out things differently for her. McCarthy remembers a happy childhood full of love and great memories. However, at the age of 11 she recalls becoming aware of the segregation and racial issues that America was experiencing. Her first exposure to racism caught her by surprise. Her story reminded me of the incident I encountered with my friend Fitzgerald:

"We were so transient for a period of time. . . . We would leave our neighborhood and walk through a neighborhood that was predominantly Italian because we walked to school . . . and I was on my way home from school one day [when] it was actually brought to my attention. [A]n elderly woman who was White turned around and called me the "n" word. I had no concept of what that was because in my neighborhood it was not used. And I came home, and I had a sense that it was something that was not good because of the face. I [would] never forget [her] face when she said it to me. We were crossing the street. Being a child, [I] may have run even faster than she was expecting and she said this word to me. And, I went home and my Nana was there waiting for me, and I turned around and I waited for my parents to come home because they both worked. And at the dinner table, I asked the profane question: I heard this word today and what [does] it mean? The [prejudiced] lady said that I was one of these, and I did not know to be proud or to be sad about this.

"My parents were stunned. And I remember them attempting to explain to me what that was supposed to mean and how I would handle this because I would probably have to hear this type of word and negative things as I continued to grow. . . . So, as an adult, I now understand [my parents'] challenge attempting to explain to such a young child. That is when I first realized there was supposed to be some kind of differences.

"I remember other Black children who were turning around and were beginning to use the word with each other. They were testing their boundaries. And we actually learned basic coping techniques testing each other, instead of getting it from the outside. The parents did the best they could . . . I was aware that the struggle was going on but I did not understand it.

"Being the second minority [in school], if not the first one, was difficult for me. I felt I was the same person just meeting a lot of new people. However, many times White America makes more difference about Black Americans than Black Americans going into the world. I was just a child going to get an education like everyone else. That's where I began to really tell the differences. I could tell when a person was looking at the window when I was walking to school . . . Where I came from everyone spoke to everyone, so I would speak to everyone and they would not talk back. These are the things that you start remembering. Well, when they would turn around and call me the word, I would reply with the definition [of the word] and tell them they are and I am not.

"In Massachusetts, we were the only Black family in the neighborhood. That was not strange to me. That was just the place where I wanted to live. . . . In Florida, I have learned there was segregation. I did not know it when I came here. I didn't know it was still here. I didn't understand the history of it. I

[was] hear[ing] other than what I had been told or seen on TV because when the civil rights period took place, I was still a young person.

"[I] thought, because I was a woman of color and I came here, I would be embraced by others. I remember that in Providence, RI, my first neighborhood, I thought they would welcome me to their neighborhood, being so far from anyone that I knew, but I had to work to establish that. That was a new experience for me. [A]lberta you don't understand. You're not from here. And, I shared with them that prejudice is alive. It helped me understand it a little better in a different perspective."

The second narrator, Joseph Bernadel, is a foreigner like myself. We both experienced a cultural shock when we came to this country and learned about America's racial issues. Born in Haiti, he remembers a joyful childhood with no racial issues. Later on in life, at an early adult age, he migrated to the United States and entered the United States military. Bernadel retired at the age of 57, after serving for 22 years as an army major, and moved to Delray Beach, FL, where he was appointed Executive Director for the Milago Center, a nonprofit art, cultural and educational facility. In March, 2000, he quit that job, envisioning the need to form a one-stop community center that would provide a litany of support services for Haitian immigrants under one roof — from English language classes, job and life skill training, to assistance in finding housing and balancing a checkbook — services that would help them to integrate more quickly into American society. In August 2001, he co-founded Toussaint L'Ouverture High School for Arts and Justice in Delray Beach. According to Bernadel, his memories of Haiti are very positive. He recalls:

"In Haiti, there is no issue of race as it is in America because the janitor is Black. So is the president. So is your teacher. So is your parent. So are your brothers, sisters, and the people on the street; and the guy begging on the highway is also a Black person. So, the issues of blackness [and] race are not predominant. In Haiti, there is mostly an issue of class, whether you are educated or you have money. [We] rejected from very early on the concept of any race being superior to us. In Haiti, the people of different ethnic groups live in harmony in terms of racial attitude. . . . There was always the presence of a multicultural environment in Haiti, so I can't remember any specific thing and just say, oh man, there are White people or there are Chinese [people] in the world because we were always in a multicultural environment.

"When I joined the military [however], the concept of Haitian was not prevalent. Most people in the military did not know anything about Haiti in 1975. . . . So, here I was, the sole apparently Black guy, and I am speaking with a different accent. I am neither White, neither African-American, nor Hispanic, so everybody was confounded [about] what kind of animal that was. So, I had

> *a lot of fun with just helping them being confused because at any point of time I could be with my African-American brothers and be African-American. When I was with my Hispanic friends in the military, because I also speak Spanish, my name and my facial [look] make me pass for Hispanic. I could never be White [but] there were some friends who were always teasing me because some of my background included this racial group of people. The majority of the officers of the United States military were predominantly White people. It was not until maybe late 1978, beginning '80s, that the military started making a consorted effort to select, identify, prepare and educate and promote African-American people. [T]hey give us General Colin Powell as the most revered and celebrated person of the African-American ancestry."*

Finally, the narrators' experiences reminded me of this anecdote that happened to me on the train headed from home school one night. It was around 7 p.m. and already dark outside. As the train sped between the Fort Lauderdale station and the next stop I stood close to the exit doors waiting for my stop which was quickly approaching. A man sitting next to the exit doors started talking to me in a loud Spanish-accented voice. He was very agitated and kept insisting that I should not be standing up while the train was in motion and should wait until it came to a complete stop. I could not care less about his advice but I politely said, "Thank you."

However, he kept on. I tried to ignore him and turned my head in another direction, but he kept on. It seemed like ten minutes went by, although it was really a two-minute situation; still, it irritated me. Soon, half of the people in the train compartment were watching the scene. By the time the train slowed down, he started insulting me since I did not respond and did not obey him. He went on saying that, "White girls are stupid," and "Your father should have told you that." A Black woman who was standing nearby told him to leave me alone, but he did not stop. By the time the train came to a full stop. I had had enough. I dashed out and ran away, quickly. I realized that he was probably mentally disturbed but, I thought, he did not have to be a racist. For that moment I definitely could relate to what a Black person might feel like being called the "n" word. It was embarrassing, insulting and degrading.

Cathleen Anderson and sister with family helper, Genie Stuart in 1940s

Professor Joseph Ely, noted principal; Attucks School

Narrathor Joseph Bernadel.
Photo by Ry Nielsen.

Hollywood narrators at Race and Change gathering.
L-R, Susan Abrams Heyder, Oliver, Pedro (Peter) Hernandez, Reeta Mills

RACE AS A MULTICULTURAL EXPERIENCE

INTRODUCTION

The following writers bring a different lens to the discussion of Race and Change and the narrators in the oral history projects. They come from other countries, from ethnic heritages where racial issues are not as easily pigeonholed, not "black or white," or they have had international experiences that provide a broader look at the issue of dealing with differences.

At the end of a project day.
Photo by Ry Nielsen

Katerina C. Nadel teaches at American High School, in Hialeah, in Miami-Dade County. When she first moved to Miami Beach in 1990, she and her husband were not sure if they would stay. Fifteen years later, the couple feels it may be time to have their address printed on their checks. The oral history experience had a very emo - tional impact on her, Nadel says. An immigrant herself, she has always been acutely aware of her biculturalism — being of two places, two lives, two minds. Sharing the experiences of the people in the oral history archives, and also having a chance to meet and talk with a number of them as an interview in the field, was a way for her to experience the true universality of humanity that links us each to the other. She will be forever grateful for the opportunity to grow as a student, a teacher, and a writer.

ETHNOLATHOSTAUTOPHOBIA*
THE FEAR OF ETHNIC MISIDENTIFICATION

Katerina C. Nadel

Tuesdays are my busy days with two other classes before this one, so I come early and sit in the quiet room catching up with myself. Like a cat, weary of protecting my back, I turn the first seat in the row around, creating a ying-yang space with the desk where I sit. Someone comes in and I glance at the clock — it's just about 4, and we would be getting under way soon.

The class is a rather representative sample of South Floridians, the faces you're likely to see on a UNICEF greeting card — all the colors of the rainbow. We're reading autobiographical essays on people's experiences with race, in preparation to write about our own. They span the country: a White man from Georgia and a White woman from Connecticut, a Puerto Rican man and woman from New York, a Chinese woman from California and a self-described "Black southern girl." We're discussing the week's readings when "it" happens.

*"Ethnolathostautophobia" is a made up word expressing "fear of ethnic misiden-tification." The word is a combination of four words derived from Greek: ethno-, derivation of "ethnic" or "ethnicity"; -lathos-, from the Greek word "laqo" meaning "mistake"; -tauto-, from the Greek word "taytotita" meaning "identity"; -phobia, from the Greek word "fobia" (phobos) meaning "a persistent, abnormal, or irrational fear of a specific thing or situation" (*American Heritage Dictionary*, 4th ed.).

The woman now sitting in the desk next to mine, just outside the bounds of my defensive cocoon, leans over and in a whisper asks me to verify the pronunciation of "café con leche." "Is that how you say it?" she wants to know. I give her a smile — my stock, polite, affable, ignorant smile — and shrug signifying "I don't know." But I don't want to be silent in the face of this affront. I want to demand, "Why ask me? How should I know?" I want the stranger sitting beside me to say why she would assume that I speak Spanish — but I know why. I have a dark complexion, olive skin — what (if I remember from my one introductory Spanish course some ten years ago) is called "morena" or "morena de tez" (I looked that up to be sure), or more appropriately in my case, "melachrini" in Greek.

I hear the voice inside my head say, in Greek, "*Min arpazese* — don't be so ready to come to blows." It's my mother's voice. But it irritates me, I tell her. "You're being thoughtless and rude," my mother scolds, but it's what I feel. A knee-jerk reaction. I hadn't meant to be put off, but I hadn't expected the question and now I'm uncomfortable that I may have offended my classmate with my curtness. The entire "café con leche" incident takes just a second, and I am called back to the reality of the classroom by the professor's voice telling us to pair up for an assignment. We look around for easy access to the face of a friend, or a welcoming stranger, and the "café con leche" woman and I turn to each other and naturally, silently, agree to work together, interviewing each other about our family cultural history.

I learn that she is from Trinidad and that she moved to New York when she was seven. Only a minute before, she was Black and I was White — but now we can talk. I discover that we have a common point of reference because I left my native country when I was seven, too. I listen intently as she paints a picture of her father as a man larger than life, reminiscing about the parties he liked to throw, how he loved to cook and to entertain family and friends. Her father's life hadn't turned out as he had hoped, she says with sadness in her voice. Careful of stepping over a line, I ask her why she thinks that, and the common ground between us grows a little: our fathers both traded homeland for exile in order to build better futures for their families. She says that her father was very creative, and outgoing, but that he had to work at all types of jobs to support his family, sending barrels of dry goods home to Trinidad, helping his community in whatever way he could — while my dad, who always loved history and politics and had been a good student, had to go to work as a young boy, barely an adolescent, apprenticed to a master carpenter, to help support his extended family of brothers and step-siblings. When he was 35, my father closed up his carpentry shop in Athens and moved us to Montreal in the late '60s, where his older brother had gone with his family a couple of years earlier.

What was it like in Trinidad, when she was growing up? I wonder. How did her life change when she went to New York? But I don't ask these questions. Instead, I let two thin strands of our common experience define who she is. I know all I need to know about her. I figure Trinidad is like Jamaica or Barbados, colonized by White Europeans, probably with some history of slavery. I surmise that her dad, whom she describes as a traditional strong island male, has White prejudice because, being Black, he must have experienced discrimination and possible subjugation under White rule. I reach the obvious conclusion that race and culture in Trinidad is a matter of Black and White.

After class I'm in a hurry to get home to write up my encounter, feeling pretty good because I asked her the probing question about racial attitudes and she had been rather open and forthcoming, her eyes bright as she thoughtfully delivered her judgment: "Cautious," she said. "My father was always cautious of other people — people not from the island. When I got to New York my teachers were White males. My father was very cautious of them. Back in Trinidad, my teachers had been Black nuns. . . . There were never any White people over at my house. Well, if ever there were, it was people I brought over. A teacher or friend from work. If I wanted to experience diversity it had to be on my own time," she had said. Her gaze shifted toward the far wall, looking for the past, trying to catch memories.

Inevitably doubt sets in, and I begin to wonder if we talked enough, if I asked enough follow-up questions, if she might not have said something really wonderful if I had only known how to prod her more. At home, sitting in front of the computer, fingers tap-tap-tapping on the keyboard, searching for words to fill the empty space that taunts me, I am resigned to the fact that indeed I don't have enough — but not yet ready to accept defeat, I decide to supplement my writing by doing some background research on Trinidad.

The next day, I spend an hour at the library scanning the history and social studies books on the Caribbean. Some six or eight books on Trinidad and Tobago with dusty scholarly titles line a shelf, along with a couple of dozen volumes on Haiti and Jamaica. Thinking the scholarly titles too complex — I'm looking for some quick insight — I choose, instead, a general interest travel book aptly named *Insight Guide,* and finding a reading spot by a window, begin the journey of discovery. Leafing through the book I come across a full spread of two facing portraits, one of an Indian man, one of a Black man, with a caption calling the reader's attention to the two faces of Trinidad. I am rather surprised to learn that half of the people are of African descent, and half of East Indian immigrants. I jot some notes and check out a couple of the dusty books, just in case.

The young man who processes my books smiles appreciatively, as he says, "That's where I'm from — Trinidad. Are you doing a project?" I briefly explain I am on a cultural journey. The Indo-Trinidadian is joined by a tall Asian-looking young man. "He's from Trinidad, too," the first clerk says by way of introduction. I ask if he's Asian, and he happily volunteers he's a mix of so many cultures. His sing-song accent has a hint of French in it, it seems to me, and I catch that Syrian is part of his heritage. I share with them what I have learned about the two faces of Trinidad, adding that now I'll enlarge my definition to include more faces, thank them for their interest, take my books and head home.

As luck would have it, I pull into our driveway as my husband is coming out our door so I offer to go with him to the bank for company. It's not our regular branch. Our animated conversation from the car ride, on this 'n' that, continues as we make our way around the velvet rope to the front of the line. No one else is waiting. A teller behind the counter is talking to a woman with a clipboard who is standing in front of her. The woman looks official, and though I think it's odd that she is holding the clipboard, I dismiss her as a local business customer. Joe and I are clearly and rather loudly speaking English to each other the entire time. The clipboard lady pivots where she stands to face us, blurting a garble of incomprehensible noise in one fluid action. Joe says, in English, that he has checks to deposit. I say, "I didn't realize we were in a different country." "*Min arpazese.* Once again, it's my mother's voice, inside my head, warning me about my quick temper. The clipboard lady laughs, "Ha! Ha! Ha! Ha!" Just like that, too. A put-on, fake, nervous laugh. She does not look at me, however, or acknowledge my presence. Switching to English and speaking only to my husband, she directs him to the counter.

By now new customers are lining up and the nervous greeter turns her Spanish attention to them. My husband rolls his eyes and tells me I'm nuts. After 20 years together, he is used to my strong opinions and even stronger reactions. Undeterred by his shushing and my mother's admonishing voice, I continue with my point. Calmly. I say something like, "It just keeps happening . . . I resent the presumption . . . this is a business . . . we're on Miami Beach . . . it's rude . . . we're obviously speaking English . . . we should change banks on principle. . . ." Although I exaggerate jokingly, I am not beyond doing that. Joe defends the clipboard lady, saying, "At least she's bilingual." The checks deposited, we leave the branch. As we walk to our car, he tries for the last word. "You probably terrified them. They're probably saying what stupid gringos we are." "Good," I retort. "Next time, let them think twice before assuming the whole world is Spanish." As we distance ourselves from the bank, the pounding in my chest dissipates and my breathing returns to normal. The ride home is markedly subdued. Joe talks quietly about going to see a movie, as I utter random "uh-huhs," here and there.

But I'm not really listening. Instead, I am reflecting. I was ready to come to blows over a simple, albeit mistaken assumption. It bugs me that it bugs me so much. Trying to deconstruct the events of the past couple of days, I replay a litany of other mistaken identity encounters I've recorded and filed in my mind for easy access and retrieval. Thinking about my interview with the Trinidadian student in class, I notice how quick I was to catalog her father's experience, looking for a simple answer — Black man under White colonialism — to a complex question. And I had arrived at a wrong conclusion. I had done "it" to someone else — what I am so sensitive about people doing to me.

I come home alone and set to work. Lost in thought, trying to make sense of my forays across cultures, too distracted to sit and write, I decide instead to give the oral history tapes a try. The tapes are part of the Race and Change Project, an archive of memories of residents of the City of Hollywood, Florida, collected in 1999. I have three narrators I want to listen to for our diversity course and I choose to start with the tape of Leonard Robbins.

Born in 1921, Leonard Robbins is the oldest, and only native-born American in my circle of cross-cultural encounters. Right away, he captures my imagination, speaking honestly about his experiences with religious and racial injustice:

> *"I'm Jewish — that's why I would empathize with many of the problems that minorities have in the United States and especially this area. . . . After I started school I became aware that I was not Christian, but I was Jewish, because I had a few classmates who called me names that were identified with being Jewish . . . Religious differences didn't become very prominent in Broward County until 1936, about the year before I got out of high school. When they built the Fort Lauderdale Beach Hotel . . . they had a big sign out front, 'Restricted Clientele.' I didn't even know what it meant until my father explained it to me and that meant that Jewish people were not welcome. And, of course, Black people weren't welcome anywhere. Even on the east side of the tracks . . . I became aware of the difference because they didn't have any ordinance about Jewish people but they sure had them about Black people. They wouldn't let them come east of the tracks after 6:00 at night unless they were vouched for by someone they worked for . . . often wondered why people made such a fuss about it. Because people are not really different."*

Hearing Robbins make glaringly direct pronouncements, I am struck by his outspoken views on injustice, prejudice, and discrimination in this country.

"I was working in my father's store in Christmas of '47 . . . selling clothes the day the telegraph came and advised me that I had passed the Bar. Now, trying to get a job, I couldn't get a job. One lawyer in Fort Lauderdale had offered me a job, but the big firms didn't . . . One of them told me, 'I don't hire any Jews' . . . Here I am, a highly decorated war veteran, I had six medals . . . flew 50 missions, a graduate of Harvard Law School which should be some recommendation and nobody wanted to hire me."

I recognize myself in Robbins, especially when he admits that, at times, he may be too direct in his approach to curing social injustice.

"My mother contributed to the opera every year and they wouldn't even let her get into the Opera Guild. I'm impatient. I'm impatient and prejudiced. It just bothers me. . . . There are more White Christians than there are Jewish people, and they have the money. If you want to succeed in their world, you have to play their game. And I say this to my Black friends, too. They want to stick with their street English or whatever. I say, 'If you want to make it in somebody else's world, you have to play somebody else's game.' That's the old story. Most people don't believe you."

Listening to Robbins reminds me of the stories my husband's grandmother would tell about the restricted shops in Quebec City and Montreal when she was growing up. In one of the more genteel confectionary shops the sign read: "No Jews, No Blacks, No Dogs." But I don't think of Montreal as having a racially segregated past — at least not a recent past of the last 50 or 75 years. Taking a mental inventory of the common points between Robbins and myself, I find we have similar outlooks, if not exactly common experiences. I put the Robbins tape aside, and turn to the tape of Vera Williams.

She is originally from Jamaica and has what is not an uncommon life experience that includes living and working in England and in Canada, and now Hollywood, FL. She calls herself a "nursing snowbird." I am drawn to her story because, like me, she knows both Canada and the US. But Williams surprises me with her frank talk of childhood memories of color tensions in Jamaica.

"[S]trange enough, there was an awareness of color. It's a gradual thing. . . . You realize that there are people with a different hue to their complexion. In my district there were no White people. We were all Black people but, as with every Black community, there are different colors and textures. People will tend to show preference for this or that color. . . . Sometimes you would hear people say like they didn't like anything too black.

> *"The first time I became aware of how profoundly color could affect you is when I left Jamaica. . . . [W]hen I went to England, the advertisement [for rental apartments] would say in the newspaper, no law against it, they would say, 'No Irish, No Blacks, No Dogs.' It was very awful. . . . I wanted my children to be able to go to school and get whatever amount of education they wanted, could handle, without having to fight tooth and nail. So, I decided to go to Canada. . . . I was working in the same place as a Canadian Black woman and a White person who was observing us said to me, 'Why are you so different than this other woman,' attitude-wise, I guess. I had to say, 'I was 19 before I encountered White people. So, I guess you haven't changed me' . . . I just go out there to meet the world."*

Williams explains that as a traveling nurse] she was provided housing by her employer, and that provided a sheltered entry into the South Florida community.

> *"[W]hen I came here, I didn't have to go out into the community. I didn't have to look for housing. I didn't have to find my own way . . . But the thing that alerted me was when I met some people and having grown up in black skin, you can sense attitude. You know when somebody has a different attitude towards you, even body language and tone. The thing I found astonishing was that people's attitude, when they saw that I was Black, I sensed a change in their attitude when they heard me speak and realized I wasn't from here. I was taken aback by that. It became more positive, more friendly. I was astonished because I thought, 'Oh, so, if I was from here you would have a more negative attitude towards me. But I'm not from here, you have a better attitude towards me.' That was interesting. I think a lot of people from the Caribbean have noticed that. We talk about it."*

I wonder how Williams's experience compares to my classmate who describes herself as a "Caribbean Black woman."

During our first talk she hadn't said anything about ethnic or racial tensions back home, talking more about island people in general, and only mentioning Whites when she moved to New York to work. This time I am careful to ask about more. "Back in Trinidad the Indian Blacks and African Blacks pretty much kept to themselves," she tells me when we talk a second time. "There was a sense, an attitude that the Indian Blacks were more superior than African Blacks. They had more advantages, they stayed closer, were more together as a race. It felt like they had preferential treatment — maybe because they were classified more Caucasian because their features were different from African features. Their features were more Caucasian than ours."

We laugh remembering how wrong each of us was about the other. "People mistake me for either African or Jamaican. Maybe because I'm dark," she says. "They don't think I look African American. My mother gets really offended at being mistaken for Jamaican because she is proud of her Trinidadian heritage. Americans don't know Trinidad as much — Jamaica is more well known because of the music, the food. People I meet are always telling me, 'You're not from here, you're from an island.' It happens at the supermarket, the dry cleaner — it happens often."

I am touched by her candor as she describes the inter-and intra-racial hostility that awaited her in New York, and how she had assimilated to American life. "I changed everything . . . the way I spoke . . . the way I dressed . . . wore my hair. I had to get rid of my accent. I stopped using island English. I changed my style of dress. I had to drop the Catholic school look — bows and ribbons . . . got extensions to be more culturally accepted . . . Americanized." I think back to our first encounter over the café con leche. I hadn't thought about how she must have felt reaching out, initiating the exchange across the racial and cultural chasm that separated us. Maybe she'd been cautious when she saw I was White: tentative, afraid of what racial or cultural insensitivity might fall out of my mouth. Certainly I had been made weary by our first exchange, before we shared our experiences and our memories. Before she became a person. I found we had more between us to connect than to divide us.

The difficult journey — one story after another of intolerance and hostility — is coming to an end. I'm on my last tape and his name is Pedro (Peter) D. Hernandez. "*I use the Peter 'cause it's easier to recognize,*" he explains. The words float like soap bubbles, barely touching the surface of his tongue as they escape his mouth, with no hard sounds, running into each other, the ends dissolving into the air. I recognize something in his voice. It's not so much the accent, characteristic in a sense of the Hispanic immigrant who came here old enough to have started school elsewhere, who learned to speak English here, and who has a strange way of mingling languages the way all of us do who were thrown into our new exile schools before ESOL. What I recognize is a degree of annoyed accommodation.

Hernandez came to Hollywood, where his uncle had settled some years before, after a two-year stopover in Spain — a sort of clearing house for Cubans fleeing the Communist regime, waiting in limbo for American sponsors and money to come through:

> "*I was about 11?. . . . We arrived at Miami International. . . . My dad's family was there, which I barely remember. My uncle Luis had a 1963 four-door Cadillac. . . . As we were driving back from the airport, the weather was humid*

*and hot and his air conditioner didn't work, but the breeze was coming in. I just
felt it was hot. A few days after moving in with Uncle Luis, his wife and two
daughters, I got a used bicycle. It was the first bicycle I ever had. I rode that
thing until I was crisp. I was so sunburned it wasn't even funny."*

Listening to Hernandez recount the scene of his arrival in South
Florida in the summer of 1974, a scene comes to my mind of another
landing, four years earlier, in 1970. That plane arriving from Athens,
Greece, at Montreal's Dorval International Airport where we are greeted
by a mob of family and new Canadian friends led by my father's brother.
On our ride home, I remember going over a bridge and how the smell
of swamp gas permeated the wood paneled station wagon. My brother,
who was four, turned up his nose. *"Kati mirizi skatila.* Something smells
shitty," he pronounced, accusingly. The plane ride had been fun, but
now he was bored and tired, and he wanted to go to our grandmother's
for his usual afternoon ice cream cone and siesta story time. Little did
he realize it would be two years before he would see her again.

I am struck by the common ground, this time between myself and
Hernandez. We're born two days apart, and though our journeys began
6,067 miles from each other, some 40 years ago, Hernandez and I now
find ourselves practically neighbors; he lives in Hollywood and I live on
Miami Beach. We've yet to meet, but already I know so much about him.
We share the experience of that carefree summer, our first, in our new
countries. I can't help but shake my head and shudder, thinking back on
it now, how akin to an alien arrival from a distant planet was the welcome to our new schools. After all, how much English did they expect
us to learn, that summer, playing hopscotch on the sidewalk, riding a
used bicycle all day in the sun?

"The language was a major barrier," Hernandez remembers.

*"I couldn't understand what people were saying to me. . . . The school was the
big monster, it seemed like . . . My dad dropped me off at school and I didn't
know where to go. I saw all the kids outside and the doors were locked. The bell
rang and everybody went in and I'm standing outside saying, 'Where do I go?'
I didn't speak any English at the time, so I went to the principal's office and
tried to talk to somebody and they didn't know. Twenty-five years ago, [the]
school system in Broward County was not set up to take children who did not
speak English . . . I went to the office and they tried to come up with somebody
who would translate for me. They didn't have any teachers. They came up with
this kid . . . [but] it became obvious to the school that I wasn't going to be able
to go through classes with [him]. He was a child and he couldn't relate [what]
I was trying to say and what the teacher was trying to say . . . I was labeled
'LD,' learning disabled. I was put in a class with what some people might call*

'misfits,' but, in my case, they were kids that were different and I felt right at home because I was different. "

"*It's funny,*" Hernandez reminisces, "*in Cuba we didn't have a racial tone as far as discrimination toward one another. Everybody was Cuban.*" When asked to describe himself racially, an obviously perturbed Hernandez asks for clarification: "*My Hispanic background? Well yeah, I'm Hispanic. That seems to be what I'm classified every time they ask you what's your name and your race. Whether you're White, Hispanic, or Asian. I'm always baffled because . . .,*" he hesitates looking for the words, and I recognize the same annoyed tone I get when I'm confronted with such questions of identity. "*[Y]eah, the — the skin of my color is white but that doesn't count as being described as White. You go by the last name so you become Hispanic. So you could classify me as Hispanic,*" he says. I notice the odd slip, the way he flips "color of my skin" and says instead "skin of my color." I could tell it bugs him, having to describe himself in such a seemingly arbitrary manner.

"*Within three months, I was speaking English. I caught on quick and the accent was getting better and better,*" Hernandez announces, triumphant.

"*I learned early in life that if you want to be successful in life you have to blend in. Even today, I go to Miami in the truck and when I speak Spanish people say, 'You don't look Cuban.' I say, 'What does a Cuban look like?' I have cousins with blonde hair and blue eyes and cousins that are African American. So, what does a Cuban look like? I never get a response to that question.*"

I wonder about that, too, Peter, when I think of all the times people have said to me, "You don't speak Spanish? But you *look* Cuban." I wonder what an American looks like. Is it, Peter, that you don't seem dark enough to be Cuban, while I don't appear light enough to be American? With these questions echoing in my head, I make another trip to the library — this time, in search of answers to the elusive identity query, "What does a — look like?"

The books have titles like *Rethinking the Color Line, Pride Against Prejudice, Coming to America, American Skin, Face to Face, Why Can't They Be Like Us?* and *Whiteness of a Different Color: European Immigrants and the Alchemy of Race.* Bringing them all home, not sure if our preoccupation with race is necessarily a good thing, I learn about the developing field of "whiteness studies."

In *Whiteness of a Different Color,* published in 1998, Matthew Frye Jacobson writes: "We tend to think of race as being indisputable, *real.* It frames our notions of kinship and descent and influences our movements in the social world; we see it plainly on one another's faces. It seems a product not of the social imagination but of biology." Working from the premise that racial classifications are arbitrary intellectual and sociological constructs, Jacobson asks, "What has become of the 19th century's Celts and Slavs . . . Hebrews, Iberics, Mediterraneans, Teutons, and Anglo-Saxons?" He points out that "the most significant revision of immigration policy, the Johnson-Reed Act of 1924, was founded upon a racial logic borrowed from biology . . . and, consequently, the civic story of assimilation (the process by which the Irish, Russian Jews, Poles, and Greeks became American) is inseparable from the cultural story of racial alchemy (the process by which Celts, Hebrews, Slavs, and Mediterraneans became Caucasian)."

Essentially, argue the "whiteness" scholars, the once divisive "racial" distinctions among "Whites" was glossed over in the face of the "greater" racial differentiation between "white" "yellow" "brown" and "black" peoples. When Hernandez is perceived as not Cuban — when Vera Williams feels more welcome as soon as she is recognized by her speech to be Jamaican — these instances confirm Jacobson's statement that "race is not just a conception but a perception." Significantly, Jacobson argues that the "history of whiteness and its fluidity is very much a history of power and its disposition."

Invariably I find myself having to defend against the characterization that it offends me to be identified as Hispanic. It does not. I readily identify as ethnic, but when my particular ethnicity is blurred I feel as though I am at risk of losing myself. When I lived in Montreal, I remember not ever having to say what I was since I was readily recognized as Greek-Canadian, one among 65,000 other Greek-Canadians living in Montreal. Then, in 1990, my husband and I, just married, moved to South Florida and the encroachment of my ethnic identity began. Now that I've had time and distance to think about it, I can admit the irony of my one-time desire to distance myself from that mass of Greek-Montrealers. Being one of them, I could afford to be different from them — I could insist on the distinct pattern of *my* spots, because it was clear I was a leopard. As I get older, and further away from the group, I find a sense of community, identity, and home in that association. This summer, I was back in Montreal, visiting family and friends. Dining out with friends — one Greek, one English — we were served by a young man claiming to be Greek. My friend Demitra and I did not believe him, flatly demanding that he provide proof of his lineage. Come to find out, he was Greek, but from Ontario — at which point, Demitra and I said, in unison, "Well, there you go — you're not a Montreal Greek."

It's our last chance to workshop our stories in class. Sitting in the requisite circle facing one another, I feel tense, unsure of my boundaries. The past three months have been grueling, but now we're laughing. I look intently at the faces around the room. More than the rainbow of colors, I now notice the expressions — interest, confusion, excitement, trepidation. We've become oddly close — the way complete strangers become close, dressing silently in the gym locker room — we've seen each other naked. Later that night, having dinner with my husband and his father at a casual restaurant, I bubble over as I relate my cross-cultural writing experience to my American father-in-law. My husband, who has heard the story a dozen times already, is insisting emphatically that I am, quite simply, American. "If my mother were traveling in China when she was pregnant and I was born there, that would not make me Chinese." He cuts the words with quick hand gestures. "People don't look at me and think I'm Israeli," he argues. "But you're not Israeli. You've never been to Israel," I say to him. "You're Canadian, regardless if you're Jewish. Your ancestry is Polish, Russian — European, like me," I explain. "Besides, you don't look Israeli."

I'd like to go back and point out that, yes, being born in China would make him Chinese, but I think better of it, not wanting to make a very big scene, especially not in front of his father. Our English words fly across the table, stopping when the young man bussing our table asks us something — in Spanish. The scene seems to play out in slow motion. Time stops as three "Anglos" fumble to understand. The bus-boy gestures to the far end of the table, out of his reach. In my best, most tolerant behavior, I hand him the salt and pepper shakers. "I think he wants to clear the condiment tray," I say to my fellow diners, in my most articulate, measured voice.

Rebecca Karimi grew up in San Antonio, Texas. Closely attached to her Mexican grandparents, she cherished the family ties shared with them and the rest of her relatives. She received a B.A. in Liter - ary Criticism/Creative Writing from the University of California, Irvine, studying under author Oakley Hall, of Down Hill Racer fame, and a Master of Art's degree in Liberal Studies from Florida Atlantic University where she is enrolled in the Ph.D. in Compa - rative Studies Public Intellectual Program. Her primary areas of interest are oral history, Mexican American studies, and creative nonfiction writing and she enjoys dabbling in radio production. In addition to her work as a writer, she has conducted oral history interviews for the Race and Change Project and produced an archival multimedia historical presentation from that research high - lighting the racial climate of early Boca Raton, FL. That work is in the archives of the African American Research Library and the Boca Raton Historical Society. She is also working on an oral history project on her family's history.

CAFÉ CON LECHE AMERICANA

Rebecca Karimi

I grew up near the San Jose Mission on San Antonio's south side in the '50s and '60s. We lived in one of the pockets of Latino neighborhoods sprinkled between the *Anglo* ones. The South side differed from the other sides of town. The West side embraced most of the Mexicans, while the East side sheltered the African Americans, and the North side claimed all the rich White people. But our side was mixed. Half and half. *Café con leche.* Salt and pepper. On our side, you heard the twang of Hank Williams' country western tunes in concert with Lola Beltran's *rancheras;* you smelled the aromas of sauerkraut and *kielbasa* intermingling with Spanish rice and pinto beans; you saw White skinned, blonde-haired *gringos* politely co-existing with brown skinned, black-haired Mexicans: and everyone lived in relative harmony.

The schools reflected the area in the same way. Harlandale School District divided each grade, except first, into three groups, based on scholastic ability. *Anglos* comprised most of the first group, while the second or middle group held *Anglo* and Mexican kids. The third group retained the Mexican children who just crossed the river and spoke only Spanish. Everyone considered them the "dumb group" because they had failed a grade or two. By the second grade, I had earned a seat in the first group.

Mexicans have a great deal of respect for those in authority, adults in command, and teachers. That notion smacked itself into my head from an early age — my father made certain he walloped it into me. "Becky Jeanne," he commanded in his broken English, "*nececitas respectar los adultos*, be *abusada*, pay attention, say 'Yes sir and Yes Ma'm' and do whatta the teachers say. *Bueno?*"

"*Si Senor*, I will, I promise," I meekly agreed.

"*Los adultos* know better," he went on, "They learn a lotta things and need to be treated with lotsa respect." Submitting to authority became second nature, though at times it was difficult to do. I was 10 and in the fifth grade at Huff Elementary when I had my first test.

Her name was Mrs. Pruitt, aka Prune Face. Arrogance dripped from her like sweat, and she sneered if you asked her a question, so I kept my mouth shut. One of only three Mexican children in my class, I never felt at ease with her. One day while studying Texas history, she proudly remarked in her syrupy Texan drawl, "Class, did ya'll know that *true Mexicans* are white-skinned, blond-haired, and blue-eyed?" A sudden gasp of surprise arose from the class. "Yes, yes, they are. The ones we see here aren't *true Mexicans*. They're . . . Indians," she snidely remarked. My face burned like fire as I tried to force my eyes up, but couldn't, I just knew she was talking about me. I felt the penetrating gazes of my classmates rest on my bronze skin and ebony hair. I slowly shrank into my seat. "Yes, the dark ones are Indians," she insisted. I glanced sideways and saw her wily cat eyes glaring right at me, her lips curled into a spiteful smile. My stomach came up to my throat.

"Liar," a voice shouted repeatedly within me, but my lips kept silent. I didn't want to fail my parent's test when it came to respecting those in authority. Mute and motionless, like a Mayan stone goddess, I could only sit and listen to her racist propaganda. The bell rang, and I ran all the way home. I didn't even stop to talk to my friends. "*Mami*," I said panting heavily as I reached the screen door, "what colors are the real *Mejicanos*," I asked.

"What color?" my mother inquired as she opened the door for me to enter. "Why, all colors, *por que?*"

"Mrs. Pruitt told the class today that the *true Mexicans* are blonde-haired and blue-eyed and that *we* were *Indios*. She looked right at me, Estella, and Esperanza when she said that. *Digame*, tell me, is that true?"

"*Pues los criollos* have white-skin, like your Daddy. They descended from the Spaniards," said Mami in her soft, Tex-Mex accented voice that sounded like a southern drawl with a Spanish accent. I thought of Papi's family, all very fair with hazel eyes. But then I thought of Papi's swarthy-looking brother who looked like one of the handsome Indian princes I would see on the Mexican calendars, scantily clad in a loin-cloth with a feathered headdress, ready to sacrifice a beautiful buxom Indian princess.

"*Y Tio Guillermo?*" I rapidly asked.

"Some Spaniards were mixed with *los Moro's*. The Moors were darker, like your *tio*, while others had lighter skin and hair," she added.

"*Y los indios?*" I asked impatiently.

"*Los aztecas y las mayas* lived in *Mejico* first. Some married the Spaniards and created a new breed, a mixture, called los *mestizos*. Did you know my grandfather was half Indian and married a Spaniard?"

Varying shades of brown and white relatives flashed through the pages of my mind as I looked at my mother's pecan-colored face and then at my bronzed forearms. I pondered her words for a moment. "So, if the *Indios* were there first, then they're the true *Mejicanos*, aren't they?" I didn't wait for an answer. A large grin slid over my face. At that instant, armed with my newly acquired knowledge, I felt a sense of superiority over Mrs. P ruitt. I knew the Indians were the true Mexicans. The White Spaniards were invaders. No longer ashamed of my color or ancestry, at least for the moment, I sat down to eat my favorite meal of *carne guisada* tacos.

After that, I treated Mrs. Pruitt politely, because of her status as an adult and teacher, but I no longer believed everything she taught us. The history of the Alamo came next in Mrs. Pruitt's class that year. I smiled to myself. We won that battle and whooped them Texans good.

Miles away and decades later, I had a chance to talk to a fellow student at Florida Atlantic University while in a writing class where we met. Of Anglo Saxon origin, she grew up in South Florida in the mid-'80s in a Hispanic neighborhood where she felt like an outsider, much like me. I can imagine her as a tiny, flaxen-haired little girl, standing alone as she wipes the tears off her translucent, milk glass colored face. She cries because her daddy lost his temper with her that day. All she did was bring her best friend home, and she couldn't understand why he had gotten so mad and had shouted at them in such a mean way. She thought he would be glad that her best friend didn't speak Spanish like the other children in her third grade class. Her parents' words echoed in her ears. They constantly complained about wanting to move out of Miami, into Fort Lauderdale, or somewhere where people spoke English. But they were just "too poor to move," her Mama had said. Unable to afford a new car, much less a new house, they were stuck in a predominantly Latino area of Miami-Dade.

Her father didn't approve of her next best friend Jason, however, and she wished so hard he would. He was nine, quiet and in the third grade, just like her. They understood one another. She tried to reason why Daddy didn't like Jason. Maybe he didn't like him because his jeans were tattered and torn, she thought. Or maybe because he always wore the same tee shirt? Maybe Daddy didn't like Jason's hair? Hers was straight and the color of vanilla ice cream — the opposite of his. He had fuzzy, dark brown hair, the color of deep, rich chocolate. Maybe that's what Daddy didn't like. Maybe that's why he had called him a name that day.

Frightened, the two innocent children trembled near the living room door, not knowing what to say. They stared at her father in amazement, then bolted outside. After this awful experience, Jason would certainly never want to be her best friend again, she thought. Her body sagging with embarrassment, she said goodbye quickly, turned around, and trudged into the house. Later, when she asked her mother what "nigger" meant and told her the day's events, she was told not to worry, that she could play with Jason as long as her father didn't find out. "Next time, go over to his house and it'll be our secret," Mama reassured her. And that's how they played together throughout their school years.

In contrast to her experience, I was the one who suffered the consequences of racial and social bigotry. Like an annoying *mosca* in a *panaderia* that ruins the sweets, I was the fly in the bakery that people shooed away. I looked like everyone else in my *barrio* on the South side, eyes as black as a cast iron skillet, hair as brown as Brer Rabbit molasses, and skin as dark as a Texas pecan. But it was *where* I lived that was poles apart from my peers. My house wasn't normal like my cousin *Miguel's casita,* or unusual like the *casa de maranito* around the corner that was shaped like a pig. It wasn't even like my neighbor Yolanda Canales' house that stood next door to her father's Conoco filling station. Nope. My house consisted of three rooms inside my *papi's* bar. "*Donde vives?*" The teacher would ask me. "I live at 3023 Roosevelt Avenue *en los* living quarters," I answered, repeating my father's words. Few Americans dared venture into my domain. Until one day.

"Zippity do dah, zippity day, Judy Jones is coming to play," I remember humming merrily that day. "I'm eig-h-t years old and in the third grade, zippity do dah, zippity ay." Judy Jones was the new girl in my class and lived in an *Anglo* neighborhood called Hot Wells, which unlike mine had big fancy houses and backyard swimming pools. She wore beautiful, puffed sleeved dresses with pretty pink petticoats underneath that made her skirts stand out like an umbrella and had matching bows for her short, chestnut brown hair. Her mother, Mrs. Jones, was a new teacher at Huff Elementary School, and Judy was the first *American* girl to come over and play. *Papi* drove us home from school in our blue '57 Chevy station wagon that had been in a wreck, but hadn't been fixed yet. Clunking along the dusty dirt road, we bounced as each pothole ejected us from our seats, until finally, we reached our destination.

Scrambling out the station wagon's doors into the parking lot, we skipped into the restaurant part of the bar where *mami* had a table waiting for us loaded with ice-cold bottles of Big Red soda water and squishy soft *carne guisada* tacos. The scent of homemade flour tortillas filled the air. Perfectly shaped like a soft, fat baby's hand, the tortillas were dripping with butter. We gobbled them up and went out to play.

The hours flew as we amused ourselves. I gave Judy a tour of my room, my parent's room and the kitchen. "Is this *all* of your house?" she asked. "Yep," I said, "but let me show you the puppies," so we scampered off to a dilapidated barn where the dogs were kept.

Full of dog hair and smelling of puppies, we returned to the house and I treated her to another bottle of Big Red soda water. We giggled and poked fun at our red moustaches and skipped arm in arm out the door of the apartment into *papi's* bar. *Mami* stood in the kitchen area and smiled through the To Go window saying, "Beckita, you look so happy with your friend." We hugged each other, and I squeaked like a sparrow, "She's my best friend, aren't cha, Judy?" "Yeah," she agreed and we started giggling as noisily as monkeys. The room had begun to thicken with customers, smoke, and beer. Tunes of Pedro Infante's *corridos* filled our ears along with the yelps and calls for more tacos and beer from *Papi's* patrons. "*Guedo, dos tacos de chorizo con otra Lone Star, y una Corona,* they requested incessantly, and kept my parents busy.

The Lone Star beer clock showed the little hand on the five and the big hand on the twelve. Five o'clock, that's the time that Judy would be picked up. We stood at the front door and stared out at the traffic that pulled into the parking lot. "There's my mommy's new white Buick. My daddy bought it for her," she said exploding like a cannon as she ran out to greet her mother. All of a sudden when I saw Judy's fancy new car pull up next to *papi's* sad looking one, I felt a funny feeling inside me. My face pressed against the glass, I peered outside. I wondered what Mrs. Jones was telling Judy. She grabbed her daughter's hand and they strode briskly towards the door. Mrs. Jones looked glamorous as she glided into our business, dressed in a beautiful white suit. I could see the look of disgust as she crinkled her nose to the stench of rotten beer that permeated the air. She hid her uneasiness behind her white cat-framed sunglasses while the accordion music blared in the background as a drunken crooner slurred the words of Jose Alfredo Jimenez' famous song, "*Llego borracho el borracho*. That crooner was my *papi*. Suddenly I heard an inebriated wolf whistle followed by a loud yelp yelling, "*Oi, oi, oi, Mamasita*."

Mrs. Jones face turned to ice and she took Judy's hand and turned around to leave. Too late. *Papi* ran to greet her. "Hello Mrs. Jones, Comeen, comeen" he blabbered happily with a thick, slightly tipsy, Spanish accent. "Woncha stay for a soda water?" Ever the polite Hispanic male, he extended his hand and I saw her hesitation. In a cold yet cordial manner, she excused herself and they left my life forever.

The day after, Judy ignored me. At recess, I asked her why and she said in her southern drawl, "My daddy says he doesn't want me to be friends with any one whose daddy owns a bar. They didn't like your neighborhood, either. 'Too many Mexicans,' Daddy says. My mommy says it's better if my friends are White, like me." "*Permiso*, I whispered as my lip began to quiver and I ran to the restroom so she wouldn't see me cry.

At the time, I didn't know why the little girl who was labeled the fly was shooed away from polite society. All I knew was like giant fly swatters, some adults attempted to rid their world of people like me. Obviously, I couldn't change my gender or race, but I could change my social status. Nestled in the cocoon of hard work and education, I morphed into a butterfly and was able to flutter up to a higher social standing. Unfortunately, I grew ashamed of my Mexican heritage, temporarily. After many years, I have finally come to accept who I truly am — a beautiful Mexican American woman from the barrios of San Antonio, embracing my *Mestizo* heritage, and sharing it with a multicultural society.

Immigrating to a new country or region requires great valor, especially when you arrive as a child or young adult. Like explorers of old, newcomers may suffer rejection, prejudice, or even worse, hostility as their ways, food, culture, and skin color appear odd to the pre-existing community. In the Race and Change oral history project, I encountered several narrators who migrated to the Lake Okeechobee area from Cuba and Georgia. During the interviews, these people share stories of hardship, heartache, and heroism as they sought to carve out new lives for themselves and to flourish like the lush vegetation of Florida.

The clock ticks back to 1960. One brave traveler who made the trip of a few hundred miles across the Atlantic to the US, was Armando Perez, Jr. Immigrating to Florida as a young boy of nine, he was born in Havana, Cuba in 1951. Living in the small town of Perico in the Mantanzas Province of Cuba, he grew up surrounded by family, and he fondly recollects holidays like Christmas, where a roasted pig fed large gatherings of over 40 people and how he would improvise with wood to make handmade toys. His father secured a position in the sugar cane industry in the US and worked in the fields cutting cane. Although only one of a few Hispanic families when they moved to the Glades area, they were later joined by their relatives which helped ease the loneliness of a new country. Currently a high school principal at Glades Day High School in Belle Glade, FL, Perez gives an account of growing up in "the Glades" and how life has changed over the years:

> *"When we drove up [from Miami], it was amazing. When you see Lake Okeechobee for the first time, from the Pahokee point of view, it looks like an*

ocean [because] you cannot see the other side of the lake. So here I am, nine years old. I thought I was like some Conquistador looking out over the Pacific Ocean for the first time. It was pretty tough; there weren't that many Cuban families in Pahokee when we moved there. [W]hen I first arrived, I was in several fights that first semester . . . I didn't speak English very well. I don't have any idea what the fights were about. I didn't know enough of the language to figure out what was going on.

"One of the things that still sticks with me is the cultural difference that we had in terms of the food. A big ticket item for me has always been the fact that in the 1960's, in high school, I remember [the] Anglo Saxon Caucasian White kids mocking the fact that we ate black beans and rice. They would say, 'Yuk, I wouldn't touch that,' because of the way it looks. [Y]ou couldn't invite somebody from your high school to come and eat because your parents were cooking Cuban food. [H]ere it is 40 years later and ethnic foods, whether it be Cuban or Japanese, is a big splash. . . . It was rejected because of ethnic and racial differences [but now those who] used to poke fun are eating black beans and rice. There's been a big cultural change [for] the acceptance — ethnically and racially — of differences.

"[I] found it odd that African Americans were not allowed to go into the places that Whites were being allowed to. . . . The Blacks were isolated, they had their own high school, so when I came in 1962 to Pahokee there was East Lake High School [which] was all Black, and Pahokee High School was all Caucasian. When I looked back to Cuba there was more of a racial mix. [I] had friends in my small town that were of different racial backgrounds. . . . [T]hey put us [the Cubans] in the White high school in Pahokee. [I] remember the first couple of days that the high school was first integrated in 1966 or 1967. That was when the federal law came down for East Lake High School to close its doors. . . . The first school in the area to be integrated was Pahokee High School. The next two years when we played Belle Glade High in football, Pahokee was integrated and Belle Glade High was not. [There] was a little bit of strife until Glades Central High School [opened].

"You kept to your own ethnic community; I socialized with other groups through the school setting, but outside of the school setting you did not socialize with other groups. [I] was a junior and I asked a girl to the prom. She was White, and her dad wouldn't let her go to the prom with me because I was Cuban. That hurt my feelings for a long time. I ended up going to the prom with another Hispanic, and had a great time. There are still racial hang-ups that people just can't get over. I have two daughters. My youngest went to the prom with a Black boy her senior year. My wife had trouble with that. I don't consider her a heavily prejudiced person, per se. She's Hispanic also, but she had trouble with that. Why? I don't know. I think it was the way you were brought up. My mother was instrumental and tried to drive into me the aspect of not being prejudiced. Look beyond the person — what's on the inside, not what they look like."

Perez coped with rejection and prejudice in the Pahokee neighborhood he colonized, but proved as resilient as a stalk of cane. Sailing over cultural, language, and racial barriers, he elevated his status within American society and now, like his Spanish forefathers, his ship has reached safe harbor.

The Glades of the 1930's, an even earlier time, was more of a rural area than the one Perez knew growing up. South Bay's oceans of bean fields shimmered in the hot Florida sun for Lexie May Childs and her husband. Childs's memories are also in the Race and Change archives. Guided by her mother, they relocated to South Bay in September of 1939 from Byronville, GA. And, though married two years, she remained childless when they ventured to the new land to seek higher wages. However, migrant workers seeking better pay spilled over a land teeming with harsh living conditions. Only the hardiest stayed. Eventually, circumstances improved for the voyagers from a little farther north.

"When I left Georgia we lived in big houses. Although they was kinda like plantations, they wouldn't [be like] quarters, but every plantation had houses and we lived in them. And my husband lived in this big house. And when we came here, and see these little huts, Oh Lord, little 10 x 10 one room shack, that's not for me. [T]hey had tin tops and when it rain, you'd hear the rain. [I]t was dark. Good Lord, it was dark. But I guess we was used to it, but I just didn't see myself staying here that night.

"[W]hen I left Georgia we was working for 60 cents a day. When I got here I would pick beans, and if you could pick a lotta beans, you make money. [You could make] $2.50 -$3.00 a day. That was a lotta money. Think about it — making $3.00 a week in Georgia, and come down here and make $1.50 per day? That was big money. So when I went to the field and made me $1.50, I said, 'No, I ain't going back to Georgia. I living in this shack from now on, I ain't going back.' So you took that 10x10 and did the best you could do with it. [We] let a bean box be everything; it was your bed, your table, your chairs and you learned to live with it, and enjoy it.

"In the old place nobody told me I had to come to work, I just did it. When I got here it was a little bit different. If you stayed in this man's camp, then he expected you to work, [S]omebody asked you why you didn't go to work if you wasn't at work, somebody's there to ask you why. But you see, in Georgia didn't nobody ask me why. That was a difference I seen. But darling, I been around White people all my life, and Black people. I don't see much difference nowhere I've ever been.

"When I was growing up, [in Georgia] we was all the same, my family, my friends. Racial didn't mean much to me. [W]e stayed around White people and their kids, we played together. . . . We knew that there was just so far to go, you was taught that. You couldn't go but so far with Miss So and So, you couldn't

go in there and play in her house. They didn't stay all night with us and we did-
n't stay all night with them.

"[T]he time racial got to be something in my life was when I was grown,
married and began to listen to racial stuff. You know, you can't do this or that.
Well, that didn't bother me cause I'd been doing it all my days. Didn't bother
me. I know when I visited, if I went to the house, hey, you knew where you was,
you didn't have to worry about it. Didn't nobody have to tell you to go to the
back door. You knew that's where you went, so it didn't bother you.[T]hey did-
n't have to enforce no law, you going into the White community; you just know
if you wasn't going to work, that wasn't the place for you. And you just didn't
go.

"We eat in the back of the restaurant or out the window. [Kids] now can't
see that. But it didn't bother us, because we did it all of our lives. I've known
that all my life, and when you're raised up under something that you've known
all your life, it doesn't make any difference. I never had no problem with it. It
don't bother you none if someone call you Black, do it? Do it bother you? Don't
bother me. Never.

"In the '60s things began to change. I'll tell you a big change. There were
bathrooms in the filling stations, and the bathrooms might say, 'white' and 'col-
ored' or they'd say 'white ladies,'and 'white men,' and 'colored.' And when those
things went to a-coming down, we didn't have a worry; change was on its way.
I used to go to Georgia and they used to have partitions in the middle of the
street [for the water fountains] and I know that one big pipe goes up with the
water and then another — pipe on this side, pipe on that side — they say,
'white' [or] 'colored.' All coming out the same pipe. And then I went there one
time and there wasn't no white, [or] colored on each side anymore."

Childs navigated the hostile waters of racism, bigotry, and segregation and like her ancestors, prevailed. Living through the tumultuous
times of Jim Crow and the Civil Rights era, she experienced a whole
new dimension to life once the manacles of prejudice were loosed.

Childs shares similarities with another African American woman
and oral history narrator, Susie Mae Brown. She also grew up in Georgia,
and moved to South Bay. The two women met there and formed a life-
long friendship. Orphaned at the tender age of 12, Brown's older brother
and his wife raised her until she married. With children of her own,
Brown entrusted them into the care of her brother in order to improve
her chances of success in the uncharted bean fields of Florida. She
remembers arriving in South Bay on the 17th day of October in 1936 as
clearly as if it were yesterday. While in South Bay, Brown has worked in
several different capacities: as a field hand, a nanny, and a waitress. She
shares many dramatic, life-changing memories of growing up in her
native Georgia along with her life in the Glades. At 85 years of age, the

traces of her Southern roots still strong in her voice, she maps out the course of her life:

> *"My grandmama come from Africa and was sold in South Carolina. [The slave-owner] put her up on that block and sold her and she had to wear [his] name. She came from [South Carolina] in a mule train. Grandmother Queen. [M]y papa died when I was nine and my mama died when I was 12. [My brother] was making me do the right thing, just like a mama would do. I try to obey, yes suh, shure enough. It brought me to 85.*
>
> *"Well, when I come up the High Sheriff had my daddy making liquor for him. That's right, named Deputy Charlie, Macon County — he was the High Sheriff. They wasn't no revenuers round then. [When the revenuers] was comin, they'd let the sheriff know in that town an den [Deputy Charlie] come out dere an tell my daddy, 'Well, Fletcher,' cuz my daddy's name was Fletcher, 'Yuh gotta git everything cleaned up.' [T]hey had the barrels of beer sitting in de kitchen door and they made liquor in the house in de wash pots. That's what I come up through. I seen some of that, you know. Yes Lawdy, yes suh. I was working on the farm. . . . My Auntie told me, 'You git your brother and sister-in-law to keep your chilluns and you go with me down to Florida to work. They was only three year old and the other was just a baby, one year old. I made 20 years old the 13th day of September and we left Georgia on the 15th day of October 1936 and got in South Bay on the 17th of October 1936 at 12 o'clock.*
>
> *"I worked with the peoples in the house keeping the chilluns for them and cooking and cleaning for 'em. We had to go in the back door. I'm talking 'bout me, cuz I'm the nanny here. . . . You'd be sittin up in de car with de lady. [S]he carry me to [her] house, an [she] go in the front, and I had to go round through the back. I started doing that and I quit. I say, 'Now I'm in there cooking, cleaning, taking care of her chilluns and I don't wanna go through the back. No suh.' So I says, 'Miss Ellen, I can go in there?' and she say 'Yea, c'mon.' Lotsa people in the city done called us niggers, but none of those chilluns done called me dat . . . 'Well Susie,' [they would say] 'you just was alright,' cuz I was taking care of dem teenage girls and I'd be done fair to them. . . . 'Don't ya'll be coming here bothering these girls,' I'd say, so [this boy would bother a girl] and I heard [her] saying, 'Susie, Susie, Susie, look here and make him turn me loose.' I know dat love, you know, and I say, 'you turn her loose, don't you rough her up like that, that's gon be your wife.' They married and they together now. Yes suh, this your Black granny. They just call an' come an' throwed their arms round me. They all treated me nice. I reckon it was why the Lawd letting me stay around here dis long.*
>
> *"But when I first came here, wasn't no cane fields, the only sugar mill was in Clewiston, um hum. That made all [South Bay] be bean farms. I picked here and [I] lived in the working camps across the railroad tracks owned by [this family]. [T]he houses we moved in, they were shanties, a tin top and sides. They had*

some little pumps — us didn't even wash our clothes in 'em cuz [the water] smelled so bad. And the water we drunk [was] from the Hoover Dike. You had to work to go in de fields. I was young then and sometimes you just don't feel like going. I had problems with my periods, and some days you don't wanna go. They bring the truck there, and wait out there until everybody go and when everybody done got on the truck, they know'd about how many because they was holding a pencil. Then he go round [the shanties] from door to door, 'Whack, Whack, Whack.' You know what he was hitting with? A blackjack. The police have them, a club. That's right, knocking on each door. Yeh, that was obedience, so I never had no problem. I had to work cuz I had something to work for, cuz I had chilluns. Yes, suh.

"We'd be in the bean fields sitting on our hampers waiting for the beans to dry, and if they was [dry], they would say, 'Okay, let's go.' [The overseer] was coming on swinging [the blackjack] and some of them didn't wanna go and walk all the way up there, but when he got on up there I had my beans where he could see 'em and smack! Yes suh, he knew I was working. [He] was real mean. The club was used to hit the Black people. Yes ma'm, shure was, that's what it was for.

"We stayed in de fields until we through or until it git night or late. Sometime we didn't finish the field exactly like we was supposed to. . . . When night come or evening come, some of us would knock off. And [a picker] come out of the bean field, and didn't wanna go back to the fields. [There] was one boss, went on out to the bean fields, and they wanted [this picker] to pick beans, [but] he didn't wanna pick. And so [the boss] shot him — so he there- lying on the side of the road. . . . I was picking beans that day in that field, too. [A]in't got no hate against them, I don't hate peoples. What bother me is them that killed the man without a cause."

All too familiar with slavery, bigotry, hostility, and violence first-hand, Brown, much like her grandmother Queen who sailed on a slave ship from Africa, has exhibited the same bravery, tenacity, and endurance. Like her ancestors, she has navigated through the rough waters of life and has never lost sight of her destination.

The Belle Glade/South Bay landscape looks different since Susie Mae Brown first immigrated. The area is no longer a migrant worker haven; football fields, prisons, and Wal Marts replace the bean fields while sugar cane farms, sod farms, and nurseries dot the horizon, keeping the local economy going. I, too, have migrated from the barrios of San Antonio. In 1996, I relocated to Wellington, FL, west of West Palm Beach, and in the process my profession changed from a pharmaceutical sales representative to an educator. Led by a compelling principle to help minority kids since I had grown up in such a racially-bigoted atmosphere, I ventured into a new teaching position at Glades Central

High School. Unfortunately, the underlying currents of racial bias act like invisible riptides for people to commit hostile acts against one another, and often we are powerless once caught in the swells.

As I recall, it was fifth period one Friday. I had a six-week test scheduled, and it was our first pep rally. The students buzzed with excitement, and whizzed through the test. Suddenly, girls began surrounding a popular football star, hugging, kissing, fondling, and practically necking with him there in the classroom. I stomped over to break up the conflagration. As I ordered them to sit down, I noticed some weren't even in my class. The talking and laughing grew louder. "Guys, sit down and keep quiet. Some are not finished with the test," I reproved them and admonished the girls saying, "We do not conduct ourselves this way in class."

"We don't gots to. We're finished with our test," they protested. "Aw, c'mon now. These girls just hanging round, ain't doing nothing wrong," retorted the player, stroking one on the back. A teammate shook his head saying "Yo, mind the lady and sit down. I'm still taking my test and it's too loud in here. Ya'll c'mon." "Shut up, m-f-," he yelled back. Before I knew it, everyone began yelling at each other. Mountains of curses tumbled down like rocks in an avalanche. Boys were confronting one another, girls were screaming, the clamor was nerve-racking. "I told you to sit down and stop, but you didn't listen," I shrieked angrily as I started filling out a referral form. "You cain't give him a referral," a horde of girls detonated. "That mean he cain't play football tonight, an he's the star." "I don't care who he is, I don't care if he plays, and I don't care if any of you go to the pep rally — and whose class are you in, anyway? You'd better get out of here," I roared, turning and reaching for the buzzer to call the office. The intercom came on, but the students yowled every time I tried to speak. Mob rule prevailed. I felt like a victim waiting for the guillotine. I ran to get backup from a coach across the hall, but by that time the throng was unstoppable. An emergency alarm sounded, kids darted out the back door, security swooped in, and I stood outside my classroom shivering convulsively, fearing for my life. A few days later, I resigned my position.

The swells of bigotry, hatred, and prejudice overpowered me that day. I sought, in earnest, to help these victims of racial hatred, but like decades before, in my classrooms as a child, I only got stuck in its mire. This time, I was the teacher, not the student, and I failed the test miserably. I still desire to help, however, in a different manner so I've retreated into the cocoon of hard work and higher education. Time heals; strength gathers and, wounded but not broken, like butterflies we can always re-emerge.

Arlene Galarza says, "the Race and Change Project forced me to analyze reasons behind my behavior and attitudes toward my Puerto Rican culture. It has also humbled me when I compare my struggles to the experiences of the narrators in the oral history proj - ect. Perhaps the most poignant effect was the realization that people of the past who are decades older than I have felt the same alien - ation. Since writing this essay, I have become an English teacher at Plantation High School in Broward County, Florida. I'm now a vegetarian, much to my family's dismay. Although I continue to question my Catholic background, I have converted to non-denom - inational Christianity and am active in my church's choir and youth group, which goes skating once a month. And occasionally, I run a search on Classmates.com for James Henry."

ATTITUDE RECEIVE

Arlene Galarza

Peter Hernandez is a 40-year-old Cuban businessman who came to Hollywood, FL, from Spain when he was 11. I encounter his archival oral history interview in the Race and Change Project during an inves- tigation into issues of identity and assimilation that have haunted me for years. I am surprised to discover that he did not have problems with identity, but I did find an older, kindred spirit as Hernandez's confident voice filled my ears with a familiar accent speaking about his first years in Hollywood. Although he often got into fights, having no other Spanish classmates to back him up, he adjusted to the new environment very quickly, and learning a new language seemed to be the worst of his struggles with identity.

"In Apollo Middle School, there was a Black kid, Anthony, and whenever I had problems with the Blacks, he would step in and say, 'No, he's my friend.' And I would have no problems. So, I've always made friends with people, no matter who they were, and when you became friends, race doesn't become an issue. It's just person to person.

"I have a good friend who doesn't care for Cubans, but we've been friends for years. He says, 'Well, you're different.' I said, 'I'm different because you've allowed me to enter your world and I've allowed you to enter my world. But you

don't do that with other Cubans. If you did, you'd find that we're all the same.'
But he won't admit to that. He says I'm still different and I respect that. It goes
back to some of the experiences he's had in the past."

Hearing this confident man speak about going to school during the mid '70s when there were no other Spanish speaking students to communicate with, I feel ungrateful. I wonder why I was vulnerable to conforming to the more popular culture when I had plenty of friends who would have appreciated my true personality. Here is a man who is Cuban but looks White, a man who was discriminated against because of the blood in his veins and the accent on his lips. Yet, he found a way to blend in without betraying his heritage.

"I learned early in life that if you want to be successful, you have to blend
in. Even today, I go to Miami in the truck and when I speak Spanish people say,
'You don't look Cuban.' I say, 'What does a Cuban look like?' I have cousins
with blonde hair and blue eyes and cousins that are African-American. So, what
does a Cuban look like? I never get a response to that question."

Hernandez stood strong in who he was, and at the same time managed to accept those people who could have never understood him. He adopted the language, and some of the traditions of the people in Hollywood, but never seemed to feel short-changed when they did not reciprocate. I envy the way he let other people's perceptions roll off his back. By contrast, I realize that I struggled a great deal with a curiosity that challenged the way that I was taught to think. And that curiosity was almost completely beaten down by the time I was 13.

Throughout elementary school, my persistent questions about my Puerto Rican traditions were never innocent; they were pointed disputes against the nature of my parents' Catholicism and double standard toward women. I was responsible for most of the chores delegated to my brother, Richard, and me. It seemed like there were no consequences for him when he failed to do his chores, yet plenty of consequences for me. In my family, my brother was allowed go out anywhere, and he got away with breaking curfews, talking back, and getting bad grades. I was kept inside, locked in. Both my mother and father adopted a "boys will be boys" attitude that they brought with them when they moved to the States from Puerto Rico.

I also questioned God, church, and the necessity for both ever since my mother dropped me off at Blessed Sacrament Church for Catholic school in Hartford, Connecticut when I six. My dispute derived from the fact that my parents forced us to go to church even though they didn't understand the English sermons as well. Any questions I had about our religion were left unanswered by my father, who did not communicate with us much. And my mother, who hated my challenging spirit, would say, "Why do you ask so many questions?"

As if I did not already feel like a black sheep, Richard called me a "disgrace to the race" one day when I was in eighth grade because I had never learned to speak Spanish. I think I was disinterested in speaking Spanish because I fell in love with poetry and the English language. My language arts teacher had recently showed the film *Dead Poets Society*, thus sparking a life long passion for teaching and writing. But my brother's taunting eventually resulted in me sacrificing my dreams for my roots. I paid the price with an identity crisis that probably stunted any growth I could have made in my writing then.

Richard made a point of making me feel ashamed for not acting like a Puerto Rican. Besides the fact that I didn't speak Spanish, I hung out with mostly White friends, listened to adult contemporary music, enjoyed school and always had my nose stuck in books. When I looked at the other Spanish people at middle school, I recognized the same street-hardened childhoods that calloused my own cousins. They needed to belong, but only with others who wore the same baggy clothes and designer sneakers with the tags left on. I wanted something deeper, to be around people who could reveal their passions and secrets unfettered.

Unfortunately, Richard was a great arguer, and even if I knew he was wrong about something, I could never win. As I curbed the questioning of my culture, I let myself fall victim to the idea that maybe I *was* a disgrace if I acted White — whatever that meant. So, I began to imitate Richard and the other Spanish people at school. I began to hate my thin, curveless figure, and snubbed some of my friends because they were White. Soon I, too, was wearing baggy clothes, even though they slipped off my frail 85-pound body, and I pretended to hate poetry and school. I fumbled with Spanish; I could never get past conjugating verbs. I tried to walk the walk, and talk the talk, but failed miserably. The once intellectual Arlene acted like a roughneck who, incidentally, was rarely allowed out of the house or else she'd get grounded. Somehow I never stopped fearing my parents. The whole persona fit as awkwardly as a one-size-fits-all hospital gown worn backwards. In the end, I was not only ashamed of how badly I failed at molding myself into an image that Richard had created; I was ashamed of myself for even trying.

These emotions resonate with the memories of Diana Wasserman-Rubin, 55, who moved to Miami Beach from Cuba at age 14. As I listen to her oral history interview, I am comforted to discover that she went through similar struggles with her identity in middle school where she was ostracized because of her race and because she did not speak English.

"That's when the culture shock hit me because now I'm among my peers for the first time [since moving to Florida] and these peers don't treat me very nicely. I

don't wear the same clothes that they wear, we didn't have the money at all to buy from the nice stores. I was wearing some hand-me-downs from friends, et cetera and I didn't communicate, obviously. I was very, very thin. I wasn't eating well. I wasn't adjusting to the diet. We had Spam in twenty different ways that my mother had figured out how to make it. . . . I remember her cooking in the hotel. The hotel had like . . . two burners, and she would make Spam because it was the cheapest thing to buy then with tomato sauce. She would cut it up in little pieces, she would mold it with her hands so I would think it would be, like, something different, like a hamburger and then put some mayonnaise on it. I mean, I can't remember how many different ways she made Spam. Needless to say, I have never touched it since."

I empathize with Wasserman, and feel relieved to know that I am not alone. I, too, grew tired of my mother's cooking — for me it was white rice and beans, or beef stew. But what I really hated was yellow rice and chicken. I don't know why, but I have never had a taste for Spanish food, especially chicken with the skin left on it. The fact that my mom made these dishes everyday worsened my distaste for them. Although I understand the misery one can endure when they don't like Mom's food, I know that a simple distaste can't compare to Wasserman's poverty and lack of nutrition.

"[A]nd the reason I went to Saint Pat's [High School] is because I was so miserable at Nautilus that I used to cry every day. I wasn't eating, I was complaining. My parents didn't have money. I think my father may have borrowed the money to put me in Saint Pat's to help me be able to concentrate on academics and, at least, maybe, to feel — that's because of the Catholic connection because I had been in Catholic school in Cuba — that I would be more open to, you know, learning and getting away more from the social dissatisfaction that I felt at the time."

Despite her trouble adjusting to a new culture and language, Wasserman's first encounter with discrimination didn't happen until many years later, long after she was an adult. She said she met some college students at Florida State University during one of her visits to Tallahassee, and they questioned her about her married name and her accent.

"'Diana what? Wasserman?' Ah. Now, I am from the Sixties, come from Cuba, speak English with an accent and I'm maybe a Jew. These boys got up from the table. They were all sitting around the table with my girlfriend and myself. And they moved away. . . . Then I went over to them and I said, 'What happened? We were talking, we were telling jokes, we were singing the songs, what happened boys?' And they said, 'Oh nothing. We just have nothing else to talk about.' I said, 'Does it have anything to do with who I am?' I said, 'Were you

*having fun with me before?' 'Yeah, but we . . .' They didn't know how to vocal-
ize it but it was quite obvious that they were disturbed by who I was and that
is, without a doubt, the first time I felt truly, truly discriminated against
because of who I was."*

I realize that I, too, have never been discriminated against for being
Puerto-Rican. I can't think of a time that anyone was ever outrightly
cruel to me, or ever called me names because of my Spanish background. I begin to wonder if I didn't cause my own struggle because of
people's comments that I acted too "White." Something that Hernandez
said in his interview echoes in my mind: "I think attitude comes a long
way when it comes to experiences. The attitude you have may very well
be the attitude you receive." I comb my hair with my fingers absently
and loosen up and laugh, remembering how I always copied the same
gesture from my White girlfriends while growing up, and still do, even
today. My hair is very curly and tangled, so I could never get my fingers
through it in one stroke without losing a ring or breaking a nail.

When it came to interracial dating, my first experience started one
afternoon late in my freshman year of high school. I ran out of the cafeteria without my book bag, and cried all the way until I got to the court-
yard in the front of the school. I rammed myself, back first, into the bark
of a tree and recounted in my mind the huge mistake I had just made
by leaving my journal on the lunch table while I got a soda. Richard got
a hold of it and started reading my poetry out loud to all his basketball
friends. I tried to get it back but he just called me a *gringa* and threw it
at my face. As I was sniffing, a boy leaned over from the other side of the
tree and asked if I wanted to join him. I wiped my tears, embarrassed,
and hated myself for having assumed I was alone. We ate lunch together,
and I felt better because he never once asked why I was crying.

Later, I found out his name was James Henry. He was a sophomore
who others called the "Cowboy" because he was a southern White boy
who wore faded brown cowboy boots. I spent the next month having
lunch with Henry because I was intrigued. He never asked me who I
hung out with, or seemed impressed when I told him who my brother
was. The only thing that piqued his interest was my contribution to
"ethnic Fridays." Every week, he asked a different person to bring in
food from his or her culture to share with our lunch bunch. But this was
actually Henry's scheme to get free Asian and Spanish food. I found
myself asking my mother for a pot of her Spanish yellow rice and chicken
to bring in. Henry loved it, and I was so taken by his affinity for ethnic
foods that I almost asked my mother to teach me how to make it.

But only a couple of weeks after we met, Henry told me he was moving away to Iowa. I was incredibly disappointed because he was the only
person I ever met who was completely unmoved by my "Spanish" front.

In fact, he never seemed to notice that I even had a front. For the next few weeks, we spent every lunch break together, and we talked over the phone on weekends. I found myself writing more poetry and even submitting one to the literary magazine. Soon, I dumped the ghetto façade and started wearing my old clothes and grew my nails long.

One day before English class, I was filing my nails when my girlfriend, Phyllis, confronted me. She said that I used to be different, and she didn't like what was happening to me. I was dressing too much like a girl; I was filing my nails, and writing poetry. I asked her, "How can those changes be for the worse? How could that make me a bad person?"

"Before, you used to be tough," she said. "You didn't listen to anybody, and you wouldn't let anyone tell you how to act." I laughed at the irony of her statement. I apparently convinced someone that the front was my true self. To this day, I don't even remember what I told her. I just know that our conversation confirmed that I was growing out of my identity crisis — as well as my friendship with Phyllis.

I felt free when I realized Henry loved me for who I was, not for how well I conformed to my culture. I was mesmerized by the way he was truly unaffected by other people's comments about his cowboy boots and thick Louisiana accent. I think he was unaware of my issues. Instead, he complimented my poetry and my smile, which I never used to show when I tried to act tough. He emphasized the importance of family and communicating to them — two foreign concepts to me since my dissention from Catholicism.

Before he moved, he invited me to a beach party for his birthday. I immediately reverted to my rote memory response of "I'm not allowed out." I explained I wasn't allowed to see guys, but Henry couldn't understand why I would not even ask. It's amazing how my American friends could not digest the idea that there was no negotiating with my parents about dating and going out to certain places. After days of Henry bugging me, I bravely approached my father with the idea, knowing I could very easily risk the privilege of seeing any guys in the future. Yet, something got into my father that day. He said yes. I once thought that Henry was too naïve, too American to ever understand the dynamics of the male-dominated Puerto Rican culture I come from. But when differences in culture are stripped away, I think we are all a microcosm of that little five-year-old begging to be let outside, free to skate on the asphalt of the open road.

Henry moved a week later, and I never heard from him again. But he left me completely reformed. I have never worn hoop earrings, sports jerseys, or baggy clothes since. Sometimes I think he was a dream, that I made him up because I needed to learn what I learned from him at that time in my life. I think again about what Peter Hernandez said, that "the attitude you have is the attitude you receive."

Henry's departure from my life did not quell the questioning of my culture, however. In an attempt to rebel against those double standards and religion, I became atheist. I started buying my own food when I began working at 16, so I did not eat dinner most nights. Against my father's wishes, I got involved in many extracurricular activities during senior year. I even held long-term relationships with guys who were attracted to my independence, not my cooking.

But one day — I was 18 by now and in college — I visited my grandmother in Miami, and she greeted me with the standard "Dios te bendiga" ("God bless you") and a tight hug that could have stopped my circulation. I sat behind the kitchen counter and watched as she ecstatically cooked me some yellow rice and chicken. For the first time in my life, the smell of cilantro and olives was welcoming, and the clang of her metal spoon hitting the cauldron made me smile. It felt like home.

The old questioning surfaced in me again, and I asked her if she ever felt demeaned by the fact that she catered to my grandfather, cooking and cleaning after him. She wasn't offended by my question the way my mom might have been. In fact, she said she loved to do it, and having a husband with an appetite gave her reason to be fulfilled. She hummed an old Puerto Rican song about bread and butter in her high-pitched soprano voice that in the past used to awake me at sunrise. I was grateful to have a loving family.

The next year, I moved out of my parents' home — with my brother, of all people. The move gave me freedom from my homebound upbringing, and I all too eagerly joined a dance academy because ice skating lessons were too expensive. I cleaned after Richard sometimes, and also started learning to cook for my boyfriend. Turns out that my grandmother was right; it actually feels good to be needed. Today, I have a strong maternal instinct to take care of my nephew when he's sick. And the first thing out of my mouth when I have a guest is: "Are you hungry?" But some things don't change. I still eat chicken without the skin.

*Serena R. Bruno has a master's degree in Intercultural Commu -
nication from Florida Atlantic University and is currently teaching
at Valencia Community College in Orlando, FL. She has enjoyed
many international excursions and job positions which have molded
and nourished her passion for cultural awareness. Hearing the
wealth of knowledge and experience wrapped up in the voices of the
oral history narrators was an activity in growth and awareness for
her, which has sparked a love for telling the creative true story.*

TALKING IN CLASS

Serena R. Bruno

There I was, roaming through a foreign airport with far too much luggage to maneuver with the purposeful posture I normally prefer to
assume. I stared blankly at direction signs with indecipherable codes
and searched for a contact person I didn't know, had never seen, and
was beginning to feel did not exist. Should I stay in one place? Should
I keep moving and searching? Should I start selling my belongings for
travel money? I had just landed in Seoul, South Korea after a painfully
long journey from my home in Orlando, Florida, and the only thing I
knew for sure was that I had already broken more social taboos than I
would ever learn in my new host country. I was certain the outfit I was
uncomfortably tugging on was not appropriate. (I swear this sweater
shrunk on the plane — was it really this tight and short when I boarded?)
What was the proper response after I bounced my 85-pound bag off one
of the many staring, motionless strangers around me? Should I have
stared back? And, by the way, *why* were they staring, and *when* would
they stop? Who could I have asked about the nearest hostel in case my
new, mysterious 'employer' is just a teenage internet junkie playing an
elaborate hoax? Who could I possibly have communicated with? I was
beginning to seriously regret not learning any of the Korean language
before embarking on this adventure. Standing in that busy airport on
the other side of the world, without a familiar face in sight and only foreign sounds in my ear, was possibly the most entirely alone I have ever
felt in my life.

A few months before, shortly after finishing my bachelor's degree,
and filled with the ever present need to escape my mundane American

existence as a young, college grad unsure of my future, I yearned to experience new and unusual cultures. I began searching the internet for teaching work abroad. My online search ended quickly when I found and accepted an English teaching position at an elementary school in Seoul, South Korea. After very little contact with the mysterious owners of the private school, I signed the one-year work contract; everything was handled by email. I received my international one-way ticket in the mail, packed a year's worth of luggage, and arrived alone at the Seoul airport one week later. Although I was eventually rescued from my initial state of fear and apprehension upon arrival, my experiences of loneliness as an English teacher in this foreign land would continue to haunt me in the days and weeks to follow.

My lack of communication skills in this new culture was the source of many disorienting moments from that first night in the airport until I finished out my contract. One example was my first solo bus ride. I was sure that I was ready for this responsibility, sure that I could get myself home from the subway stop without incident, despite my limited experience and the complete lack of traffic or street signs on the roads of downtown Seoul. Sadly, I was mistaken. I boarded the correct bus; I just did it on the wrong side of the street. I realized my mistake when the driver took a right and then a left instead of two rights to get to my neighborhood. Sitting quietly in the third row, I watched as people rang the bell for their stops and the once packed bus emptied. The slowly darkening view outside my window seat was becoming less and less familiar as we drove farther from my destination. The driver finally stopped at what appeared to be a resting point for the metro employees and I was the only passenger on the bus. I tried to appear natural, pretending to read the colorful advertisement on the back of the seat ahead of me, hoping my anxiety was not obvious. I had not gone unnoticed. The driver fired several questions at me in a voice as rough as it was foreign. His words were as unfamiliar as the lines and dashes on the text I was still staring at. I simply repeated the one word I knew he would recognize: *"yangjae,"* the name of my neighborhood, along with the subway stop where I started this adventure.

The driver put me on a returning bus and gave the second driver some instructions for my situation. After waiting several awkward minutes for the driver to begin his route, we headed back to where I had come from, picking up several new passengers on the way. After much confusion along the route between myself and the driver, stares and, no doubt, unflattering comments from the other passengers, and the utter loss of my confidence as an independent traveler, I gladly exited the bus at my neighborhood stop. I am sure that there were plenty of "clueless foreigner" jokes made at my expense that night. Although frustrating, the trial of that first Korean bus ride would prove to be simply a precursor to the tribulations of teaching English to Korean kindergarteners.

The inability to communicate can be extremely discouraging in what is supposed to be the healthy educational environment of the classroom. A new school with a new language can be terribly challenging to adapt to. Many immigrants to the United States have experienced this frustration upon first arriving in America and joining society. I became more familiar with this as I listened to the audiotaped narrative of Jose "Pepe" Lopez among many other longtime residents of South Florida during a graduate course on the cultural diversity of the region. Lopez immigrated to Miami in 1961 with his family at the age of 13 to escape the Cuban Castro regime. In an interview conducted in Hollywood as part of an oral history project in 1999, Lopez describes his first few weeks in a Miami school as being extremely hard because of his inability to speak English. He was unable to understand the lessons or read and write and, although he had help from a Dominican girl who served as his translator, this time period was very daunting. He tells the story of a day when his brother and he were riding the bus and talking with each other in Spanish. The driver suddenly stopped the bus and forced them off because their foreign language conversation offended him. Lopez soon learned to communicate in English and fit in well at school, but he said he would never forget those first few weeks as an outsider. Lopez is now serving the community as a retired law enforcement officer and the Executive Director for the Broward County Latin Chamber of Commerce, having successfully overcome his inability to express himself.

My first few weeks as an English teacher in South Korea gave me the same isolated feelings that Lopez details in his interview. I remember my first day in the classroom so vividly because I was terrified. Here were 12 five-year-olds staring up at me with fear, confusion, and expectation, mirroring my desperation. My attempts at a greeting were met with little response, barely a whispered "hel-lo" from the back of the class. The cramped room felt suffocatingly hot in the typical South Korean un-air conditioned building and I tried to buy some time by opening several windows and allowing the cool autumn air to ease our collective stress. I turned back to the class to find all of their tiny, almond eyes on me in anticipation. Although I was not sure what a raised head and puffed out chest communicated in the Korean culture, I tried to display a show of confidence and begin with my first "lesson.'" This consisted of hand gestures and silly faces in a vain effort to elicit any reactions from my young students. Even taking attendance was torture since the students were assigned Western names by the school for the benefit of us American teachers, and many of them did not know that they should respond to

"Ryan," "Sally," or "Peter." That first class session was spent in exasperation trying to communicate with a crowd of non-English-speaking children, some of whom had never been this close to a "round eye" before. I had never felt so foreign.

Fortunately, some people are able to use these frustrating experiences with communication problems to inform their careers and become even better at relating to multilingual students. Armando "Mandy" Perez, Jr., learned from his difficulties as a non-English-speaking student to become a more understanding and patient teacher later in life. Perez, who describes his life in the 2001 Race and Change oral history project conducted in the Lake Okeechobee area of South Florida, first came to the United States from Cuba when he was nine years old. It was 1961 and, like Jose Lopez, his family was also escaping the Castro regime. But rather than settle in Miami as many Cubans did, Perez' family went north towards the land of sugar plantations and agriculture surrounding Florida's largest lake, in the area known as the Glades. He describes candidly the conflicts that resulted from trying to fit in at an entirely White school as a Latin middle school student with little English skills.

> *"When I first arrived, I was in a bunch of fights as a seventh grader. I was in two or three fights that semester. I didn't speak English very well so to this day I don't have any idea what the fights were about . . . I know I was involved in fights — I don't know if I pinched the wrong girl or said hello to somebody's girlfriend or what had happened, or if it was just because I was Cuban, but you know . . . I didn't know enough of the language to figure out what was going on."*

The conflicts that can arise from an inability to communicate are apparent from Perez' experiences as a struggling young student. Not only did he not understand the language of his aggressors, but he also was unable to understand the social rules of conduct for this new culture. So he felt forced to react physically to compensate for his lack of comprehension.

Perez, now a successful educator, has remained in the same community where he encountered these conflicts. He eventually learned to speak English, developing a unique accent mixed with the melody of his cultural heritage and the Southern twang of his adopted home. He has also adapted successfully to the social norms of his community.

> *"I try to come off and let people know what's inside, and . . . treat others the way I expect to be treated. I think I've changed . . . I've mellowed as a person, as a teacher. I think that I've changed . . . probably in my speech pattern, in my language, in the words that I choose . . . [S]ometimes, it's hard for me to communicate my feelings because English is my second language, but I'm not any*

better at Spanish because I was so little when I came here. So I'm caught in between. So in terms of what I've changed [it's] the way of expressing myself."

The difficulty my students and I had in expressing our feelings adequately proved to be the most frustrating part of teaching children in South Korea. As we outgrew our initial apprehension and adapted to each other's differences, we encountered a greater need for expression. On many occasions a student would try to tell me a story about their weekend or about an encounter with a fellow student during lunch break. The young child would begin full of emotion and anticipation of my reaction, with an animated face and wildly moving hands. Soon, he or she would meet with frustration over a word he did not know or a sound she could not pronounce, and abruptly give up, throwing tiny hands in the air and moaning with irritation. I would try to encourage a second attempt, hoping for more success, but most often the student was convinced that communication was impossible. Of course, being children they would have an entirely new story in just a few minutes and the effort would begin again. As their schooling progressed they became more successful at communicating with me, but inevitably there were still those moments of absolute frustration.

Parents Day arrived at the school and everyone, students and teachers alike, was feeling the stress. It is very important for the Korean child not to fail in front of his parents and to show a high degree of mastery among his classmates. My students and I were nervous as this day approached, and we had practiced our lessons for a week. Peter, my brightest and most helpful pupil, was particularly excited to show his mother the things he had learned and accomplished in class. As the parents filed in and the class began, I noticed that Peter was visibly upset and refused to participate. I was confused and concerned since this was totally out of character for him, a student who consistently finished his work early and helped his fellow classmates. We made it through the 40-minute period without incident and we were all proud and relieved — except for Peter who had kept his head on the table for the majority of the class. I tried to talk to him through his tightly folded arms and spiky, black hair to figure out what had made him so upset. Through tears he told me, "No here, teacha, I don' know. No here." I was still very confused as he earnestly repeated whatever it was he was trying to tell me. He was becoming more upset and progressively less comprehensible to me. I soon gave up, standing to dutifully bow and thank each parent as they filed out of the classroom, connecting them with their child. It suddenly became obvious why Peter was so upset — his mother was not here on Parents Day, a day he had been working toward for weeks. He felt tremendously disappointed and abandoned, and to add to his frustration, I had not understood him when he desperately needed me to. Peter went home early that day, and I went home later feeling a sense of failure, worrying that he would not be the same vibrant young boy I enjoyed having in class. But with the resilience of a bright and loving child, he came into class the next day as cheerful as ever and simply told me, "Teacha, she forget. She sorry. I okay." I understood him clearly, and from then on I, too, felt that we would all be "okay."

Although I did not share their problems with the English language, I did encounter difficulties in knowing how to express the emotions I felt for these remarkable children. Not only was I aware of the limitations of their English comprehension, I also did not want to act in a culturally inappropriate manner. I had not received any information or training from my employers to guide my behavior or assist me in my relationship with my students. In addition, I had not seen the Korean people share more than a minimal amount of affection, and I was unsure of what the children would be comfortable with. But my worry proved to be fruitless as they slowly began to initiate hugs and cheek kissing, and affection became a normal part of our interaction. Though our verbal communication may have been limited to learning the colors of the rainbow or counting to 10, we were able to express our proud moments and affection through a basic language of bright smiles, excited hand clapping, and spontaneous group hugs.

Much can be learned about the art of communication while educating children. Jeannette Dexter has spent a lifetime teaching and is well aware of the frustrations and rewards in the classroom, especially when it is filled with various languages and cultures. Dexter, who is White and tells her story during the 2001 Glades area oral history project, has been an educator since 1960. She arrived in South Florida in 1965, the first year in which the schools in the area were integrated. Not only did she face the difficulty of teaching African American students who were in unfamiliar surroundings, she also had students who had recently immigrated to the country from places such as Cuba and Puerto Rico who were unable to communicate in English.

> *"I remember having Puerto Ricans, Mexicans, and Cubans [in our school], and the reason I remember that was because we had to teach 15 minutes a day of Spanish and the kids would get in an argument, the ones from Cuba, and the ones from Puerto Rico, and the ones from Mexico would argue . . . because they don't all pronounce things or talk, you know, [the same]. And here I am, I don't even know Spanish. I took French!"*

Dexter's difficult beginnings teaching in a multilingual classroom did not discourage her from continuing her work with non-English speakers, however. *"For a number of years I taught English as a Second Language when we first started getting in the Haitian population here. I worked in night school with the Haitian population teaching them, basically getting them to speak and then teaching them to read."* She became very active in these efforts, even tutoring the seasonal sugarcane workers from Jamaica. *"We had a night school and three nights a week the sugar companies would load them on buses, and we had classes for them because most of these Jamaicans could not read or write."*

Dexter is still active in the education of children and adults in the Glades area. She feels that now, more than ever, it is important to recognize and celebrate the diversity of their community. *"In the Glades area we have identified about 18 different cultures here."* She describes proudly how the community and its schools have improved over the years. *"[Y]ears ago we didn't [teach about other cultures] as a curriculum, never thought about doing that. But now we . . . do celebrate the differences of all the different cultures that we have."*

Although few foreign countries have such a variety of cultures within their schools, they often include the instruction of several foreign languages in their grade school curriculum. South Korea is an extremely homogenous culture, with few immigrant students, but the mastery of a foreign language is highly encouraged. The opposite seems to be true in American schools, with many new immigrant students losing their native language as they are immersed in English instruction.

My Korean students and I struggled through many frustrating English classes, but their early introduction to bilingual communication provided them with an even greater ability to express themselves. It may have seemed like a slow and arduous process at the time, but looking back I am amazed at how quickly they were able to learn how to communicate with me. One precious student, Emily, stands out in my memory today. She was the youngest child in the class at barely four years old, and this was her first school experience. She had no English skills, but was the most accomplished competitor for my attention. For the first two months of instruction she did not verbally communicate with me, and refused to follow the strict "no Korean" rule when interacting with her classmates. She became frustrated quite often and gave up on many class projects. I knew she was intelligent; many times she would climb onto my lap and articulately and earnestly explain her feelings, entirely in Korean. I decided it was up to her, that she would choose when she wanted to express herself to me in English. So I waited.

One day in class, as often occurred in our room, we were all sitting together at the table coloring a picture of dancing elephants. We made the color decision as a class: "What color should the elephant's shirt be?" I asked, "Green, teacha, green!" they answered. Emily always fought for the seat next to me and so, like always, she was at my elbow. Watching intently, she would dutifully color her picture in the exact shade and manner as I did mine. I resolved not to color the little singing bird that the class had decided should be blue. Emily waited. I was not coloring, and this was the chance she needed to make her move. She reached her small hand across the table and gingerly picked up a crayon she had been studying. She turned to me with beautiful, questioning eyes, showed me the broken, blue crayon she had chosen, and spoke without pause or a hint of doubt, "Is it dee brue color, yes teacha?" "Yes, Emily, it is," I answered, trying to hide my shock and choking on unexpected emotion. "Very good job!" The other children did not seem to notice her accomplishment and carried on with their coloring, but that day would start the rewarding communication I would continue to share with one of my brightest and most treasured students.

There were many of these rewarding moments in the small classroom I shared with 12 delightful and absolutely unforgettable Korean kindergarten students. Throughout my year with them I would continue to be surprised at how proud and emotional their achievements made me feel. As our communication improved, we became not only more successful as a class, but we were also able to express ourselves more fully in our daily contact. My day was filled with excited stories of weekend trips to Grandma's and narrations of silly arguments at lunch break, along with cherished expressions of love through bear hugs and the soft feel of a timid hand coming to rest in mine. Our interaction grew and adapted to fulfill the need we had to express ourselves and discover each other.

I call South Florida my home now and as I complete my graduate studies I value the exposure I have received to so many foreign cultures, and the chances I have had to share my culture with others — both here and abroad. I will always remember the children who were my students, and who taught me so much. As we sat in a small, huddled circle on the floor of the empty playroom the last day of school, we tried to express how much we would miss singing songs and planting apple seeds together. In our year together I had given them the powerful tool of bilingualism, but even more important, I knew that they had given me something I would always cherish.

Jennifer Hayden Epperson graduated summa cum laude with a bachelor's degree in French Literature and Music from Wheaton College, Norton, MA. She was awarded a master's degree in Broadcast Management from Bob Jones University, Greenville, SC. She has worked in various capacities in broadcasting in New England and currently she is station manager at WRMB-FM, Boynton Beach, FL. She has also served in international broadcast-ing as the executive producer and host of Trans World Radio's "Women of Hope" program that targets oppressed women around the world. Her love of the media has also taken her into the class-room at Palm Beach Atlantic University, West Palm Beach, FL, where she taught radio, and she has been published in NRB *and* Wireless Age *magazines. She enjoys flute performance, drawing, archery, genealogical research, and lives with her husband, Jack, and three pug dogs in Wellington, FL.*

FINDING A FACE

Jennifer Hayden Epperson

Like most children, I first learned about myself from a mirror. Mirrors don't lie. Nor do they comment on the reflection. What's there is there and it is up to the viewer to pass judgment on the image staring back. At age three, curiosity about my own appearance got the best of me. I had always been told that my eyes were blue, but I needed to know for myself. I remember pulling myself up onto the toilet, then the vanity, and steadying myself by pressing my knees into the rim of the sink. I carefully examined the face in the mirror looking back at me. My skin was smooth and pink, like my dolly, Pudding. My hair was dark brown and gently turned up at the ends. Then there were my eyes. They were blue. I sighed with satisfaction. I knew that there was something good about blue eyes. The ocean was blue, and the sky was blue. I knew my eye color pleased my parents. And besides, it was my favorite color crayon in the whole box.

Balanced on my grandfather's knee, I later learned more about myself when I looked into his face. As he told me stories about our Rhode Island family, the image I saw of myself became clearer and clearer. One day, a question had come up during a conversation among my childhood friends after a game of kick the can. "I'm part Polish and part English," said one. "My mom's French Canadian, and my dad is Swedish," said another. The discussion left me puzzled.

The next time I went with my mother to her parents' house, I found Grampy, smoking his pipe and sitting in his rocking chair in the kitchen. When I entered, he said, "Kooky, go get me a beer from the 'fridge," in his deep Rhode Island accent. Carrying the cold, slippery wet can in my little hand, I climbed onto my usual perch, his strong right thigh. I asked him, "What are *we*?" Grampy didn't hesitate. His voice boomed. "When anyone asks about you, you tell 'em you're Swamp Yankee." It sounded gross, especially the "swamp" part. But Grampy explained with authority, "It means that the family goes so far back that we have no idea when they came over on the boat." I later found that Swamp Yankee is the term for descendants of Rhode Island colonists who engaged England's Redcoats during the American Revolution. They fought guerilla style, choosing bogs as their battleground. They knew the lay of the land, hid behind trees, and picked them off, one-by-one. The Yanks held their breath and waited, firing only when they saw "the whites of their eyes." I also discovered the names of some of the boats on which my family crossed the Atlantic Ocean. One of them was christened the Mayflower. Like Grampy, I became very proud of being a "Swampah," even though I had nothing to do with choosing my heritage.

Grampy's affinity for Cap'n Black pipe tobacco and Narragansett beer soon took its toll on his body. A genetic disposition for circulatory problems didn't help, either. His toes grew cold, and soon we learned that he would lose a leg. After the surgery, I was allowed to spend the night at my grandparent's house. Grampy came to the breakfast table on crutches with his khaki pant-leg pinned up to the stump. After he ate, he declared, "Time to strap on the monstrosity." But I didn't care about Grampy's monstrosity. Whenever I saw him, I continued to eagerly hop up on the prosthesis to hear more of his stories. I did notice that it wasn't warm and soft like his real leg had been. It was hard, slippery and cold, and I had a hard time balancing on it.

When he wasn't telling stories, sometimes we would play a game. I would name a people group and Grampy would tell me what they were called. But these were derogatory names, I would later learn. Here I learned that Chinese people were Chinks, and Japanese people were Japs. Black people were Niggers, the French were Frogs, and Polish people were Pollocks. Even the English were not exempt; they were Jickeys. It seemed that Grandmother knew how to play the game Grampy's way, too. When she confided in me that she was part Canadian French, or "Canuck," she commented, "That's not so good." Later, I asked Grampy what was wrong with being French. He snapped, "Can't trust 'em." Whether he knew this from personal experience or from centuries of animosity between the English and the French, I don't know, but I knew I would continue to trust my grandmother.

Early one morning in my sixteenth year, the phone rang. It was my grandmother. "Betty, I think your father is gone," she said to my mother. She had heard the television in the kitchen still blaring before dawn, which was odd, and found Grampy lying on his bed. Somehow she knew that he was dead, but she didn't want to touch his skin. She didn't want to remove any hope that lingered. Grampy's body was lowered into a grave in Riverside Cemetery in Providence, near his father and grandfather's family, and I grieved. Just two nights before I declined an invitation to attend a great uncle's birthday party where I could have seen him, choosing instead to go out with a new boyfriend. Grampy liked my new boyfriend. He had a two syllable English family name that easily rolled off the tongue. "Palmer, that's a good one," he said. I pictured my grandfather at the party laughing, drinking beer, and smoking his pipe. Those moments may have been the last I would have with him. Now he was gone. I would never be able to ask him any more questions about *us*.?A window to the past had closed.

Interestingly, on the other hand, a part of me was relieved — not that Grampy was gone, but that I no longer had to closely interact with him. As I grew older, I increasingly found Grampy's gruff mannerisms and cutting remarks intolerable. They were like high grit sandpaper scratching away at my soul. I didn't like how he called, "Hey, you!" to my grandmother. What's more, I had met a Black boy named Tommy at school. He was smart and well mannered. And certainly, he wasn't a "nigger." I grew to dislike the names Grampy taught me. The game we had played when I was a child was no longer funny.

Later, as I entered college, I was required to complete a certain amount of credits in a foreign language. Because my grandmother's grandfather was Canadian French, I chose to continue my French studies in his honor. Ever since I was a young girl, I had heard that his Swamp Yankee wife forbade him to speak French in their home. How ironic that I would spend so much time masticating "er" verbs that were never even tasted by his own daughters. I not only found that I was a quick study, but thoroughly enjoyed it. Was it possible that I could possibly be fluent one day? I dared to dream that perhaps I might actually communicate with a person from a Francophone culture.

One evening, while still a college sophomore, I told my family at dinner that I had declared a double major in music and French Literature. My father stopped eating his pot roast and mashed potatoes. "Why the hell are you majoring in French?" My first inclination was to slide under the table. But then, something rose up within me, something that defied generations of antagonism between Anglophone and Francophone nations. I had an answer for my Anglophone father — and grandfathers, and great grandfathers for that matter — and I spoke it. I wanted to communicate with people who spoke a different language, I said. And besides, I was getting pretty good grades. My father quietly resumed eating his pot roast. I imagine that he was wondering if his daughter was going to end up in gay Paris. Instead, I ended up in the heart of predominantly Black Haiti, visiting not once, but three times. Two decades have passed, and I have continued to expand my understanding of other cultures.

Shortly after Grampy died in 1983, I drew a portrait of him. It was an artistic breakthrough for me, the first piece I had ever created that resembled the face I was studying. Perhaps love and grief were the dual passions that drove me to perfect his likeness with paper and pencil. But maybe I was also struggling to maintain some connection with him despite the growing gap between us that widened as I matured. Would Grampy have accepted my French major and visits to Haiti? Would he have encouraged me to explore other cultures? I can hear him, huffing and criticizing my choices. "That's a pip, Kookie," he'd say, with disapproval in his voice.

Through these eyes that I discovered in the mirror at such a young age, however, images have been burned in my memory that I will never forget: sparkling blue eyes set in the ruddy creased skin of my grandfather's face; also shiny mahogany skin of Haitian girls in starched blue gingham dresses on their way to school; and being a small white speck swirling in the middle of an undulating molasses brown crowd outside of the Aeroport International in Port-au-Prince, shocked as the word *"blanc"* was hurled at me to get my attention.

I am aware that I have changed. But how? When I look into the mirror each day, I see the same blue eyes, rosy skin, and dark hair, though now I am covering the gray that has begun to blanket my scalp. As I see others, I am still aware of black or white skin. However, I am conscious that there has been a change in how I interpret the images I see. This process has become a choice, a conscious effort to understand others. I have learned to resist a knee jerk assessment of others based on familial and cultural conditioning. As a result, I have learned to find pleasure in my own reflection, beyond the mirror, in the face of others.

Families definitely have an impact on how we view ourselves, and, as our world expands, how we view others. The following women come from diverse backgrounds but they share unique perspectives on how family has taught them to evaluate themselves and others. Their memories were recorded for Race and Change oral history projects in Delray Beach and Hollywood, FL. As each matured, she learned to find her own way — down the path her family directed or a more difficult one she may have carved out on her own.

As I turn the mirror away from my own life, it rests on the image of Jolene Fenelon. Like me, Fenelon was born in 1966. But she is a native of Jacmel, Haiti, and considers herself Black. She works as a substitute teacher in Broward County. In addition to being a teacher, she has done a lot of learning, too. Despite our cultural differences, she and I both realize that our families have had an impact on how we view skin color and we both have encountered frustrations with our own people who are unable to escape the restrictions of their confining mindset. As Fenelon recalls:

"I had a wonderful childhood. I had everything I wanted — Mom, Dad, my grandmother my grandfather, aunts and uncles, [and] lots of cousins. [I was] brought up in a house with a lot of people, with a lot of love. The racial climate where I grew up [in Jacmel, Haiti] was fine. My mother has a fair complexion, my father's [was] dark, and on my grandmother's side some are really light and some are really dark, and some are in between. I had an uncle . . . he was the commissioner for Jean Claude [Duvalier]. He used to write speeches. I used to visit him. He was a very popular guy, well known. He was very White. You used to feel it was different . . . I knew because my mother would tell me that he would visit her and two of my aunts. My grandmother had six kids. Of the six, four of them are light and two in between and he would favor the [lighter ones.] I mean, there was a little resentment, but it wasn't a big deal. But it would carry over until now. As we get older we realize that. We knew there was a problem, but we never made a big deal about it.

"In Haiti, the darker you are the less fortunate you are compared to the fair complexion and the 'in betweens,' unless you are very intelligent and get a break. The darker people were treated differently. They will call [darker people names]. You can go to any school you want, but there was always [that type] of resentment. [For me], I had different races in my family . . . so it didn't matter to me. I was brought up to respect people, regardless of the color.

"On my father's side, my grandfather's [family] way back were slaves. On my mother's side they were Spanish. She's a product of a mixed marriage back in the early days of Haiti. We were a really close family, and up to today we still are. When I moved to Delray Beach, I found the type of Haitians that I wasn't used to. I used to volunteer at the church, at Pompey Park, to help them. It became a problem because they didn't trust anyone. I remember when I used to help fill out income tax [forms] for them. They would be very disrespectful coming in here [saying things] like, 'Who do you think you are telling me what to

do?' *But they didn't understand that they are living in a different country now and they had to adjust.*

"*You still find five to six in one bedroom and, to me, that's, I dunno, usually [supposed to be] two people in a room. And I don't think the American community is used to that. If you drop by a house here in Delray [you see] five or 10 cars [parked in front of] a one or two bedroom house. I mean, they're all in there. They still have the same mentality as if they were in Haiti, playing dominos, and I don't think that the Americans appreciate that. But [the Haitians] feel like that since they live in a democracy, they can do whatever they want, but they don't understand that democracy has a limit, social wise . . . I want to help them to see what other people see . . . [but] they don't want to listen. It's a different type of social problem, but it's like me against the world . . . I feel like it's a losing battle.*"

Jolene Fenelon received a beautiful gift from her family. She learned racial tolerance at a young age. She saw many different shades of people on the branches of her family tree, and in her community. As for me, eight years of my life would pass before I would meet a person with dark skin. Racism was not absent from Fenelon's life, however. It was like a slow drip that leaked throughout her Haitian community in Jacmel and her extended family. In my family, racism was more like a poorly built dike. Once the topic came up in conversation, denigrations would come crashing through the walls of propriety, soaking the participants in the mire of prejudice.

Fenelon and I, however, share the surprise of entering a foreign culture. She entered mine, and I entered hers. Upon arriving in Haiti, I felt like I had left the picture of my own environment, and walked into its negative. White becomes black, and black becomes white. While it is uncomfortable for anyone making this passage, it poses challenges that both Fenelon and I embraced. Fenelon experienced frustration because Haitian immigrants often have difficulty adapting to the United States, and some never make the adjustment. Having interacted with Haitians both in her native country and the United States, I understand her exasperation. However, I continue to pursue interaction, probably because I am an outsider and have not been overwhelmed by the magnitude of challenges most Haitians face.

From the white sandy beaches of Jacmel, moving east through the Parc Nacional Forêt des Pins, we find a change in language, government and culture. The Dominican Republic is the other nation, along with Haiti, which occupies the island of Hispanola. It is also the native land of Evelyn Baez-Rojas. Born in 1951, she migrated to the United States through New York City in 1963. From there, she moved to Hollywood,

Florida in 1992 and works as a clinical psychiatrist. In her Race and Change oral history, she talks about her family and the role it played in how she would come to view her unique physical traits.

> *"My father lost his job and we had to leave [the Dominican Republic] because we were poor. We all lived fairly close to one another. I grew up around both sides of my parents' family. My father was a carpenter. My mother stayed at home and was a seamstress. I was to be a lab technician. I had to go to school and university. I was expected to have my own profession so I would not have to rely upon a man in case things did not go well with the man you chose.*
>
> *"In the DR, there is always striving to be whiter. People want to marry people with light skin, straight hair. My grandmother was always with a brush after me. She would ask, 'Why do you have kinky hair, when everyone else in the family has straight hair?' And I grew up with that complex. To this day, I still blow dry my hair. However, there are a lot of people in power who are dark-skinned, so I would say that there is an aesthetic desire to be like the White race, but Blacks are kind of equal in intelligence. The family members who were light skinned, blued eyed are deemed beautiful . . . not smarter. I was always thought of as very, very smart in my family, even back then. [They] would say, 'Evelyn is very smart. She's not pretty, but she's smart.' Compared to other relatives, I'm not considered white, white. I am considered [a] wheat [color.] My nose is not straight enough, and my hair is not straight enough to be White. In my family, my first cousins range from very dark to blue eyed, blond hair. I'm in the middle of this mix. My grandmother always said, though, it was better marry a Black professional than to marry a White garbage collector. So, I think there is this high value placed on intelligence and achievement. To become a professional and to marry a professional . . . they are doctors, lawyers, architects, lab technicians — anything that was a trade that earned a living.*
>
> *"Looking back, I surpassed my father's expectations, and my mother had no inkling of what I was doing, not even when I graduated with my Ph.D. Now she does. My husband is a physician; he was Dominican, too. I met him in my first year of college. We married in 1973.*
>
> *"You know how I have become aware of race relations changes? Through my kids. I have wonderful kids, and they have a good mix of friends. [But] I have those remnants of [wanting to have] a pretty nose and straight hair. I would like for them to marry someone who doesn't have a flat nose and kinky hair. And that's my prejudice. They will say things like, 'Mommy, you're so prejudiced.' You know, I guess I am. My oldest daughter had a Dominican boyfriend who was dark skinned. I just wish his nose wasn't that flat. I kept saying that and she said, "Mommy how can you keep saying that? Why is that important to you?' And I couldn't answer her. It's ingrained in me from way back. So I am a racist if you want to call me that. My kids are very good for me that way [though]."*

Baez-Rojas is a good example of how malleable a small child can be. To this day, she struggles with certain facets of her physical appearance, and I empathize with her feelings. In my family I was the "smart one," and my younger sister was the "pretty one." I will be the first to say that my sister is "pretty smart," but I still continue to seek assurance that I am not ugly. It's an uphill climb, but women can find their worth beyond the reflection in the mirror. Shedding such negative self-images, as well as prejudice, can be a lifelong struggle, especially if callous adult hands have branded them into minds of little children in their care. The wound may heal over but the scar tissue remains. Some, like Baez-Rojas, see the lesion and are unable to overcome the ugliness of it. However, I view it as a beauty mark, thrust upon me as a yearling. Now it is healing and is a reminder of how far I have come in my journey of accepting and understanding others who are not like me.

Sometimes, cultural differences are not evident. Beneath the skin lies a plethora of ideals, religious beliefs and moral standards that are shaped by the community. Such is the case with Susan Abrams Heyder, a native of Hollywood, Florida. Born in 1948, she describes herself as Caucasian. Even so, she is no stranger to bigotry, as she is Jewish. She begins by recounting her youth, and how she was able to accept those of other colors and beliefs during a time when segregation was the norm.

"My family life was pretty close to perfect. My parents were wonderful people. I have two brothers. My father was an attorney in Hollywood, and my mother was a housewife. We had a woman who worked for us five days a week — Artie Gregory. She was my second mother. She still is, [though we lived a] separate existence. She came, she worked, she went home. But when I had started at South Broward High School, she had a nephew, Benny Johnson who went to Attucks [High School.] Benny was in a play, so I went with Artie to this play, and I was the only White face at this play. I loved it. I thrived on it. It was exciting. It was MacBeth, and I never thought anything of it, except for the fact that I realized that Attucks was virtually across the street from South Broward. I thought it was so stupid. Certainly, I have never been a prejudiced person. I just remember that you would never see Black people anywhere, unless they were working at a White person's house. In my case, I would go to Artie's house and I would play with her nieces and nephews. It wasn't a problem at all with my parents.

"I honestly have to say that I think that my parents were very fair minded and there was never a [racist] verbal attitude to me. I am certain that if I were to have dated anyone of a different color as my kids do, things would have been halted a lot sooner. My oldest daughter has been dating a Black young man for five years, and one of the first things my mom said [was], 'Maybe you had better talk to her about that.' And I said 'Why? We've always welcomed everyone

into our house all these years.' Even when we were hesitant in the beginning, we said, 'You should think about your children if you're going to take it that far.' And our three daughters said to us, 'Mom and Dad, you've always welcomed everyone into our home. Don't start changing things now,' and we said that we wouldn't. And we haven't. So obviously, whatever I grew up with blended very well with my life later on.

"*I don't know that I really felt [racism.] [T]o say that I was sheltered or kept from it, I don't feel that I was, but I think that was just the way it was. There were just very separate venues. Where Blacks would be, where Whites would be was just separate. I didn't see it as a negative. Now, I look back on it and I see it is a negative. As I have said, I did wonder why there was a separate school right across the street from another school, but it wasn't at all discussed. I didn't feel it, I think, because I didn't want to. I never thought there was anything to be different between myself and anyone else.*"

The Constitution of the United States asserts that all [people] are created equal and are endowed by their Creator with certain inalienable rights. Despite this declaration by the Founding Fathers, very rarely does a child grow up in an American home in which all people are viewed equals. According to Heyder, she was reared in such an environment and she has been able to pass this precious heirloom down to her children. As a White Jewish girl, she doesn't remember the signs forbidding Blacks to a cool drink from a "white" fountain on a hot day. Still, although she did a fair amount of wondering why she didn't interact with Blacks in school, she accepted the segregation as the norm. I wonder if I would have behaved any differently, having matured at the same time and in the same environment as she did.

My dear mother passed away a year ago after a 24-year battle with breast cancer and I picked up scrapbooking as a means to grieve. That was something I once swore I would never get involved in. As an artist with some ability, I saw the exercise as crafty, frou-frou, mere pabulum. But, as the saying goes, "Never say 'never.'" As mothers in my scrapbook group pasted digital images of their children onto colorful pages, I picked through old photos of myself as a baby, taken when having a Kodak color camera was the latest in technology. There I was in a baby carriage, bundled up tightly to keep me warm in the early New England springtime. Above me is the budding pink dogwood, which still blooms at my childhood home. And though she wasn't in the picture, my mother's presence is there. I imagine she took the photo while on a short walk with me up and down Vaughn Lane where we lived. And there are my blue eyes, peeking out from under a knit white bonnet she probably purchased at Cherry and Webb department store where my grandmother worked at the time.

The wheels on the baby carriage have given way to the wheels of cars, trains, and wings of planes, as I have journeyed around the world. I have pictures of the many places I have been and the people I have met. Each photo is like a little mirror image staring back at me, reminding me of who I was then, and how I have become who I am today. This voyage of oral history writing has also provided me with images of the person I am vis-à-vis the cultural experiences of others. I am an Anglo Saxon who grew up with prejudice in my own family, and have broken free to make my own way. Each cross-cultural encounter in my life has been like a small reflecting pool and I am always the better for having looked in.

Vera Williams with infant son in 1965 in England

Narrator Jeannette Dexter
Photo by Natasha Pierre-Louis.

Armando (Mandy) Perez bids goodbye at the end of interview.
Photo by Natasha Pierre-Louis

STARTING A "RACE AND CHANGE PROJECT"

The Race and Change Project has become the focus of new dialogues across cultures in a number of communities. The discussion centers on race and the conflicts that arise, but other issues also naturally arise, including ethnicity, class, language, religion, migration, and cultural heritage. Bringing people together from different, even antagonistic backgrounds, and giving them an opportunity to share their personal stories can be a healing experience — for the speaker and the listener.

The use of oral history techniques helps to frame the dialogue in a compelling way that unearths memories that give new insight into the evolution of our national history. Creative writing exercises allow participants to find ways to bring the discussion into the present and relate it to their lives today. Here are some approaches to launching a Race and Change project or course that have proven effective with a wide range of cultural audiences.

Collecting Oral Histories on Race

☙ Be inclusive — Seek out a range of narrators who represent different racial, ethnic and/or cultural groups and/or different perspectives within a particular group. Look for generational representation as well. Include "voices" from the perspective of pivotal social events or eras: for example, people who grew up during the Depression, during the '40s and '50s, and during the Civil Rights Movement and start of the Women's Movement; people who arrived in the community during major immigration periods; and people who migrated into the community from other parts of the country. In addition to race relations include questions about: male and female roles and expectations that change with different generations and within cultures; routines of daily life including such activities as food preparation, housing, chores and recreation that change with different eras; and specific cultural stories, rituals, and customs that may vary even within groups of the same race or ethnicity, depending upon where they grew up or economic or religious background.

☙ Trigger memories — Ask questions designed to elicit detailed recall and storytelling. For example: Tell me what you remember about growing up in _____; What are your memories of growing up female/male? What do you remember about your earliest awareness of people who were different from you? What was the attitude in your community towards people who were different? The interviewer may sound repetitive but the purpose is to trigger a sequence of memory in the narrator. Memory builds on memory. Often a small seemingly inconsequential recollection of a scent or scene opens the door to suprising stories and revelations.

☜ Follow life patterns — Group questions to focus on experiences at different stages of personal development and awareness because the type of stories changes. The order of questions is important. Start with "Early Life." This is where the most detailed, and nostalgic stories are recalled focusing on childhood memories including actions, impressions, and imaginative activities. Then move to "Family and Community." Here, narrators will recall a wide range of day-to-day routines; special events, including holidays; religious or social observances; and colorful insights regarding places and people who would otherwise be lost to history. Next, comes "Work and Career." At this stage, the narrator gives more factual information than stories, shedding light on individual work history and the economic struggles and successes of the community, the work lives of its people and the shifts in the country's racial and social climate that affected employment. End with questions about "Later Life." Here, the narrator can share adult experiences that have influenced his or her view of how society has changed over time in terms of social and economic opportunity, and how he or she has changed in terms of attitudes. Within each of these life stages you can ask questions about memorable racial encounters.

The "3R's of Writing" Exercises
☜ Reminisce: Explore your racial history — Write an autobiography in two pages answering the following questions: Who are you in terms of the racial/ethnic culture you are a part of? What were you taught about people who were different from you? Who were your influences? How have you changed? The goal of this exercise is to tell your life story, beginning in childhood, with a theme in mind that allows you to be selective about the parts of your life that you will include.

☜ Reach Out: The Cultural Inventory Encounter — If doing this in a group or class, break into pairs, preferably with two people who do not know each other. Each person conducts an interview for a maximum of 15 minutes (a time limit keeps the interview focused). The leader keeps the time and announces when the interviewing role switches (you can be a little flexible if necessary). If doing this on your own, find someone you don't know well — but would like to know better; this is a good chance to interact with someone from a different culture, for instance, under the guise that you are, after all, a writer. In either case, the interviewer asks one of the following questions to start the interview: Tell me your earliest memories of growing up in ____; Tell me about your earliest memories of awareness of the racial climate where you grew up; What do you remember about life in your family or community as you were growing up? What do you remember about attitudes towards people outside of your family or community? All of the questions may be eventually asked or new ones may come up during the course of the interview. As interviewer, try not to interrupt; just listen.

ℭ Reflect: Ways to put it all together — Write a story, maximum six pages, combining the autobiography in Step One and the Cultural Inventory Encounter followed by a personal anecdote that responds in some way to the issues raised in the encounter interview. The point is to come to some new realization after the interview experience. From this point, oral history voices can be added to the story using interviews that you record or interviews you uncover in an archive that also explore the issue of race and race relations. After each voice, or story, add your own reflections to what has been said. What emerges is a blend of historical and present-day perspectives where the writer, in the process of the journey, comes to some new conclusions. Trust me. We are by nature storytellers, and we are wired to make connections. Readers, in turn, bring their own experiences and perspectives to the issues raised, creating further dialogue.

Projects for Public Presentation
ℭ Sharing the stories collected or written is the most important part of the process. Public programs can provide a way to honor narrators for their participation in a project and show the continuing relevancy of history. Projects can include, but are not limited to: publications such as articles and books; video productions; websites; multimedia exhibits of photographs and excerpts of recorded interviews; public readings of transcripts of interviews. For historical preservation, consider donating interviews to a local archive where researchers and future generations will have access to them, or starting one at a local library or through a community organization if one does not yet exist. And, hold onto those seemingly trivial artifacts from the past that you may think no longer have any use. Grandmother's tea set; Dad's uniform and time card; Mom's old photos; yearbooks; report cards. Write down your memories. The bits and pieces of ordinary lives, placed in history-loving hands, can be woven into valuable new tapestries.

ℭ

For more information about the Race and Change Oral History Project and archive and the Lift Every Voice Project for community audiences, contact Kitty Oliver, Kitty O. Enterprises, Inc., 1323 SE 17th Street, Fort Lauderdale, FL, 33316; kittyo@kittyoliveronline.com; or visit www.kittyoliveronline.com.

Cover photos: Race and Change Project narrators Vera Williams and Bob Gossett
Photo credit: The Miami Herald

AFRICAN AMERICAN RESEARCH LIBRARY
AND CULTURAL CENTER — SPECIAL COLLECTIONS
A BROWARD COUNTY LIBRARIES DIVISION

Holdings in the Special Collections encompass primary and secondary resources on African, African American and Caribbean history and culture.

Alex Haley Collection
Alcee Hastings Collection
B. Carleton Bryant Collection
Black Heritage Library (Fisk University)
Burnett Roth Collection
Cato & Margaret Roach Collection
Charles Mills Record Album Collection
Clinton Mack Photograph Collection (Pompano Beach c1930s)
Coretta Scott King Award Books
Daniel M. Johnson Collection
Doris Avner Ethnic Dance Collection
Dorothy Porter Wesley Collection
Earl Chesler Collection
Emridge Jones Collection
Eric Rawlins Record Album Collection
Ferris Family Collection
Frederic G. Cassidy Collection
Jack Abramowitz Collection
Kitty Oliver Oral History Collection
Libraries-In-Action (Broward County)
Library of the Spoken Word
Maurice Dawkins Collection
Nana Sarpong Collection (Ghana)
Niara Sudarkasa Collection
Negro League Baseball Memorabilia
Pettis Family Collection
Philip Rappaport Pamphlet Collection
Samuel F. Morrison Collection
Sixto Campano Sheet Music
Urban League of Broward County
Vivian and John Hewitt Haitian Collection

New Acquisition (October 2005)
Esther Rolle Memorabilia

Miscellaneous
African, African American and Caribbean Artwork
Dissertations and Theses relating to the history of Blacks in Florida
Microfilm & Microfiche (Black newspapers and periodicals)
Stereoscopic Cards & Viewer

For more information, call 954–625–2819 or visit www.browardlibrary.org.

BORDIGHERA PRESS is

BORDIGHERA POETRY PRIZE

The bi-lingual prize for poetry, including book publication, is sponsored by the Sonia Raiziss-Giop Charitable Foundation. The prize was established to foster the Italian language among Italian-American poets and to offer publication to the best English manuscript by an identifiably Italian-American poet each year.

MOST RECENT

6 (2004) Gerry LaFemina; trans. by Elisa Biagini; *The Parakeets of Brooklyn*

7 (2005) Carolyn Guinzio; *West Pullman*

CROSSINGS: AN INTERSECTION OF CULTURES

A refereed series, *Crossings* is dedicted to the publicaion of bilingual editions of creative works from Italian to English. Open to all genres, the editors invite prospective translators to send detailed proposals.

MOST RECENT

14 (2003) Roberto Bertoldo; trans. Emanuel di Pasquale; *The Calvary of the Cranes*

15 (2005) Paolo Ruffilli; trans. Ruth Feldmann and James Laughlin; *Like It or Not*

VIA FOLIOS

VIA FOLIOS is a refereed "small-book" series dedicated to critical studies on Italian and Italian/American culture. *VIA* FOLIOS also publishes works of poetry, fiction, theatre, and translations from the Italian.

MOST RECENT

36 (2005) Anthony Julian Tamburri, ed.; *Italian Cultural Studies 2002*

37 (2005) Steven Belluscio; *Constructing a Bibliography*

38 (2005) Fred Misurella; *Lies to Live by*

39 (2006) Daniella Gioseffi; *Blood Autumn*

ITALIANA

ITALIANA is series devoted to the publishing of conference proceedings.

MOST RECENT

XI (2005) *Medusa's Gaze: Essays in Italian Renaissance Literature, Art, and Gender Studies. Essays in Honor of Robert J. Rodini*